ROUTLEDGE LIBRARY EDITIONS:
JUNG

Volume 2



# IN SEARCH OF JUNG

# IN SEARCH OF JUNG

## Historical and philosophical enquiries

J.J. CLARKE

Routledge
Taylor & Francis Group
LONDON AND NEW YORK

First published in 1992

This edition first published in 2015
by Routledge
27 Church Road, Hove BN3 2FA

and by Routledge
711 Third Avenue, New York, NY 10017

*Routledge is an imprint of the Taylor & Francis Group, an informa business*



*British Library Cataloguing in Publication Data*
A catalogue record for this book is available from the British Library

ISBN: 978-0-415-82179-7 (Set)
eISBN: 978-1-315-75425-3 (Set)
ISBN: 978-1-138-79474-0 (Volume 2)
eISBN: 978-1-315-75428-4 (Volume 2)
Pb ISBN: 978-1-138-80209-4 (Volume 2)

# IN SEARCH OF JUNG

## Historical and philosophical enquiries

*J.J. Clarke*

ROUTLEDGE

London and New York

First published 1992
by Routledge
11 New Fetter Lane, London EC4P 4EE

Simultaneously published in the USA and Canada
by Routledge
a division of Routledge, Chapman and Hall, Inc.
29 West 35th Street, New York, NY 10001



Typeset in Times by
Columns Design and Production Services Ltd., Reading
Printed in Great Britain by Mackays of Chatham PLC, Kent



*British Library Cataloguing in Publication Data*
Clarke, J.J. *1937–*
In search of Jung.
1. Philosophy. Jung, C.G. (Carl Gustav) 1875–1961
I. Title
150

*Library of Congress Cataloging in Publication Data*
Clarke, J.J. (John James), 1937–
In search of Jung/J.J. Clarke.
p. cm.
Includes bibliographical references and index.
1. Jung. C.G. (Carl Gustav), 1875–1961.
2. Philosophy.
I. Title.
BF109.J8C53 1992
150.19'54–dc20
91–13304
CIP

ISBN 0–415–05007–3

To the memory of my father,
Harry Clarke, 1906–89

# CONTENTS

CONTENTS

# ABBREVIATIONS

CW *The Collected Works of C.G. Jung*. The first number refers to the volume number, the second to the paragraph number. Thus CW8.243 refers to *Collected Works*, Volume 8, Paragraph 243. CWA refers to Supplementary Volume A of the *Collected Works*.

AJ *Answer to Job*

JS *C.G. Jung Speaking*

MDR *Memories, Dreams, Reflections*

MM *Modern Man in Search of a Soul*

MS *Man and his Symbols*

NZ *Nietzsche's Zarathustra*

SY *Synchronicity*

US *The Undiscovered Self*

# CHRONOLOGY

1875 Carl Gustav Jung born in Kesswill, Switzerland, son of a Reformed Protestant pastor, Johann Paul Jung, and Emilie Preiswerk.
1895 Enters Basel University to study science and medicine.
1900 Appointed assistant at the Burghölzli Psychiatric Hospital, Zürich, under Professor Eugen Bleuler.
1902 Doctoral dissertation 'On the Psychology and Pathology of So-Called Occult Phenomena'.
1903 Marriage to Emma Rauschenberg. Five children.
1907 First meeting with Freud. *The Psychology of Dementia Praecox.*
1909 Resigns from Burghölzli. Visits USA with Freud.
1910 Elected President of International Psychoanalytic Association. *Symbols of Transformation.* Lectures at Fordham University.
1913 Resigns as President. Final break with Freud.
1921 *Psychological Types.*
1924 Visits Pueblo Indians in North America.
1925 Study trip to the Elgonyi of Mount Elgon, East Africa.
1929 Commentary on Taoist text *The Secret of the Golden Flower.*
1934 Begins series of seminars on Nietzsche's *Zarathustra.* President (until 1939) of International Society for Medical Psychotherapy.
1935 Tavistock Lectures, London, on 'Analytical Psychology'.
1937 Terry Lectures, Yale University, on 'Psychology and Religion'.
1937 Study trip to India.
1944 *Psychology and Alchemy.*
1948 Founding of C.G. Jung Institute, Zürich.
1951 Lecture 'On Synchronicity'.
1952 *Answer to Job.*
1955 *Mysterium Coniunctionis.*
1961 Death after a short illness at his home in Küsnacht, near Zürich.

# PREFACE

Jung once remarked that

> Because I am an empiricist first and foremost, and my views are grounded in experience, I had to deny myself the pleasure of reducing them to a well ordered system and of placing them in their historical and ideological context. From the philosophical standpoint, of whose requirements I am very well aware, this is indeed a painful omission.
>
> (CW18.1731)

It is unlikely that we would learn much from attempting to reduce his ideas to a 'well ordered system', and indeed Jung frequently expressed doubts about the desirability of any such task. On the other hand there is a great need to place his ideas 'in their historical and ideological context'. Despite ever-increasing fame, and an ever-growing band of devoted followers, both the public and the scholarly perception of him is still largely that of a maverick and a 'mystic', something of a deviant who stands outside the mainstream of our culture. Jung himself foresaw this fate when, very late in his life, he lamented the widespread misunderstanding of his work which was, he believed, the result of being 'isolated between the faculties' (*Letters II*, p.629).

The aim of this book is to help to release Jung from this isolation and to show that, even though he may fall between academic disciplines, he has an important and honoured place at the heart of the great debates of modern times. By contrast with Freud, Jung has not yet achieved the status which he deserves, and I believe that this must be rectified by re-examing the part he has played in the history of modern thought. Freud's place in our culture is secure. Though his ideas and theories have by no means received universal acclaim, and are the subject of continued controversy, his influence and status are assured and can be observed in a wide variety of fields ranging from philosophy and sociology to art and literary criticism. Jung, on the other hand, though founder of a world-wide therapeutic community, and despite a powerful impact on theology, and a high reputation amongst 'New Age' thinkers, has for the most part been looked upon with disfavour, and even with contempt, by the academic guardians of our culture. It is the aim of this book to show that Jung, as much as Freud, deserves a secure place in the history of ideas of the twentieth century, that he is not to be viewed as a minor act in the Freudian saga but as part of that great tradition of philosophical anthropology which, since Plato and Aristotle, has wrestled with the central issue of human nature and human destiny.

Jung's most important contribution to modern thought, in my opinion, lies in his recognition of the reality of mind and in his recovery of the idea of the psyche as a cosmos equal and complementary to the physical world. Without falling into a dualism of mind versus body, a division which has dogged Western thought since the time of Descartes, he has reconstructed with modern tools and in modern terms the traditional concept of the mind as something that has a place in the natural order of things, 'set up in accordance with the structure of the universe', as he put it. At the same time he rejected the modern tendency to reduce mind to purely physical processes, and while arguing that the roots of the psyche are firmly planted in physical nature, he constructed a model of the human psyche which also found a place for the need for some higher purpose and spiritual fulfilment.

In this book we will explore his view of the psyche, showing how it is interwoven into the themes and counter-themes of modern thought. It will be our aim in the first place to grasp the nature of Jung's thinking, the peculiarities of his approach and method, his attitude to science and philosophy, and to examine the influences on and sources of his thought, East as well as West, ancient as well as modern. This will occupy us in Part I. In Part II we will look more closely at Jung's renewed conception of self-hood and his idea of an inner cosmos which is as rich and as worthy of exploration as the outer world of nature, while at the same time continuing to link his ideas to the broader traditions of Western thought. We will discover that for Jung the self or psyche is a kind of organic being which has its natural cycle of development and growth and which, while springing from the deep soil of the collective unconscious, and an integral part of the living processes of nature as a whole, reaches its flowering in the life of the fully self-conscious and self-activating individual.

Emphasis on the spiritual goal in Jung's work has alienated him from some intellectuals and scholars, and has helped to confirm the belief that he is little more than a cult figure. Part of my aim in this book is iconoclastic, to demystify Jung, to show that he is not a mystic or religious guru shrouded in incense, but a thinker who can stand alongside other great twentieth century figures. It is probably true, judging by the witness of his autobiography, that he had what might be called 'mystical experiences', and it is also undeniable, judging by the devotion of his followers, that he had personal charisma. But these aspects of the man will not be my concern. I want to see Jung, not as some timeless, universal figure who stands above history, nor as a backward-looking figure seeking refuge in outworn creeds, but as a man who was deeply involved in the great issues and debates of his time, certainly not without many faults and deficiencies, but nevertheless a challenging and original thinker. Some have sought to bury Jung under a weight of criticism, others to exalt him on a cloud of praise. My own aim as an historian of ideas is to steer a course between these two by, on the one hand, arguing for his importance as a modern thinker, while at the same time drawing attention to the evident difficulties and weaknesses in his thought.

Jung began his professional life towards the end of the last century with a natural antagonism towards the growing materialism and positivism of that age, and a natural affinity with those so-called *fin-de-siècle* thinkers, such as Nietzsche, Bergson, Butler and Vaihinger, who exalted freedom and self-expression in an age which elevated determinism into a dogma. This brief spring of optimism in European thought was swept aside by the dark winter of two world wars and widespread economic turmoil, a winter which is perhaps only now beginning to give way to the glimmerings of spring again. Throughout this dark period Jung, while recognizing the negativities and contradictions that lie within the human soul, managed to maintain his early optimistic view of human nature and to build it into a rich conception of the infinite potentialities that lie within us, the development of which give life some sense of purpose and hope. History has come full circle, and now at the end of our own century the spirit of optimism seems once more alive, and Jung's philosophy seems able to speak to us in terms that we are increasingly able to understand. In his autobiography he remarked that 'we stand in need of a reorientation'; this present book is dedicated to that goal in the belief that such a reorientation is indeed now beginning to take place, and that Jung has made a significant contribution towards its enactment.

My book is designed to appeal to several types of reader: in the first place, to those who already sympathize with Jung's outlook and who seek to place their understanding of his ideas in a wider context; secondly to those, amongst whom I count many of my students over the past two and a half decades, who believe that the story of modern thought is exciting and of vital concern to us, and that Jung has something of more than passing interest to say at this time; finally I hope my book will be read by those guardians of our culture and intellectual life who have tended to view Jung as a deviant disciple of Freud, sunk irretrievably in obscurantism, and who are invited to give Jung a fresh hearing at the very least. For the sake of all these readers I have attempted to convey Jung's ideas as honestly and as clearly as possible, and to discuss the wide range of intellectual concerns that surround his thought in a way that presupposes in my readers intelligent commitment to these matters rather than any deep technical knowledge, and which will appeal to the intelligent and educated reader without at the same time patronizing the scholar. For this reason, although I have drawn on the whole spectrum of Jung's collected writings, I have sought wherever possible to quote from readily available sources, and in such cases have made reference to popular editions rather than to corresponding locations in the collected works. Readers looking for a general introduction to Jung's life and thought are warned that, though this book discusses a wide range of his ideas, and often relates these to his own personal development, its approach is essentially thematic, and does not attempt a systematic presentation of his thought.

In the course of my investigations I have taken into account a wide range of Jung's immense literary output, including works published by him in his lifetime, transcripts of lectures and seminars, letters, broadcasts, and in some cases recorded conversations. I have also taken into account a wide range of critics both friendly and hostile in relation to whose ideas I have sought to clarify my own. In the end I can offer only an interpretation, a view of Jung from my own standpoint. Though I take issue with a number of critics and commentators, and argue strongly for my own case, I doubt if there is any final or definitive end to this search for Jung, but only the possibility of further travel and enrichment, and further argument, all of which I trust that the present work will encourage. Perhaps the best way to approach this task is to echo Jung's own admission that 'the only question is whether what I tell is *my* fable, *my* truth' (MDR, p.17).

# ACKNOWLEDGEMENTS

I wish to expresss my thanks to Routledge and to Princeton University Press for permission to quote from *The Collected Works of C.G. Jung*, to Routledge for permission to quote from *Modern Man in Search of a Soul* by C.G. Jung, and to Collins and to Random House for permission to quote from *Memories, Dreams and Reflections* by C.G. Jung, recorded and edited by Aniela Jaffé.

My intellectual debts are many, and are acknowledged in the appropriate places in the text, but particular mention must be made of Peter Homans, Ira Progoff, Andrew Samuels, Walter Shelburne, and Anthony Stevens, whose writings have been especially helpful to me in my 'search for Jung'. I am also grateful to many friends and colleagues, including Elaine Beadle, Peter Conradi, Dina Glouberman, Jean Hardy, Beryl Hartley, John Ibbett, Mary Anne Perkins, and Michael Whan, who have read and commented on the text at various stages of its evolution, and to Jill Boezalt who helped with the final editing of the text; all have given me invaluable criticisms and encouragement.

# Part I

# THE PHILOSOPHIC JOURNEY

# 1

# FREUD AND JUNG

> The contrast between Freud and myself goes back to essential differences in our basic assumptions.
>
> (C.G. Jung)

The rediscovery and exploration of the human psyche in the twentieth century was as much the work of Freud (1856–1939) as of Jung. But to understand fully the latter's contribution it is important to separate him clearly from the former. The linking of their two names (often along with Adler's in an incantational trinity), has engendered much confusion, and has obscured the distinctive nature of Jung's own contribution. Before penetrating more deeply into the historical roots of Jung's thought, therefore, we must first address the question of their intellectual relationship.

At the heart of the problem lies the myth that Jung was Freud's 'pupil', and that he was little more than a deviant disciple of the founder of psychoanalysis. This myth was given early credence by Freud himself who accused Jung of 'making changes', of 'throwing over all the fundamental theories', of 'modifying', and of 'offering a corrected version' of orthodox psychoanalysis. Jung had, it is alleged, been led astray by his own personal visions and by an unhealthy fascination for Gnosticism, astrology and flying saucers, and unlike Freud, had failed to develop a consistent and systematic theory to back up the insights derived from his therapeutic practice. His association with mysticism and the occult, while attractive to followers of New Age philosophy, is something of an embarrassment to 'serious' scholars. Thus, while in purely numerical terms Jung seems to have a much wider following than Freud, it is Freud who has found favour with the intellectual establishment.

It is true that not many have been eager to count themselves as Freudians, but even his enemies and critics such as Eysenck, Masson and Thornton seem to have given him a status in our debates not unlike that accorded by Nietzsche to God whose death now appears perpetually interesting. Moreover in such fields as philosophy and the human sciences Freud has become a widely exploited test-bed for all kinds of theories and thinkers ranging from the Logical Positivists, Popper, and Wittgenstein to post-structuralists, hermeneuticists and feminists. Added to this there have been serious attempts to rethink, reread and reinterpret Freud – for example in the work of Ricoeur, Lacan, Kaufmann and Bettelheim. No equivalent attention has been lavished on Jung. His influence is undoubtedly growing, though it remains largely unacknowledged, and he is still frequently consigned to neglect, or referred to in passing with a patronizing sneer.[1]

Here are a few examples of what I mean. In a recent comprehensive survey of psychological theories Hearnshaw refers in a few rather grudging paragraphs on Jung to 'the strongly mystical strain in his outlook' and to his 'flirtations with alchemy, oriental cults and occultism' (1987, p.166). Hughes in an important book on social criticism generously allows that 'it would be wrong to dismiss Jung as a charlatan', but goes on to aver that '[Jung's] mind was profoundly confused, and his writings are a trial to anyone who attempts to discover in them a logical sequence of ideas', and characterizes him as a 'mystagogue' parading in the guise of a man of science (1979, p.160). In a similar vein, but more summarily, Peters, in his contribution to *Brett's History of Psychology*, dismisses Jung's work as 'so mysterious as to be almost undiscussable' (1962, p.730), a remark which echoes Freud's own comment of 1914 that Jung's views were 'so obscure, unintelligible and confused as to make it difficult to take up any position upon (them)' (Freud 1914, p.121). Rycroft is barely more charitable when he observes that he (Rycroft) 'suffers from the not uncommon constitutional defect of being incapable of understanding Jung's writings' (1972, p.ix). Fromm, a Freudian sympathizer, was a particularly trenchant critic of Jung, referring to him as 'a reactionary romantic', accusing him of lacking 'commitment and authenticity', and of replacing the search for truth with 'a seductive spirituality and brilliant obscurantism' (quoted in G. Wehr, 1987, p.475). The 'official' Freudian view of Jung is expressed by Ernest Jones, Freud's disciple and biographer, who commented that after his early important studies in word-association techniques and in schizophrenia, Jung descended 'into pseudo-philosophy out of which he never emerged'. And perhaps most unfriendly of all was Glover's dismissal of Jung's work as 'a mishmash of oriental philosophy with bowdlerised psychology' (1950, p.134).

In the face of this concerted attack, can any good be said to come out of Jung? He is perhaps not a major front-rank thinker of our century, but neither is he as negligible as some of the authorities just quoted would lead us to imagine. I believe that Jung has an important, and so far underrated, place in the intellectual debates of our time, and deserves to be rescued from the shadow of Freud.

We need to begin with a sketch of their relationship. They first met in 1907 after a brief exchange of letters, and quickly established a close personal and professional relationship which lasted until 1913, and which involved a number of meetings, including a long visit together to the USA, and a voluminous correspondence amounting to more than 360 letters. At the time they met, Freud was a well-established if controversial figure of fifty, whereas Jung, twenty years Freud's junior, had been qualified as a medical practitioner for only seven years. There can be no doubt that Jung learned much from Freud, and throughout their friendship, though never in any sense Freud's pupil, he was happy to cast himself in a junior role, and even after the break repeatedly acknowledged his debt to the older man. The myth has it that Jung learned his trade, from both the theoretical and the practical standpoint, from Freud, and then, like many an ambitious and clever young apprentice, broke away to set up his own derivative school, that he was in effect a renegade disciple of Freud, a revisionist who started his career as a loyal and adept pupil of the master, even became his appointed successor and 'crown prince', but due perhaps to intellectual *hubris* or to a father complex (Freud accused him of both) broke away to follow his own mystical road.

It may have been the case that Jung was ambitious and clever, but in other respects the myth is mistaken. During the time of their friendship Freud certainly never treated him as a pupil, seeing him rather as a respected and highly valued junior partner in his attempt to establish the professional credentials of psychoanalysis. Jung's own attitude towards his senior colleague, though deferential in the prescribed manner of the day, was always one of intellectual and professional independence. Let us explore the relationship further.

There are well-marked differences between Freud's teaching and that of the mature Jung, which can be traced to profound differences of temperament, background and intellectual inheritance. '[My] upbringing, my milieu and my scientific premises', Jung noted in an early letter to Freud, 'are utterly different from your own' (McGuire, 1988, p.14), and in his autobiography Jung recalled experiencing these differences acutely during their trip to America in 1909. He noted that 'During this period I became aware of how keenly I felt the difference between Freud's intellectual attitude and my own' (MDR, p.184), and went on to observe that the major cultural influence on his life was that which derived from the humanistic atmosphere of Basel, which in his youth was still permeated with the ideas and personalities of Burckhardt and Nietzsche. In addition to these broad cultural factors it is important to note that within psychology itself the influences on Jung were far from being confined to that of Freud. Jung himself insisted that he 'did not start from Freud, but from Eugen Bleuler and Pierre Janet' (CW10.1034n). Thus,

Bleuler, who was Jung's clinical chief at the Burghölzli Hospital, was important in helping to shape his views concerning schizophrenia. Janet, who was also an influence on Freud, was the leading French psychiatrist at the turn of the century, and contributed to Jung's thought the notion of psychological automatism, and the idea of the lowering of the threshold of consciousness, a state in which subconsious elements of the personality well up into consciousness. He also acknowledged his debt to Theodore Flournoy, whose investigation of spiritualist mediumship helped to shape his idea of fragmentary personalities as constituents of the total psyche.

Freud's education, by contrast, was dominated by the naturalism of Darwin and by the positivism of his revered teacher, Brücke, a pupil of Helmholtz who was a pioneer in the attempt to apply the principles of physics to the study of physiology and psychology. By the time that Jung entered medical school at the University of Basel, he had read widely amongst the philosophers, and was steeped in the German Idealist/Romantic tradition from Kant and Goethe through Schelling and Schopenhauer to von Hartmann and Nietzsche. This early education, which was largely carried out in the solitude of his father's study, was almost certainly the major factor which helped to shape his mature thought, for not only are his later writings suffused with references and acknowledgements to these writers, but it is evident, as I shall argue later, that his conception of the unconscious and of the dynamics of the psyche, as well as his whole attitude and methodology, spring from this source rather than from the rival tradition of scientific rationalism. Indeed, given these differences of background and influence, the surprising thing is, not that Freud and Jung parted company, but that they ever became associates at all.

Nevertheless, their paths did converge. What was it then that brought them together? The simple answer to this is that they found, to their mutual pleasure, that their work had for some years being progressing along parallel paths. Two factors must be mentioned. The first is connected with Freud's great work, *The Interpretation of Dreams*. Jung read it shortly after it was published in 1900, and on second reading, and despite the fact that, as he reports, he covered the pages with question marks, he was much taken with the book, claiming later that it 'linked up with my own ideas' (MDR, p.170). Jung was later to differ in certain important respects from Freud in his approach to dreams, but it must be said that this is one area in which the older man's influence was indelibly marked on the mind of the younger, and for which the one was perpetually in the other's debt, a debt frequently and fulsomely acknowledged. The second factor which brought them together was Freud's own appreciation of Jung's work and his recognition that it offered potential support to and confirmation of his own. This involved two distinct, but connected, areas in which Jung was currently conducting research under Bleuler, and in which he was already building up a substantial list of publications.

The first area is that of word-association tests. The technique was not new. It can be traced back firstly to Wundt and Galton, both late nineteenth century pioneers in the early days of psychology, and beyond them to the British empiricist tradition of which Jung was aware through its French representative, Condillac. During his first few years at the Burghölzli Hospital Jung helped to refine and develop these tests. They consisted of reading out a list of words to patients, inviting them to react to each word with the first word which came into their heads, and then noting the reaction-time by means of a stop-watch. In the course of the ten papers on this topic published between 1904 and 1909, Jung elaborated on the basis of these tests an important and in many respects novel conception of the psyche which provided the foundation for his later theories. These were fully developed only after his break with Freud, but at this early stage they were centred on the idea of what he called 'feeling-toned complexes'.

In conducting his word-association tests Jung had hit upon the idea that some associations, in particular those which were evinced after a more than average reaction-time, could be linked together in a significant way, and could be shown to provide a clue to some area of psychic disturbance within the patient's psyche. This in turn gave rise to the idea of a *complex* which Jung saw as a meaningful network of mental dispositions, of thoughts and feelings, which held an identifiable and relatively independent place within the psyche as a whole; thus for example a father complex might comprise the interdependent thoughts and feelings that are associated, consciously or unconsciously, with a particularly difficult father relationship. The psyches of even normal people possess elements which behave with a relative degree of autonomy, but in certain circumstances a complex might assume pathological significance to the extent that it comes to operate independently of the controlling authority of the ego, and thereby to constitute a threat to psychic unity. Thus against a background of standard clinical observation and face-to-face questioning Jung claimed to be able to identify distressing mental contents, which were often hidden from the patient's consciousness. This claim parallels the contemporaneous efforts of Freud to show that dreams, slips of the tongue, jokes, and other psychic fragments could be used to penetrate the unconscious of an hysteric or neurotic patient. Both men, quite independently and using different approaches and techniques, had come to the conclusion that unconscious contents could be elicited by using as clues apparently chance scraps of behaviour, and that these contents could be seen to constitute perfectly meaningful constellations of thoughts and feelings.

The association tests led straight to the other area in which Jung was concerned when he met Freud, namely that of schizophrenia, which was then called 'dementia praecox'. Here again, in collaboration with Bleuler and other colleagues, Jung had begun to make some important contributions to an understanding of this mental condition, and these he published in 1907 in a book entitled *The Psychology of Dementia Praecox*. The book was widely and favourably reviewed, and brought the author recognition as an authority in the field, and as well as endearing him to Freud it attracted the notice of colleagues in America who invited him to visit Clark University in 1909 in the company of, and as an equal with, Freud.

One of the most important ideas contained in this work is the claim that the apparently absurd delusions of psychotics made perfectly good sense when systematically probed and interpreted, and that these delusions and the accompanying patterns of behaviour could be seen as playing a positive role in the life of the psyche. In other words even a person who displays the most bizarre and irrational forms of behaviour is aiming in a quite sensible and comprehensible, albeit unconscious and often painful, way towards their own well-being; they are seeking their own good without knowing it. As C.A. Meier has put it: 'For the first time in the history of psychiatry delusional material is treated as more than just unintelligible stuff and is looked upon as something worthy of interpretation' (quoted in Dry, 1961, p.32). It is true that in *The Interpretation of Dreams* Freud had argued along similar lines, namely that the crazy sleep-world of the dreamer, like the crazy waking-world of Jung's psychotic patients, made perfectly good sense provided that one treated it as a cryptogram that needed to be deciphered. But before drawing the conclusion that Jung's work was merely an extension of the insights contained in the dream book, a few points must be underlined.

The first is that Freud, despite his early enthusiasm, never fully accepted the underlying argument of Jung's book on schizophrenia and continued to maintain that the psychoanalytic method was not really a suitable tool for understanding and treating that condition. Indeed it was clear to both that there were major differences between the hysterias and neuroses which formed the basis of Freud's work and the condition of dementia praecox, and Jung was displaying great independence and originality in attempting in some measure to conflate the two.

But more important is the fact that Freud did not draw the full implications of his work on dreams. He failed to see that the causal/mechanistic model of the psyche, which he had drawn up in his 1895 *Project for a Scientific Psychology* (Freud, 1895), was at odds with the symbolic/hermeneutical view of the psyche which lay behind the 1900 work on dreams. He continued to maintain in theory that the psyche is a causal nexus analogous to a physical system, while in practice adopting a method which could more properly be called *hermeneutical* which construes the psyche as a domain of meanings.[2] Jung by contrast clearly and explicitly conceived his method as a hermeneutical one (see CW7.131), seeing in the latter something like his method of 'amplification' whereby a symbol or fantasy is enriched by elaborating a connected web of meanings (see CW7.493). It also appears implicitly in his frequent references to his method as akin to the interpretation of a text, for example: 'When we are dealing with unconscious material [e.g. dreams] we are obliged to adopt the method we would use in deciphering a fragmentary text or one containing unknown words' (CW12.48). As we shall see later, he quite explicitly rejected the causal/mechanistic model of the psyche in favour of one which viewed the mind, not as a causal network, but as a domain of meanings and purposes. This idea is clearly present in his pre-Freud writings, even in his undergraduate lectures to the Zofingia Club (see CWA.83f), and though in this first decade of his professional life he sometimes dallied with a mechanistic view, the general tendency of his thinking, from youth to old age, was consistently orientated in the opposite direction.

This view is reinforced by the fact that the ideas lying behind his work on schizophrenia had already taken shape in his mind even before he embarked on his professional work at the Burghölzli Hospital in 1900. Between 1895 and 1900 he was a medical student at the University of Basel. The period was one of great intellectual excitement for him and he took an interest in many matters beyond the medical curriculum. One of these matters was psychic phenomena, and he not only read widely on the subject, but also attended a number of séances involving his cousin, Helen Preiswerk, who appeared to be taken over by several deceased personalities of whom she had no conscious knowledge. Jung's studies of this case formed the core of his doctoral dissertation, 'On the Psychology and Pathology of So-Called Occult Phenomena' which he presented to the University of Zürich in 1902. The study is essentially one of psychic automatism in which the subject enters a trance-like state and assumes the character of another person with a wholly different personality.

The study of such cases from a scientific standpoint was by no means novel at that period, and the importance of Jung's work lay not so much in the material he adduced as in the theoretical stance he adopted to explain it. In the first place he explicitly rejected any explanation which drew upon supernatural causes. He consistently refused right to the end of his life to give any place to metaphysical explanations in his formal psychological work. His interest in the occult, which was certainly lifelong, has frequently been cited in support of the appellation 'mystic', but this is to confuse the study of the occult as a psychological phenomenon with an active sympathy with and theoretical commitment to it. As Jung himself noted: 'If you call me an occultist because I am seriously investigating religious, mythological, and philosophical fantasies

. . . then you are bound to diagnose Freud as a sexual pervert since he is doing likewise with sexual fantasies' (*Letters II*, p.186).

Furthermore, the 1902 dissertation first suggested to him an idea of extraordinary power and originality that was to play a central role in his subsequent thinking, namely that the psyche is capable of splitting off into what might be called 'sub-personalities', or autonomous psychic centres. He came to see the human psyche, not as the dynamic interplay of two or three drives or principles as in Freud's case, but rather as a highly complex relationship of psychic factors, or personality fragments, both conscious and unconscious, centred upon a conscious ego, and constituting a teleological system whose aim was the achievement of a balance between its various components. This model, which we will examine in more detail in Part II, was very different from that of Freud, and was one which he had already begun to develop before they became acquainted.

This difference of starting point, along with the differences of background and temperament which I have referred to, meant that their relationship from 1906 onwards was far from being a simple one of teacher and pupil. This is particularly evident on the question of sexuality, for though Jung adopted the term 'libido' from Freud, he construed it in a different way, so radically different that it was to become one of the major ingredients of their explosive separation in 1913. But the divergences were there right from the start, and were spelled out by both men clearly and repeatedly in their correspondence and in their public writings. Thus in an early exchange of letters in 1906 Jung wrote that 'it seems to me that though the genesis of hysteria is predominantly, it is not exclusively, sexual', and Freud replied that 'Your writings have long led me to suspect that your appreciation of my psychology does not extend to all my views on hysteria and the problem of sexuality' (McGuire, 1988, pp.4–5). Jung clearly wanted to stay close to Freud on this question, but he never at any time capitulated to Freud on this point or lapsed into bad faith, but always sought to maintain a clear, though respectful, distance from the other man. Thus in another early letter to Freud he pleaded that 'If I confine myself to advocating the bare minimum, this is simply because I can advocate only so much as I myself have unquestioningly experienced' (pp.10–11). As he expressed it in 1934: 'My collaboration [with Freud] was qualified by an objection in principle to the sexual theory' (CW10.1034n).

In his writings, which at that time were openly advocating the Freudian approach, he displayed a noticeable embarrassment when speaking of the sexual theory and often hedged it round with qualifications and reservations. Thus, to give one example, in an article published in 1908 he wrote that 'Freud's conception of sexuality is uncommonly wide. . . . When [he] speaks of sexuality it must not be understood merely as the sexual instinct' (CW4.49). But it was precisely this rather open-ended construal of sexuality by Jung, and his wish to define the libido more broadly, which led to the bitterest recriminations between them in the final stages of their correspondence five years later. Freud accused Jung of seeking to water down his theories for the sake of making them palatable to the public, but it does not seem to have occurred to him that Jung simply could not in all conscience defend a theory in which he did not wholeheartedly believe. One must conjecture that, despite the growing chasm between them on this central issue, their need for each other, personal as well as professional, was enough for a while to enable them to keep their theoretical differences in check.

Part of the legend which I am concerned to question here has it that the direction of influence between the two was all one-way – from Freud to Jung. There is something in this. Yet in the crucial area of mythology it is clear that Jung took the lead, and indeed, in a rare moment of generosity towards his erstwhile colleague, Freud admitted that Jung was the first to draw attention to the striking similarity between the disordered fantasies of sufferers from schizophrenia and the myth of primitive peoples. It was in 1909 that Jung first disclosed his interest in the history of religion and mythology, declaring in a letter to Freud that 'mythology has got me in his grip', and urging his friend and colleague to 'cast a beam of light in that direction'. Freud's initial response was cool, and he warned Jung, prophetically as it turned out, that if he persisted he would be accused of 'mysticism', but he quickly warmed to the idea and wrote to Jung of his 'delight' that he was 'going into mythology' (McGuire, 1988, p.260). It is true that Freud had already recognized the relevance of mythology to psychoanalytic investigation, but the letters indicate that it was Jung who was more acutely aware of the links between ancient myth and the modern psyche, who goaded him on to a deeper interest in the subject, and stimulated a competitive spirit between them.

Jung's commitment and interest was always the greater of the two, and his own first major work on the subject, *Wandlungen und Symbole der Libido*, later translated as *Symbols of Transformation*, appeared in 1911; Freud's first significant contribution to this field, *Totem and Taboo*, appeared one year later. Jung's marginal victory in the competition matters less than the fact that right from the start his theoretical standpoint was quite distinctive. Freud saw myth as centring on 'the same nuclear complex as the neurosis', a view which he expressed in 1909 and which was fully developed in *The Future of an Illusion* (1927) in which he propounded the view that religion is a universal obsessional neurosis. After some initial hesitation, Jung moved in a quite different direction, namely towards the view that myth and religion arise from essentially healthy and positive functions of the psyche and are not necessarily connected with either sexual or neurotic impulses. Furthermore he suggested that myth-making is a normal psychological function which links the modern individual with ancient and primitive cultures. Jung was fully aware that he was elaborating a quite distinctive conception of the unconscious, and that he was moving sharply away from Freud's position, and indeed it was over this, as much as the question of sexuality, that they finally became estranged.

Jung's exploration of what might be called the archaic roots of the psyche through his study of mythology is indicative of an early difference between them on the crucial question of the nature of the unconscious. Freud tended to see the unconscious as a kind of repository for undesirable mental garbage and held that the individual unconscious was largely the product of the repression of sexual desires in early childhood. From about 1909 onwards, namely at the height of their friendship and collaboration, Jung began to construct a quite different view. According to Jung the divergence between them was precipitated by a dream he had when crossing the Atlantic with Freud on their joint visit to the USA. In this dream Jung imagined himself exploring a house from the top downwards, and as he descended he seemed to be going back in time, until he reached what seemed like a primitive cave where he found two disintegrating human skulls. The two men had adopted the habit of analysing each other's dreams during the voyage, and Freud interpreted the dream as a repressed death wish. For Jung, on the other hand, it suggested that the psyche has an historical structure, like a series of archaeological layers, in which consciousness is underpinned by unconscious psychic levels that reach back into the past of the human race itself. This view owed little to Freud, though it is worth noting that at about the same time the latter was speculating that the Oedipus complex had its origins in some primal prehistoric event.

The intellectual origins of Jung's conception of the unconscious lay rather, as we shall see in more detail later, with the German Romantic philosophers, in particular with the ideas of Schelling, Schopenhauer and Eduard von Hartmann, which had captured his youthful imagination in his sojourns in his father's study, and also with Goethe for whom he had a lifelong reverence. The association of Jung with these German thinkers might reinforce the impression in some peoples' minds that he was a rather backward-looking figure, another world-weary despiser of rationalism and progress, and that his reaction against Freud was really a reaction against the rigour and discipline of science. This would be a mistake, for while he certainly reacted against Freud's scientism, and explicitly rejected his reductionist approach, he was in many ways closer to the ethos of twentieth century science than was Freud. In fact one might go so far as to suggest that, whereas Freud remained an adherent of the Enlightenment, and accepted unquestioningly the nineteenth century view of science, Jung's outlook was more in tune with the critical reflectiveness and conceptual openness of the sciences of our own time. As a friend of Albert Einstein and of Wolfgang Pauli (a major figure in the development of quantum theory), and as an early admirer of Karl Popper (see Brome, 1980, p.14), he was not only in touch with the revolutions taking place in physics in his lifetime, but was also sensitive to the implications these had for our understanding of the very nature and method of the sciences.

On the question of methodology he clearly differentiated himself from Freud subsequent to their rupture. But sharp differences emerged quite early on. By 1906 Freud had become convinced that he had established his psychoanalytic theories on a firm scientific basis; indeed a couple of years later he was to characterize his theory of infantile sexuality to Jung as 'a dogma . . . an unshakeable bulwark' against what he described as the black tide of occultism (MDR, p.173). Jung appears to have been deeply shocked by this. His own approach to theory, whether his own or Freud's, was much more conjectural and pragmatic. Thus, writing in 1906 he said that in his personal opinion 'Freud's psychoanalysis is only one of several possible therapies', and appeared content with very modest claims such as that '[It] has never yet been proved that Freud's theory of hysteria is erroneous in all cases'. He adopted a similar tone with regard to his own work of that period, and in the epilogue to his book on dementia praecox he wrote: 'I do not imagine that I have offered anything conclusive in this [book]; this whole field is much too broad and at present much too obscure for that', and went on to conclude that he had done little more than to 'start the ball rolling' (CW3.315–16). This might seem like conventional modesty on the part of someone at the bottom of the professional ladder, but in fact this cautious self-deprecating approach became a hallmark of all his mature writings. He always saw his work as subject to revision and reassessment, often speaking of it as a personal confession or a personal myth, and rejected the possibility that his thoughts might be fabricated into a system.

For the reasons offered in this chapter it is time that we stopped linking Freud and Jung in a symbiotic coupling, and ceased the practice, still evident in a number of recent publications, of referring to Jung as Freud's 'pupil'. Jung has for too long stood under the shadow of Freud, and his contribution to modern thought is too important to be viewed as a series of qualifying footnotes to the work of his older colleague. In order to begin to make this case plausible we will need to examine more closely Jung's distinctive method and approach, and to that task we turn in the next chapter.

# 2

# STYLE AND METHOD

> My work consists of a series of different approaches, or as one might call it a circumambulation of unknown factors.
>
> (C.G. Jung)

What kind of thinker was Jung? His narrow classification as a lapsed disciple of Freud, or as a mystic, or simply as a psychologist, has often tended to blur and obscure this question, and if we are adequately to comprehend the scope of his contribution to modern thought we must confront it before proceeding to elaborate his ideas in detail.

We must first of all recognize that there were many Jungs. I mean this in several senses. The first is that Jung himself tacked and turned and modified his views throughout his long life, and it would simply be an error of hindsight to reconstruct his whole thought as a self-consistent, monolithic whole. There were certainly themes and threads which can be traced throughout his long career, and there was no major *volte-face* or change of direction in his thought, but at the same time there were growth and development as well as periodic innovations, new enthusiasms, and fresh insights. The fact that he persisted in re-editing his own earlier work throughout his life indicates that he saw it as an ever-developing process rather than as a finished and perfected whole.

The second sense concerns the complexity of Jung's own character. From an early age he saw himself as two distinct personalities, the one rational, conventional, everyday, the other close to nature, to dreams, to the unconscious (see MDR, pp.61–2). In trying to understand Jung, we need to take seriously this fact about him. Like Kierkegaard, the great nineteenth century Danish philosopher who addressed his public through a variety of carefully contrived pseudonyms, he speaks to us not with just two but with many voices, with the voice of the philosopher, the psychologist, the scientist, the theologian, the mythologist, the seer. We need to be aware in Jung of a multi-layering of discourse, and not seek to reduce him to a single layer that conforms to our own predilections, for, as he himself expressed it, 'Everything I say is double-bottomed' (quoted in von Franz, 1975, p. 4). This is not just an irritating accidental fact about his style of writing, but, as we shall see shortly, is central to his thinking.

A further factor relates to my own approach which is essentially *hermeneutical*. Hermeneutics is the art of interpreting texts, and what I mean by using the term in this context is, to put it simply, that Jung himself is a text which requires interpretation. And as with any text, Jung is susceptible to many different renderings and meanings, depending on the point of view and assumptions of the interpreter. According to the philosophical hermeneutics of Gadamer (1979), it is a mistake to treat an author as if he or she were a kind of physical phenomenon concerning which it is possible to construct a generally agreed theoretical explanation, or a final definitive meaning. Texts, authors, human beings, works of art, they can all be approached and understood only from a particular relative historical standpoint, from within a certain conceptual framework, and by recognizing their own relative historical condition. We can engage in a conversation with them, learn from and be illuminated by them. But constantly we must be aware that our view of them is shaped from the standpoint of our own prejudices and preconceptions; we can become aware of these, but we cannot expunge them. The horizon of my understanding, to use a typical hermeneutical metaphor, may overlap with another's, but I can never completely abandon my own outlook and view the world from inside another's.

Furthermore Jung – my 'text' – is for me, not a being with whom I am acquainted, but a set of writings that I must read and interpret. He – whatever 'he' is – is mediated to me through language, in this case translated from the (mostly) original German into English, and hence in talking about 'Jung's thought' I am talking, not about some Jungian essence, but about a recovered and reconstructed Jung. There can, therefore, be no single authentic Jung awaiting discolosure, any more than there can be a single authentic rendering of a Haydn symphony. We shall see again that this observation, though of general validity when dealing with the ideas of an historical thinker, is of especial relevance in the case of Jung.

For these reasons, the 'search' expressed in the title of this book is my, the author's, own personal search, and the 'Jung' thereby discovered is shaped by the assumptions and questions with which I have approached his writings.

There have, though, been many attempts to characterize Jung in univocal terms, to docket and pigeonhole him. Some regard him as a mystic who has simply abandoned the traditions of Western rationalism and returned to some ancient form of Gnosticism, whether Eastern or Western, or a combination of both (see Hoeller, 1982, p.xxi, and Buber, 1953). Some regard him as a modern prophet, a latter-day seer or magician (see Wilson, 1984, p.8f). Others have construed his work as having a place, albeit a somewhat unorthodox one, within the tradition of Christian theology (see Stein, 1985, p.18, and White, 1952). Still others have seen in Jung the self-appointed founder of a new post-Christian religion centred on the self and psyche (see Edinger, 1979, and Stern, 1976). Finally there is the view that Jung's work can best be understood as that of an empirical scientist (see Fordham, 1958, and Hostie, 1957).

I find myself in agreement with Homans who has argued that Jung has been ill-served by what he calls 'specialist appropriation', namely the tendency on the part of scholars to appropriate Jung to their own specialism (1979, p.16). Such views as the above are not completely mistaken, for they each succeed in illuminating one of the various dimensions of his work, one of the aspects of his complex personality, one textual perspective. But what they fail to grasp is the fundamentally *dialectical* nature of Jung's thinking. The term 'dialectic' is usually associated with Hegel who used it as a somewhat rigid instrument with which to demonstrate the logical structure of the growth of consciousness and spirit. I use it here in its broader connotation to refer to someone who recognizes the partialness of any viewpoint and the partiality of any thinker – including him or herself. It implies that any theory or viewpoint must inevitably break down and give rise to an alternative viewpoint, and that no single theory or viewpoint can by itself adequately grasp any phenomenon. It may also refer, in its essential meaning, to a dialogue between two persons in which the position of one is successively modified by the responses of the other. In this latter sense Jung was very happy to use the term, and while explicitly rejecting any association with Hegel's attempt to build a dialectical system, he frequently referred to his own psychotherapeutic method as a 'dialectical' one (see for example CW16.1f).

Jung's thinking was dialectical in the sense that he himself viewed it as radically provisional, as ever open to further interpretation and further elaboration and amplification. I say 'radically' provisional, for there is a kind of provisionality which anticipates a final resolution some time in the future of all inadequacies and shortcomings. Jung, however, did not envisage this as a realistic possibility. His theories could be nothing other than provisional, for their subject matter – the human psyche – was essentially and intractably elusive. I believe it is necessary to take seriously his oft-repeated claim that he was 'not a Jungian' and to view him, not as propounding any doctrine or single viewpoint, but rather as engaging in a prolonged and complex series of experiments. These experiments were, of course, related to a particular discipline, namely psychology, and to a specific subject matter, namely the human psyche. And looked at overall they also tend to return to, and to adumbrate, certain distinctive attitudes and values. But we should not therefore try to distil from them a doctrine, a system, or a single unequivocal purpose. To do so would be quite contrary to the spirit, and indeed the stated intentions, of Jung's work.

Nevertheless we must face up to the fact that there is a commonly perceived problem with Jung's style of writing, and that this has sometimes obscured and distorted his reputation as a thinker. Not all his readers suffer from Charles Rycroft's 'constitutional defect of being incapable of understanding Jung's writings' (1972, p.ix), or would concur with Rieff's lamentation of 'downright unreadability' (1973, p.98). But even sympathetic commentators like Demaris Wehr describe him as 'shrouded in ambiguity', and suggest that the responsibility for popular misconceptions about Jung must be placed firmly at his door (1988, p.27). It was Freud, though, who first opened up the issue by unkindly describing his erstwhile colleague's views as 'obscure, unintelligible and confused' (Freud, 1914, p.121).

Such accusations are not entirely without foundation. Jung himself admitted that 'not everything I bring forth is written out of my head, but much of it comes from the heart also' (CW7.200), and while a powerful sense of urgency, commitment and polemic pervades his work, his style is often idiosyncratic and his meaning elusive. As his colleague Aniela Jaffé puts it: 'it cannot escape the attentive reader that the application of concepts and terminology is not always carried through consistently [and] occasional contradictions and obscurities arise' (1983, p.27), a comment which reflects Jung's own admission of the 'apparent carelessness and vagueness of my own concepts when it comes to systematic formulation' (CW18.1732).

The comparison with Freud is once again instructive here, for the immense gulf which separated the two men is nowhere more evident than in their respective methods of exposition, a point alluded to by Ricoeur who confesses that 'this firmness and vigour [of Freud's style] makes me prefer Freud to Jung. With Freud I know where I am and where I am going; with Jung everything risks being confused' (1970, p.176). Freud wrote with the limpid clarity of a man of the Enlightenment, in a style which befitted his aim to make psychoanalysis a science. Jung on the other hand wrote with all the struggle and passion of a Romantic, and the reader is often obliged to suffer along with him. The difference in style is, in effect, not just a personal one, but an expression of a difference of *Weltanschauung*, of the way in which each viewed and lived in the world.

A comparison with Nietzsche is equally instructive. From the turn of this century, and even earlier, Nietzsche's works were widely read and his ideas were beginning to have an impact on the broad educated public. But his reception amongst philosophers and scholars has proved more problematic – at any rate until relatively recently. His wayward and idiosyncratic style for long irritated, even outraged, scholars who refused to take him seriously and assigned him to the margins of intellectual life. His ideas were seen to be brilliant but ill thought-out and unsystematic, frequently contradictory, poetry at best. His seeming lack of philosophical seriousness, his terminal lapse into madness, and his posthumous association with the Nazis, all conspired to exclude him from the debates and syllabuses of the academies.

All that has now changed. Following the pioneering work of Walter Kaufmann (1956), a whole new generation of scholars and writers during the past twenty years or so has been busy rewriting Nietzsche's intellectual obituary. His supposed affinity with Nazi attitudes and the slur of anti-semitism have been wiped off the record. His image of the *Übermensch*, often in the past misleadingly translated as 'superman', and seen as his most unpalatable creation, has been reinterpreted in terms of more acceptable psychological notions such as 'self-overcoming' and 'self-actualization'. His ideas are seen by many as the most radical critique of the underlying assumptions of Western thought and philosophy, and his wayward style as a supreme example of intellectual and personal honesty. In all these ways his path back to 'respectability' has been smoothed, and his ideas have come to be seen to be, if not quite harmless, at any rate an important contribution to some of the central debates of our times. In a recent collection of authoritative essays on Nietzsche he is described by the editor as 'one of the prodigious thinkers of the modern age . . . one of the underlying figures of our intellectual epoch . . . a model for the tasks and decisions of the present epoch' (Allison, 1985, p.ix).

Jung's reputation has suffered in a similar way, and for similar reasons: a prolix and unsystematic style, a lack of clarity and coherence, and a supposed anti-semitic and pro-Nazi attitude. The latter accusations, which are discussed in more detail in Chapter 10 below, have now been conclusively rebutted, and as with the similar accusations against Nietzsche will undoubtedly disappear from the agenda.

But does Jung's avoidance of system and his tendency towards unclarity mean that everything thereby risks falling into confusion in the way that Ricoeur suggests? Does the confusing style betray a confused thinker? Is there more to his thought than a jumble of brilliant insights that have simply failed to cohere? The answer to this question will become clearer if we make use of a distinction, first formulated by Nocolai Hartmann in 1936, between *system thinkers* on the one hand and *problem thinkers* on the other (referred to in Kaufmann, 1956, p.68.)

In the West we have less difficulty with the system thinkers. These can be identified as the ones who attempt, or appear to attempt, to construct a complete edifice of thought in which all the various parts are made to cohere in a logically consistent whole. Such thinkers appeal and appear worthy of study because they seem to give us answers which are both clear and relate one with another in a consistent way. A model sometimes used in such cases is that of an axiomatic system, first conceived by the Greek geometer Euclid who, in his *Elements*, sought to systematize geometry by establishing a set of foundational definitions and axioms from which all other geometrical propositions could be proved. As with a French formal garden, we get a clear picture of the shape of the land, of how we might move around within it, of which moves are possible and which not, of where the internal and external boundaries lie. I would place into this category thinkers like Aristotle, Aquinas, Spinoza, Kant, Hegel and the early Wittgenstein.

By contrast with this category there are the problem thinkers, namely those who, while possibly seeking to elaborate an overall viewpoint, nevertheless put into play a variety of subordinate and sometimes mutually contradictory notions, and who seek to encourage open-ended exploration rather than to close off possibilities. Unlike the system thinker, who likes to reach clear and definitive solutions, the problem thinker is more interested in experimenting with different ideas and in exploring different routes through a problem than in reaching a solution, and is often more fascinated with the process of searching than with any final outcome. Here the analogy might be with an English landscape garden which, though it has an overall shape, and is indeed carefully planned, does not seek to clarify every detail and relationship but allows through ill-defined boundaries the possibility of change and growth, and of an endless variety of perspectives, opens up the possibility of surprises, and in the end leaves many things tantalizingly but deliberately obscure. In this category we could locate Plato, Kierkegaard, Nietzsche, the later Wittgenstein – and Jung.

In the first place we need to reiterate Jung's own explicit rejection of any claim to be either a philosopher or a system-builder. Like Nietzsche ('the will to a system is a lack of integrity') (1968, p.25), he felt a strong disinclination to construct a systematic account of his thought, partly due to personal antipathy towards this mode of thinking, but also because he believed that the very complexity of the psyche precluded any such enterprise, for 'the more deeply we penetrate the nature of the psyche, the more the conviction grows upon us that the diversity, the multi-dimensionality of human nature requires the greatest variety of standpoints and methods' (CW16.11).

Towards the end of his life he felt the need to resist the demand made on him by some of his associates to provide a comprehensive account of his thought. This was not a matter of mere personal whim but reflected a deep opposition to such an enterprise which could give support to the mistaken opinion 'that my researches constitute a doctrinal system', and, as he put it, 'slip all too easily into a dogmatic style which is wholly inappropriate to my views' (CW18.1122). At one time he saw himself as doing little more than 'carrying further certain problems and lines of investigation that had been the concern of those thinkers of the past to whom he felt a particular inner connection' (Progoff, 1953, p.xiv), and at another he remarked that everything he did was 'pioneer work which has still to be followed by a real laying of foundations' (*Letters I*, pp.231–2). And in words that have a Nietzschean ring, he made it clear in a conversation with Progoff that 'I am not a Jungian and I never could be' (p.xv).

But despite this refusal to construct a system, there is, in his case as in Nietzsche's, a coherence and an overall unity of conception and direction which remained constant from about 1920 onwards, and which can be traced right back to the beginning of his professional career in 1900. This unity in his thinking does not arise from any sequential logical structure whereby we can follow his thought from step to step; this form of thinking, which corresponds to the category of system thinking, was alien to Jung's whole mentality. But the alternative is not randomness or mysticism, as various critics have suggested. A useful way of looking at this would be to see Jung's writing as analogous to a painting which invites the reader to move back and forth over an idea or set of ideas in the way that the eye moves back and forward over a picture, and has the effect of building up a general viewpoint rather than a logical structure. An analogy might also be drawn with Nietzsche's aphoristic style, and also with Wittgenstein who in his later work offered, not a sequential argument, but a seemingly random parade of images, stories and analogies.

This method is very similar to the process of *amplification* which Jung developed as a technique for interpreting the images and dreams of patients. In contrast with Freud's method of free association, which encouraged the patient to follow the train of thought wherever it led, and which was aimed at revealing some hidden meaning behind the thought, Jung's method required the patient to concentrate on the image or thought in question and to explore its inner possibilities by building up a series of closely linked images and symbols. It involved, as he put it, 'a careful and conscious illumination of interconnected associations objectively grouped round particular images' (CW16.319), a process which is as much one of creation as of discovery.

His own writing is like this in so far as it takes a nuclear idea and amplifies it, allows it to grow and to develop, often in what are initially unpredictable ways, always full of surprises, yet always related to the initial image. In his clinical practice Jung encouraged his patients to explore mythic, historical and cultural analogies and correspondences with their images or dreams, thereby embedding the latter in a symbolic matrix. The aim was always to illuminate the central psychic core, or 'complex' as he called it, by relating it to a web of interconnected meanings that are expressed through a variety of symbolic media.

Similarly in his writings we find, not a sequential logic, but an organic logic which 'circumambulates', as he put it, a central idea which is thereby enriched and illuminated from the store of mankind's cultural and intellectual artefacts. As Hillman suggests, the method of amplification 'is rather like the methods of the humanities and the arts. By revolving round the matter under surveillance, one amplifies a problem exhaustively', an activity which 'is like a prolonged meditation, or variation on a theme of music' (1972, p.31n).

This organic mode of thinking, in which ideas build up radially from a central image or insight, gives a much more important role to the imagination than is typical in linear or systemic thinking. The process of amplification does not just mean the intellectual activity of making conceptual connections, but involves the capacity to see things in their totality, to make new interpretations, and above all to create symbols whose meaning can never be made fully explicit. It is important, therefore, to see that Jung was an *imaginative* thinker, one who thought, primarily, in images rather than words, whose typical mode of reflection was symbolic rather than verbal, and whose typical approach to an issue was intuitive rather than logical. The role of imagination in thinking, and indeed in psychic life in general, was something upon which Jung placed great emphasis. He believed that modern Western culture woefully undervalued it, along with its subordination of symbolism and myth to the power of rational understanding. Imagination, he wrote, 'is present everywhere, it is tabooed and dreaded, so that it even appears to be a risky experiment or a questionable adventure to entrust oneself to the uncertain path that leads into the depths of the unconscious' (MDR, p.213).

Furthermore, as he pointed out, imagination and intuition are not the exclusive province of poets and artists but 'are in fact equally vital in all the higher grades of science [where they] play a role which supplements that of the "rational" intellect', an observation which, he believed, applies especially to physics (MS, p.82). This observation is particularly significant in view of the weight that has been given in recent years by philosophers of science to the role of non-rational factors, such as imagination and intuition, in the process of scientific discovery.

It would be a mistake to suppose that Jung believed that the intellect could somehow be dispensed with and be replaced by the seductive wiles of the irrational. Despite the accusations of hostile critics, Jung was in no sense an irrationalist, for he had a profound respect for the importance of intellect and the need for hard logic, and his aim was not to destroy or downgrade the latter, but to achieve some sort of balance between over-exalted intellect and tabooed imagination. Thus while 'imagination and intuition are vital to our understanding', and provide the seed-bed of discovery and invention, they do not give a complete account of knowledge. Philosophers of science nowadays make a distinction between the 'context of discovery' and the 'context of justification'. Thus, to take a familiar example, the insight into universal gravitation which inspired Newton as he sat in his garden at Woolsthorpe watching the apples fall needed the hard intellectual work of the *Principia* in order to transform it into a scientific law. Jung's own 'context of discovery' was the period of 'confrontation with the unconscious' which followed his break with Freud when powerful images and thoughts flooded in on him, and it required the mature reflection of a lifetime to transform the insights of this period into some sort of psychological theory. Intuition and imagination, then, though necessary, are not sufficient for knowledge, as he makes clear in the following passage written in his last years:

> The safe basis of real intellectual knowledge and moral understanding gets lost if one is content with the vague satisfaction of having understood by 'hunch'. One can explain and know only if one has reduced intuitions to an exact knowledge of facts and their logical connections.
>
> (MS, p.82)

This point has important bearing on those critics of Jung, such as Philip Rieff, who are inclined to dismiss him as being more a religious seer than a scientist. 'Jung's was a language of faith', Rieff claims, 'revelatory, and therefore beyond the danger of being invalidated by argument or contradicted by experience', and concludes that 'Jung's theory amounts at once to a private religion and an anti-science' (1973, pp.97–8). While it may be the case that Jung, like many great scientists, made his important discoveries in a context that transcends logic, his life was devoted to the hard intellectual work of testing out these discoveries through clinical and historical investigation.

The characterization of Jung as an imaginative and intuitive thinker arises, inevitably, from the primacy of personal experience in his own intellectual formation and the extraordinary intensity of imagery and fantasy which he experienced at various crucial periods in his life. This led him to give much greater emphasis in his thought and writings to experience rather than theory, and to reiterate his empirical at the expense of his philosophical credentials. But the matter goes much deeper than this, for in addition to his own experiential approach, driven by a rich inner fantasy life, he was convinced that any knowledge of the psyche must be rooted in personal experience. He stood firmly against the view that psychology would one day become a science on the model of the physical sciences because, unlike the natural sciences, at any rate as traditionally conceived, psychology had as its subject matter the very being attempting to carry out the investigation, and hence it is impossible to eradicate the subjective element. 'Our way of looking at things is conditioned by what we are. . . . Every psychology', he argued, 'has the character of a subjective confession, my own included'. Indeed he was convinced that *all* human knowledge is tied to the individual perspective of the knowing subject, who in turn is locked into a network of culturally and historically conditioned structures. 'I know well enough', he went on, 'that every word I utter carries with it something of myself – of my special and unique self with its peculiar history and its own particular world. Even when I deal with empirical data, I am necessarily speaking about myself' (MM, pp.134–8), a view in harmony with Nietzsche's claim in *Beyond Good and Evil* that 'every great philosophy . . . [is] the personal confession of its originator, a type of involuntary and unawares memoirs' (1973, para.6).

The emphasis on the unsystematic nature and subjective orientation of Jung's work has sometimes led critics to see it as, if not irrational, at any rate essentially unscientific, despite his own protestations to the contrary. Judged by the standards of nineteenth century philosophies of science the accusation of unscientific is perfectly justified. Prior to the great intellectual revolutions within and around science in our own century, science was viewed as a discipline qualitatively different from all others. Its method was seen as pre-eminently rational and objective, based on the canons of inductive logic, its outcome a set of laws which mirrored as nearly as possible the structure of nature itself. The history of science viewed at the turn of the century was a story of continuing and inevitable progress towards truth, and was seen in marked contrast to competing disciplines such as philosophy and theology with their evident inability to command the sort of universal consent which characterized the empirical sciences. In his widely translated best-selling book, *The Riddles of the Universe*, Ernst Haeckel spoke for the spirit of his age when he argued that in the century just ended – his book was published in 1901 – the natural sciences had brought about an expansion of knowledge unequalled in the history of mankind, and that the fundamental riddles of nature – matter, energy, life, etc. – had virtually been solved.

This was an attitude towards science which Freud inherited and perpetuated. Reared as he was in the positivistic philosophy of nineteenth century thinkers such as Comte, Helmholtz and Brücke, which identified empirical science as the supreme arbiter of knowledge and as the final outcome of historical progress, he tended to see science as a one-way ticket to truth and as the steady accumulation of universal objective knowledge.

Jung was a thinker much more in tune with the methodologies of the twentieth century, which have profoundly altered our conception of science. In many respects he anticipated attitudes towards science which, under the impact of such thinkers as Karl Popper, Michael Polanyi and Thomas Kuhn, have only in recent decades become widely accepted.

Science for him was not the final word about nature, its approach was only one of several competing methods, and its deliverances were by no means guaranteed eternal validity. He recognized the essentially contingent nature of all of knowledge, including that of even the most exact sciences, and argued that no claims to knowledge and no methods of observation can escape from the relativizing effects of the historical and individual perspectives of the investigator. The mind for him was no pure white light searching out truths from within the darkness, but was inescapably involved in the world it was attempting to grasp. Its function, as we shall see in the next chapter, was not to penetrate into the inner nature of things, but to construct models, convenient ways of getting around and making sense of the world, to provide, in Nietzsche's words, 'a regulative fiction'.

Jung's attunement to the revolutions taking place in physics during the early decades of this century had important implications for his own work, and are embodied in a vision summed up in the following remarks made in 1938:

> I would not be surprised if one day we saw a far-reaching agreement between the basic formulations of psychology and physics. I am convinced that if the two sciences pursue their goals with the utmost consistency and right into the ultimate depths of man they must hit upon a common formula.
>
> (*Letters I*, p.246)

Although he never acquired a technical understanding of the developments taking place in science (he had little knowledge of mathematics), he was suffiently close to them through his friendships with Albert Einstein and Wolfgang Pauli to grasp some of the wider epistemological implications of relativity and quantum physics. He realized, long before most philosophers had woken up to the fact, that the ambition enshrined in classical physics for the construction of a single, objective and unambiguous picture of the world could no longer be realized. The new physics offered such a bizarre and paradoxical view of reality that no single self-consistent set of concepts can be deemed to match it accurately. The value of quantum theory, at least according to the most widely accepted interpretation, lies not in any supposed 'fit' with reality but in the fact that it offers a mathematical model with which predictions can successfully be made. Furthermore the ambition of classical physics to offer an objective account of the world free from subjective influences and prejudices was further undermined by quantum theory in its view that the process of observation is itself part of the system to be observed; as David Bohm has put it: 'The primary emphasis is now on *undivided wholeness*, in which the observing instrument is not separable from what is observed' (1981, p.134, Bohm's emphasis).

The paradoxical nature of the models of reality offered by quantum physics encouraged Jung in his belief that the psyche should not necessarily be viewed in terms of traditional two-valued logic (it must be either *this* or *that* but not *both*), but could be seen as possessing apparently contradictory features. Physics has come to live with the fact that some of the fundamental processes of the subatomic world had to be described in terms of two apparently contradictory models, the one based on the concept of the wave, the other on the concept of the particle. Thus according to the complementarity principle of Niels Bohr, particles of light and matter and quanta of energy can be described both as waves and as particles, such descriptions being internally consistent but mutually incompatible.

Jung sought to illuminate his own studies in the light of this, arguing that 'modern physics has shown the psychologist that it can cope with an apparent *contradictio in adiecto*' (CW8.381). The old common sense picture of the world associated with Newton and the idea of a clockwork universe has given way to one in which, not only is uncertainty intrinsic to nature at the subatomic level, but our very attempts to understand it lead to what Paul Davies has characterized as 'like something from *Alice in Wonderland*' (1982, p.9), a world in which 'intuition deserts us, and seemingly absurd or miraculous events can occur' (p.75). Our attempts to understand the human psyche, as with the physical world, inevitably lead us into making use of conceptual models which often seem bizarre and paradoxical and which run quite counter to common sense. 'The language I speak', wrote Jung, 'must be ambiguous, must have two meanings in order to do justice to the dual aspects of our psychic nature' (*Letters II*, p.70).

In examining the nature of the psyche Jung concluded that the image of the mind as subject to rational decision and in the control of a conscious ego must necessarily be supplemented by another and quite different account in terms of unconscious processes which are not only opaque to consciousness but appear to operate in accordance with quite different principles. The study of the psyche takes us simultaneously in two opposing and seemingly mutually contradictory directions, the one towards the freedom of spirit, the other towards the organic world of instinct: 'Just as, in its lower reaches, the psyche loses itself in the organic-material substrate, so in its upper reaches it resolves itself into a "spiritual" form about which we know as little as we do about the functional basis of instinct' (CW8.380). A complete account of the psyche, therefore, as of the atom, seems inevitably to lead to paradox and to a puzzling diversity of explanatory models, from which our traditional methodologies afford us no escape.

Furthermore the inextricability of observer and observed, which is a corollary of quantum theory, confirmed Jung in his belief that no science, least of all psychology, can discount human subjectivity. He clearly had this in mind when he wrote that between 'the conscious and the unconscious there is a kind of "uncertainty relationship", because the observer is inseparable from the observed and always disturbs it by the act of observation' (CW9ii.355).

No model of the psyche, then, can be freed from the subjective influences of its creator. Whereas under the old dispensation the laws of nature were believed to have been arrived at by a method which guaranteed their objectivity and freedom from subjective bias, the new physics has taught us that the observer inevitably influences the processes being investigated; 'the external world', as Davies puts it, 'is intimately bound up with our perception of the world – our presence as conscious observers', a view which taken to its extreme 'implies that the universe only achieves a concrete existence as a result of this perception' (1982, pp.12–13).

Writing of the new developments in physics which led to this view, Jung commented on 'the uncontrollable effects the observer has upon the system observed, the result being that reality forfeits something of its objective character and that a subjective element attaches to the physicist's picture of the world', such an outcome having 'a noteworthy correspondence in psychology' (CW8.438–9). Indeed the situation is much more crucial in the case of the human psyche, for whereas in observing the physical world we are observing something which, in an obvious sense, is external to us, in the case of the psyche the object of investigation is identical with the very person investigating it. In such a case there is no independent or neutral standpoint from which we can carry out our investigations, no 'Archimedian point', to use a favourite image of Jung's, to act as a firm and independent point of reference from which to study the psyche.

This emphasis on the role of the subject, his recognition that there is no pure unmediated access to the world, and his belief that all knowledge must be understood in relation to a particular perspective, inevitably led Jung to adopt a relativistic standpoint with regard to knowledge, to the view that there had been a 'shift in man's consciousness' in the modern age which has rendered obsolete any acceptance of absolute or dogmatic truth. As far as he was concerned the best that could be said of a theory or judgement was that it was *useful*. Philosophy itself is no exception for it 'still has to learn that it is *made by human beings* and depends to an alarming degree on their psychic constitution' (*Letters I*, p.331, Jung's emphasis). This is the case even with science for 'Nothing is more vulnerable and ephemeral than scientific theories which are mere tools and not everlasting truths' (CW8.697). This relativistic attitude, which will be discussed more fully in subsequent chapters, should help to make sense of some of the peculiarities of Jung's style and method. The variety of seemingly contradictory approaches he adopted, his teasingly elusive method of 'circumambulation', and his dialectical sinuosity, these can be seen not just as quirks of a confused mind and an overheated imagination, but as appropriate modes of discourse for someone who sees the world, not as a monochromatic whole, but as a kaleidoscope of colours arising from our very manner of seeing and being-in the world.

But in spite of all this, and accepting that there are some affinities between Jung's approach and that of twentieth century science, there are still disquieted voices who will say that the problem with Jung is not his wayward style, nor even the fact that as a 'problem thinker' he permitted himself a rather open-ended conception of knowledge and truth, but that he permitted himself to fall into all kinds of metaphysical and mystical obscurities. For all its rejection of traditional epistemological assumptions, modern science has not opened the floodgates to any and every speculation. Jung on the contrary appears to many to have permitted himself the luxury of adopting mystical and metaphysical ideas from all kinds of sources, Eastern and Western, Christian and pagan, while at the same time claiming the status of scientist. This, they would claim, is evidence of the profoundest confusion. In order to deal with this question we will need to investigate more fully the philosophical assumptions underlying Jung's thinking, and it is to this that we turn our attention in the next chapter.

# 3

# PHILOSOPHICAL FOUNDATIONS

> It is unprofitable to speculate about things we cannot know. I therefore refrain from making assertions that go beyond the bounds of science.
>
> (C.G. Jung)

An investigation of the philosophical assumptions underlying Jung's work takes us back to the great eighteenth century philosopher, Immanuel Kant (1724–1804). Jung had in his earliest days, prior to medical school, been deeply impressed with the philosophy of Kant, and the latter's influence pervades his life's work, to the extent that in 1941 he was able to claim that 'epistemologically I take my stand on Kant' (*Letters I*, p.294).

Responding to the sceptical challenge of David Hume (1711–76), Kant accepted that the world as it is in itself cannot be known. Our claims to knowledge are necessarily limited by the way things appear to our five senses. Nevertheless, according to Kant this should not lead to the sceptical subjectivism of Hume whereby we seem to be locked in our own private worlds, for our ways of perceiving the world are not individual but are structured by forms of perception and thought which are universally true for all rational beings. This structure includes our perception of a world of physical entities causally related within the dimensions of space and time. To understand the world in this way is, for a rational being, a necessary condition of any knowledge whatsoever, and hence not a mere contingency or accident of nature. What we cannot know is whether this structure corresponds to the structure of the world as it is independently of our perception of it. Objective knowledge, therefore, is to be understood, not as correspondence between phenomena (how things appear to us) and reality (how things are independently of the way things appear to us), for we can never have access to one side of this equation, but rather as the ordering of our perceptions in terms of universal rules which are necessarily built into the minds of all knowers. This is the heart of what Kant called his 'Copernican Revolution' which, like the earlier cosmological episode, shifted the fundamental viewpoint from which the world is comprehended, for now we seem, to use Kant's word, more like 'legislators' to the world than passive recipients of its messages.

The starting point for Jung was not altogether different from that of Hume and Kant, namely the belief that the mind itself, rather than the world beyond the mind, is the most immediate object of awareness, and that everything we claim to know is in some sense derived therefrom. Thus he typically argued that 'there is, in a certain sense, nothing that is directly experienced except the mind itself. Everything is mediated through the mind, translated, filtered, allegorized, twisted, even falsified by it' (CW8.623). This does not mean that we have direct access to mind in its innermost nature; Jung, like Kant, consistently remained agnostic on this point. Rather he meant that the mind's *contents* were the objects of direct awareness, that the only things which we directly experience 'are the contents of consciousness' (CW8.284).

> All that I experience is psychic . . . My sense-impressions . . . are psychic images, and these alone are my immediate objects of experience. . . . We are in all truth so enclosed by psychic images that we cannot penetrate to the essence of things external to ourselves. All our knowledge is conditioned by the psyche which, because it alone is immediate, is superlatively real.
>
> (MM, pp.219–20)

But what is the nature of these psychic contents? For Jung the answer is that we 'immediately live only in a world of images' (ibid.), where by 'images' he meant, not just mental pictures, but any kind of conscious content, anything of which the mind is aware. To all intents and purposes our world is constituted by these images, and 'to the extent that the world does not assume the form of psychic images, it is virtually non-existent' (CW11.769).

There is much room for philosophical confusion here, and recent discussions in the philosophy of mind, especially after Ryle and Wittgenstein, have shown that the whole language of mental images and contents is fraught with ambiguity. Jung, however, did not have the benefit of these developments and stuck to what now seems the rather dated notion that there is some kind of chasm between mental contents and physical objects, and hence that the very existence of the latter depends on a questionable inference from the known to the unknown.

How, then, on these premises is it possible to establish the existence of a world external to our mental images? Is Jung committed to a form of subjective idealism or of solipsism, namely to the belief that the only things which can be known are the contents of one's own mind? Some commentators have suggested that Jung's affinity with the Kantian philosophical tradition not only brought him 'dangerously close to the brink of solipsism' (Stevens, 1982, p.58), but also reinforced his own predisposition towards narcissistic absorption in 'the endless proliferation of his own consciousness' (Homans, 1979, p.111).

Now, there is a sense in which Jung made no systematic attempt to tackle the epistemological issues thus posed, true to his stated refusal to engage in philosophy. One might say that solipsism was simply not an issue for him since, despite Homan's comment, it is evident from his autobiography that he felt unquestioningly the impact of a world external to him, and to question this would be to lapse into fruitless quibbling. Indeed he sometimes suggested that the existence of the external world, independent of our knowing minds, could not be demonstrated by rational argument, but is an assumption we make on purely pragmatic grounds. Nevertheless, it is possible to discern a more substantial line of thinking in this regard, however unsystematically worked out, which again corresponds at certain points to the thinking of Kant.

What, then, constituted for Jung objective knowledge, as opposed to subjective fantasy? Clearly not anything that takes us beyond the bounds of possible experience; here he was at one with Kant. However, from the impossibility of human reason legitimately going beyond experience, Kant did not conclude that objective knowledge is impossible. What characterizes such knowledge, and constitutes a necessary condition for its possibility, is the fact that it is organized and articulated in terms of *categories*, general, formal or structural concepts – such as substance, necessity and causality – which are not themselves derived from experience but exist *a priori* in the mind, and which constitute a set of rules governing the way we experience and understand the world. Without such a conceptual framework knowledge would be impossible and our experience of the world would comprise a random jumble of unconnected sensations. Furthermore, Kant argued, such a framework is not to be understood as a kind of biological or historical contingency or accident which could vary from one person or one epoch to another, but is rather a logically necessary condition of knowledge for all rational beings.

Jung also maintained that our individual experiences were set within a structure which was common to mankind and which thereby provided a criterion of objectivity. 'Living reality', he argued, 'is the product neither of the actual, objective behaviour of things nor of the formulated idea exclusively, but rather of the combination of both in the living psychological process' (CW6.77), an echo of Kant's famous remark that 'Thoughts without content are empty, perceptions without concepts are blind' (Kant, 1956, B75). Furthermore for Jung this structure is not a purely abstract or theoretical thing but an actual psychic process in which the role of the psyche is essentially one of active integration, a view which bears comparison with Kant's view that the very possibility of knowledge depends on the spontaneous synthesizing activity of the subject, that, in Kant's words, 'it must be possible for the "I think" to accompany all my representations' (Kant, 1956, B131).

But while for Kant the shared framework comprised abstract categories such as 'causation' and 'necessity', for Jung on the other hand it comprised in addition a much richer tapestry of mental dispositions which he called *archetypes*. A fuller account of the theory of archetypes will be given in Chapter 9, but for the moment it will suffice to point out that for Jung they represented the underlying structure of the psyche, a common inheritance of mankind composed of a network of formal, shaping elements, that predisposed us to think and experience and feel in certain determinate ways. It is true that these patterns are manifested in different ways in different cultures, but Jung's researches in mythology as well as his study of dreams led him to conclude that the archetypes represented an *a priori* psychic structure that was present, at least potentially, in every human being.

Jung explicitly related his own theory to that of Kant. 'Among [the] inherited psychic factors', he argued, 'there is a special class which is not confined either to family or to race. These are the universal dispositions of the mind . . . in accordance with which the mind organizes its contents', and he goes on to say that one could 'describe these forms as *categories* analogous to the logical categories which are always and everywhere present as the basic postulates of reason' (CW11.845, Jung's emphasis). Furthermore the archetypes, like the categories, do not extend the bounds of our knowledge but, in the words of Kant quoted by Jung, are 'of service to the understanding as a canon for its extended and consistent employment' (CW6.733, quoted from Kant's *Critique of Pure Reason*).

In another respect, too, Jung, while remaining fundamentally Kantian in his outlook, took a decisive step beyond him. Kant's standpoint was essentially *a*-historical: he viewed the categories as timeless, universal embodiments of reason-as-such. For Jung, as for Hegel and other successors to Kant during the Romantic period, human understanding had to be understood in historical terms. Kant, on the basis of his famous 'transcendental argument', claimed that the categories of the understanding are not merely contingent facts shaped by history, but have a kind of logical necessity: the principle of universal causation, for example, is not just a fact of nature, which might conceivably be otherwise, but a necessary condition for our understanding of nature. For Jung, on the other hand, the structure of consciousness was a precipitate of human evolution, a contingent fact of the human psyche, shaped over time, and related to its historical conditions. In other words, the archetypes are contingent facts of human history and human experience which, however deeply embedded in the human psyche, however ancient and rooted in history, might conceivably have been different had human history, biological as well as cultural, been different. Indeed in his later years Jung was emboldened to attack Kant at the very heart of his theory by arguing that the concepts of space, time, and causation embedded in Newtonian physics were not, as Kant had believed, universal *a priori* principles, but were the products of a human consciousness that changes and evolves with history. One of the consequences of this view is that for Jung different cultures may not share a single universal outlook or world-view but, to use a phrase from modern philosophy, understand the world *via* different conceptual frameworks.

Thus, while Jung clearly derived much of his philosophical inspiration from Kant, he cannot strictly speaking be thought of as a Kantian. It would in fact be more correct to describe him as a *Neo*-Kantian, and to place him in the line of thinkers, such as Windelband, Rickert and Dilthey, who revived, extended, and modified the great Enlightenment thinker's ideas in the subsequent age. The Neo-Kantian philosopher with whom Jung had most in common in the present context was perhaps his contemporary Ernst Cassirer (1874–1945), 'the philosophical counterpart' of Jungian psychology, as one commentator has put it (Avens, 1980, p.19). According to this great Jewish-German philosopher our experience of the world does not give us direct access to reality, and indeed in a special sense we do not experience the world at all, for reality is covered, as it were, with a veil of language, symbol and myth, and it is only through the mediation of these that knowledge is possible at all. Furthermore this veil is not static and timeless, but is itself the product of history and cultural evolution, so that each culture possesses a distinct symbolic structure which shapes both its perception of the world and its own unique identity. Thus Cassirer writes: 'man lives in a symbolic universe. Language, myth, religion, and art are parts of this universe. They are the varied threads which weave the symbolic net. . . . No longer can man confront reality immediately' (1962, p.25).

For Jung, as for Cassirer, the world of common, shared experience is not a world into which we have direct insight, or which contains truths waiting to be apprehended, but one in which we are incorporated by virtue of a shared symbolic language. Although Jung did not intend to offer anything like an epistemological theory, he consistently maintained that our world is shaped by our psychological predispositions, from which we cannot simply divest ourselves by an act of will: 'Whatever we touch or come into contact with immediately changes into a psychic content, so we are enclosed by a world of psychic images' (*Letters I*, p.255). Thus strictly speaking we are not locked into our own private *individual* worlds, but rather into the *common* world of the human psyche. This common world is shared by all members of our species by virtue of our commonly inherited archetypal endowment. We may of course still wonder whether the world outside that symbolic framework is 'really' matter, or 'really' spirit, or Platonic ideas, or energy, or whatever, but such speculations, according to Jung, are quite fruitless.

This, then, constitutes in broad outline the philosophical basis of Jung's thinking, the absolute presuppositions, often alluded to albeit never fully worked out, that underlay his psychological thinking. One of the corollaries of this way of thinking was for Jung, as for Kant, a scepticism with regard to metaphysics, or any claims to knowledge that transcend the limits of experience. Although Jung was not always consistent on this point and sometimes strayed into metaphysical territory, in the main he took the view that knowledge was limited within the bounds of human experience. In view of Jung's reputation as a mystic and dabbler in esoteric and occult forms of knowledge, we need to spell out this point in more detail.

'Every statement about the transcendent', he wrote, 'is to be avoided because it is only a laughable assumption on the part of the human mind unconscious of its limitations' (CW13.82). This applies to traditional philosophical questions such as the issue between materialism and idealism, for, he argued, materialism – the belief that matter is the fundamental constituent of reality – is as much a metaphysical belief as its seemingly more outlandish counterpart, idealism. Hence '[the] materialist is a metaphysician *malgré lui*' (CW11.763).[1]

But equally questions about God and the spirit world succumb to the same kind of analysis, for 'my aim as a psychologist is to dismiss without mercy the metaphysical claims of all esoteric teachings' (CW13.73). Contrary to some common misconceptions, therefore, Jung held a strictly agnostic view with regard to religious belief, maintaining that 'epistemological criticism proves the impossibility of knowing God' (CW8.625). It makes no difference that the idea of God (or the idea that we live in a material world, come to that) is firmly implanted in the human psyche, for 'the fact that metaphysical ideas exist and are believed in does nothing to prove the actual existence of the content, or the object they refer to' (CW9ii.65). Even if psychological investigation were to establish that the idea of God was impressed on the human psyche as a universal archetypal image, 'nothing positive or negative has thereby been asserted about the possible existence of God' (CW12.15).

But he was always careful not to confuse these matters with the question of the objective truth or falsity of religious beliefs, and sought to distance his own scientific discipline of psychology both from the realm of religious faith and from the realm of his own personal beliefs. Phenomenologically, he thought, it is impossible to distinguish between God as a transcendent being and God as an experience of the collective unconscious: 'We cannot tell whether God and the unconscious are two different entities. Both are borderline concepts for transcendental contents'. All we can establish empirically is that 'there is in the unconscious an archetype of wholeness', namely the God-image (AJ, p.177), and that therefore at the heart of the religious quest lies a need which is embedded in the psyche itself.

Some commentators have been worried that Jung himself often professed a personal belief in a transcendent reality of some form or other, and that these beliefs became increasingly intrusive in his later writings. Wilson goes so far as to suggest that the whole of his scientific work was something of a cover-up disguising his true metaphysical intentions (1984, p.8f). But an elementary distinction can surely be made between a person's publicly stated views on the one hand, put forward in the name of science and backed by evidence and argument, and on the other their personal and privately held beliefs. It is worth pointing out that Newton and Einstein also had strong personal beliefs of a metaphysical kind which, while explicitly excluded from their strictly scientific teachings, also had a tendency to intrude themselves on, and may even have helped to shape, their 'official' philosophies.

The same general line of argument is applied to psychological concepts. Jung maintained that the unconscious mind, like the 'transcendent', is knowable, not in itself, but only by its manifestations, i.e. in terms of observable phenomena. It was, he said, making use of a Kantian term, a 'boundary concept', which offers no insight into the hidden workings of nature, but merely points to the limits of what can be known. Thus the analyst has no insight into the unconscious over and above the words and images conveyed by the patient. We should not, he warned, 'labour under the illusion that we have now discovered the real nature of the unconscious processes, for we never succeed in getting further than the hypothetical "as if"' (CW7.272) (probably a reference to the work of the nineteenth-century Neo-Kantian philosopher, Vaihinger, who, in his book *The Philosophy of 'As If'*, (1924) argued that the Kantian categories had merely hypothetical and relative value: we perceive the world 'as if' it were in space and time). And as we shall see in a later chapter this argument applied equally to that supposedly mysterious concept, the *collective* unconscious, which is similarly a boundary concept to be understood in purely phenomenological or experiential terms.

In spite of these oft-repeated disclaimers, critics of Jung persist in accusing him of falling into all kinds of mystical and metaphysical obscurities, especially with regard to his notorious excursions into mystical and occultist traditions. He appeared to them to have permitted himself the luxury of adopting bizarre pre-scientific beliefs from all kinds of sources, Eastern and Western, Christian and pagan, while at the same time claiming the status of scientist. This, they would claim, is evidence of the profoundest confusion. Anthony Storr, for example, who is by no means a hostile critic, felt obliged to dismiss Jung's 'preoccupation with the occult, with his views on synchronicity, and the ghosts and poltergeist which throng the pages of his autobiography' (1973, p.117), in order to save Jung's reputation as an empiricist, and D. Bakan speaks for many when he claims that Jung 'arises from a clearly mystical tradition within Christianity' (1958, p.58).

It must now be evident that this sort of objection is mistaken. Jung certainly took the experiences and beliefs associated with metaphysical and religious systems seriously; indeed a large part of his writings is devoted to the study of themes from Christian theology, alchemy, astrology, Gnosticism, Taoism, and yoga, and he devoted many years of work and considerable scholastic skill to an understanding of these beliefs. But his approach to these systems of thought was always explicitly *phenomenological*, and he was always careful to leave on one side as irrelevant to his enterprise the truth-claims contained in them. That is, his interest in, say, Christian beliefs lay, not in the question of whether they were true or false, a matter on which he pronounced himself officially agnostic, but rather in the role that they played within the psychic life of the individual or the group. Thus at the start of a series of lectures on religion delivered in America in 1938 he made the following disclaimers:

> I approach psychological matters from a scientific and not from a philosophical standpoint. Inasmuch as religion has a very important psychological aspect, I deal with it from a purely empirical point of view, that is, I restrict myself to the observation of phenomena and I eschew any metaphysical or philosophical considerations.
>
> (CW11.2)

> My standpoint is exclusively phenomenological, that is, it is concerned with occurrences, events, experiences – in a word with facts. When psychology speaks, for example, of the motif of the virgin birth, it is only concerned with the fact that there is such an idea, but it is not concerned with the question whether such an idea is true or false in any other sense.
>
> (CW11.4)

The term 'phenomenology' began to enter his vocabulary in the 1930s, and is clearly an important one. What exactly did he mean by it? Negatively, as we have just seen, he meant that his psychology made no transcendent or metaphysical claims; in that sense it is a boundary concept that delimited his field of inquiry. 'Psychology cannot establish any metaphysical "truths", nor does it try to. It is concerned solely with the *phenomenology of the psyche*' (CW18.742, Jung's emphasis). On the positive side it is 'sheer experience' (CW18.1738), the direct awareness that an individual has of themselves and of the world prior to any theorizing. In this sense it is similar to Husserl's notion of *Erlebnis*, by which he meant the lived experience of the individual consciousness prior to any shaping by scientific or other theory (1958, pp.102–16), and we saw at the beginning of this chapter that for Jung 'the only things we experience immediately are the contents of consciousness' (CW8.284). A good example of Jung's phenomenological approach is to be found in his book *Psychological Types* which was essentially about the 'various attitudes the conscious mind might take towards the world' (MDR, p.233), and which sought to categorize the human personality, not in externally observable terms, but in terms of the various dispositions of human consciousness towards reality. Thus in a sense an 'introverted' person actually experiences the world differently from an 'extraverted' one, and the world of a 'thinking' type is in a sense different from the world of a 'feeling' type.

Jung was often uncritical of this notion of immediate experience and speaks as if the idea of a basic datum, untrammelled by theory, is self-evident, an assumption of Husserlian phenomenology that has received much unfavourable attention in recent years. This is brought out in remarks such as 'Facts are facts and contain no falsity. It is our judgement that introduces the element of deception' (CW18.1584), and 'the interpretation must guard against making use of any other viewpoints than those manifestly given by the content itself' (CW17.162). Moreover he criticized the Freudian theory of dream interpretation for being too theory-based, and appeared to hanker for a kind of pure phenomenology of the dream from which all theory has been expelled (see CW9i.112). On this view psychology can claim to be a pure study of psyche without any reference to theory, whether scientific or metaphysical.

At other times, however, he demonstrated considerable suspicion of the immediate deliverances of consciousness, and appeared to come close to recognizing what most recent philosophers of science have come to take for granted, namely that all experience, however 'basic', is in some sense 'theory-laden', that data and theory are mutually inextricable, and there is no meaningful way in which we can sharply distinguish between them. When dealing with the deliverances of consciousness, as expressed through the words and behaviour of patients, it is impossible, Jung realized, to detach the personal prejudices and assumptions of the observer – in this case the doctor or therapist, for 'our way of looking at things is conditioned by what we are' (MM, p.134). Assumptions are unavoidable. The apparently self-evident procedure of procuring factual evidence in the natural sciences ceases to be self evident when the psyche itself is the object of investigation, for 'in no field of experience is the eye for facts so myopic as in the psyche's perception and observation of itself. Nowhere do prejudices, misconceptions, value-judgements, idiosyncrasies, and projections trot themselves out more glibly and unashamedly' (CW17.60). For Jung this constituted one of the fundamental dilemmas of psychology, for in this field above all others the object to be investigated mirrors the investigator, and introduces, as was pointed out in the last chapter, an 'uncertainty relationship' between observer and observed.

One consequence of this is that, by contrast with Freud, Jung's methodology does not lay itself open to the charge that the evidence on which his theories are based lacks the objectivity and certainty that is to be expected in the natural sciences. Whereas Freud believed that, in the clinical setting in which patients' dreams and fantasies are analysed, something approximating to the rigour of experimental testing could be achieved, Jung suffered from no such illusion. Indeed he went even further and suggested that even in the physical sciences an element of uncertainty and subjectivity inevitably creeps into its observational data.

Whatever the uncertainties and distortions that inevitably arise in studying the phenomena of consciousness, these remained, Jung believed, strictly *empirical* in nature. He frequently reiterated the claim that he was first and foremost an empiricist, and throughout his life stood by the belief that his study of the psyche was not philosophy but an empirical science. He himself was reared in an empiricist tradition, and the early development of his theories while at the Burghölzli Hospital, especially those connected with the idea of autonomous complexes, were entirely based on empirical research, some of it involving experiments that would not be out of place in a modern psychology laboratory.

Nevertheless his use of the term, as with the parallel term 'phenomenology', requires some explanation, especially in view of the fact that the phrase 'empirical psychology' has acquired a meaning quite distant from that which Jung used in reference to his own studies. Historically the issue was a pressing one for him in the light of the cultural hegemony in his lifetime of positivism, with its commitment to a fundamental empiricism. In addition to this broader consideration, Jung was in general very wary of *a priori* theorizing. This attitude no doubt had its foundation in his own personality with its powerful orientation towards personal experience, but it is also evident in his rejection of Freud's sexual theory which he came to see as the unwarranted imposition of theory upon evidence, and in his insistence as a therapist on treating the individual case rather than in attempting to apply general theories indiscriminately.

When we come to examine his theory of archetypes in Part II we will observe two sorts of empirical evidence adduced in support of the theory. The first is clearly *phenomenological* in the sense just discussed, namely the sort of information provided by patients in recounting dreams, fantasies, and so forth. For Jung psychic data such as dreams were regarded as empirical facts in the same way that natural scientists regarded specimens and instrument readings. Such data are no doubt subject to a variety of distortions, but as I have suggested Jung was fully aware of this; such distortions represent a congenital defect which, though rendering psychology a very imperfect science, does not alter in principle its empirical credentials. The second sort of evidence is *cultural*, namely the publicly observable and recordable activities of groups of people expressed in the form of myth, religion, art and literature. Thus Jung's study of alchemy is essentially empirical in the unexceptionable sense that it is based on a study of records of a specific class of cultural activity. In this sense Jung's work is no more nor less empirical than the work of enthnologists, anthropologists, historians and sociologists, and indeed draws on work from all these specialisms.

However, despite his oft-affirmed devotion to the 'phenomena', his claim to the title of 'empiricist', and his conscious tendency to want to avoid theoretical abstractions – 'how difficult and thankless is the task of theory-building in psychology' (CW16.203) – Jung's writings do in fact display a marked inclination towards speculation and to the formulation of conjectures and hypotheses. It is important to see that this tendency in no way conflicted with his basic Kantian assumptions. In 1937 he noted that 'Although I have often been called a philosopher, I am an empiricist and adhere to the phenomenological standpoint'. But he immediately proceeded to qualify this remark in the following terms: 'I trust that it does not conflict with the principles of scientific empiricism if one occasionally makes certain reflections which go beyond a mere accumulation and classification of experience' (CW11.2), and elsewhere he remarked that 'science cannot exist without hypotheses' (CW10.1041). Thus his theory of archetypes, formulated shortly after his break with Freud, was by no means a mere 'accumulation and classification of experience', but was put forward as a bold and speculative hypothesis designed to explain a wide range of phenomena. This speculative spirit became even more marked in the later years of his life, following the Second World War and a critical illness, most obviously in his theory of *synchronicity*, the hypothesis that in addition to the principle of mechanical causation it was necessary to postulate a principle to explain meaningful coincidences. But even here the aim was to offer, not some metaphysical insight, but rather an explanatory hypothesis to explain certain observable phenomena. It is true that he was not prepared to accept the constraints of a materialist world-view, and thus to explain everything in terms of matter and physical energy, but this world-view itself, as we saw, was for him a metaphysical assumption rather than an unchallengeable truth. Even his theory of *individuation*, which as we shall see in Chapter 12 goes beyond the domain of orthodox scientific psychology, can be described as metaphysical, not because it makes claims to knowledge of a transcendent kind, but because it deals in ends and purposes.

In this respect Jung's understanding of the scientific method was well in advance of his time; indeed he was, as Rychlak puts it, 'the most sophisticated of the classical analysts when it comes to issues of theory construction' (1984, p.34). The traditional view, that scientific progress takes place by the steady accumulation of factual evidence upon which a secure structure of laws is built by means of the logic of induction, has been challenged in recent years, most conspicuously by Popper. During Jung's lifetime only a few daring spirits such as Nietzsche, C.S. Pierce, and Ernst Mach felt able to attack the prevailing wisdom and to suggest that scientific discovery involves a speculative, creative, even an irrational, element, and that scientific theories are not so much copies of nature as projections onto it. Although Jung's ideas on this were by no means adequately worked out, his acquaintance with the twentieth century revolutions in physics led him to see that scientific knowledge was much more like an interpretation of or a perspective on the world, than a structure of logically attested truths, and that scientific theories are creations of the mind, not mirrors of the inner workings of nature.

This attitude to scientific method is clearly illustrated in his claim that in his psychological work he was offering, not a set of truths about the psyche, but rather a *model*. In 1924 he wrote: 'It is not a question of . . . *asserting* anything, but of constructing a *model* which opens up a promising and useful field of inquiry. A model does not assert that something is so, it simply illustrates a particular mode of observation' (CW8.381, Jung's emphases). Even as early as 1912 he was admitting that 'the libido . . . is not only not concrete or known, but is a complete X, a pure hypothesis, a model or counter, and is no more conceivable than the energy known to the world of physics' (CW4.282).

A model does not give us any new information about what lies beyond experience but gives us a hypothetical picture, an articulated perspective, which enables us to fit together and make sense of the data of experience – the phenomena. In this sense the theoretical entities of physics such as electrons and photons are models. We have already begun to see this in the case of the idea of the unconscious. We noted above that in making use of this concept Jung was not claiming to have revealed something that was hitherto hidden from sight. As he put it, having laid out the various observable 'symptoms, actions, affects, fantasies and dreams', we should not then 'labour under the illusion that we have now discovered the real nature of the unconscious process' (CW7.272).

Furthermore, like Nietzsche Jung believed that in this regard there is no essential difference between psychology and the natural sciences for they too are concerned, not with discovering timeless truths concerning reality, but rather with constructing convenient models with which to cope with it. 'If on the basis of observations', he wrote, 'psychology assumes the existence of certain irrepresentable [psychic] factors, it is doing the same thing in principle as physics does when the physicist constructs an atomic model' (CW8.417). The point of such a model, whether in psychology or in physics, lies in its function as a useful picture of the world: 'The conception we form of the world is our picture of what we call world. And it is in accordance with this picture that we orient ourselves and adapt to reality' (CW8.697). In both fields, furthermore, theories come and go, come into and fall out of favour. They are like tools which we fabricate, retain so long as they perform a useful function, and discard when they cease to do so: 'Nothing is more vulnerable and ephemeral than scientific theories, which are mere tools and not everlasting truths' (CW18.577), a view expressed by Jung in 1961 and which has become widely held by both scientists and philosophers of science in recent years.

Many examples of this approach can be found in Jung's writings. Thus, in speaking of the idea of the 'self', he wrote that it 'is no more than a psychological concept, a construct that serves to express an unknowable essence which we cannot grasp as such' (CW7.399). As we have seen, he treated the notion of archetypes in a similar way, and made quite explicit the relationship between this concept and those of physics: 'We must . . . constantly bear in mind that what we mean by "archetype" is in itself irrepresentable, but has effects which make visualizations of it possible . . . . We meet with a similar situation in physics: there the smallest particles are themselves irrepresentable but have effects from the nature of which we can build up a model' (CW8.417). His theory of psychological types bears a similar imprint. He offered it, not as a final definitive truth, but rather as the one out of many possible candidates which best suited his purposes, as 'my way of solving the problem'. There are, he allowed, many different possible ways in which to categorize the human personality, and he declined to offer his own as 'the only true or possible type-theory' (MM, pp.98–9). The value of his typology lay, therefore, not in its theoretical finality, but in the fact that it offered 'a system of comparison and orientation' (MM, p.108).

Jung's thinking on this matter is closely linked to the concept of *projection*, for in a sense models are not so much discovered in nature as projected onto it. It seems that this idea occurred to him at a relatively early age. In a letter written in 1942 he described how in his high school days he made collections of inkblots whose 'irrational configurations stimulated my fantasy activity so delightfully that they afforded me day-long enjoyment', an idea which was, as Jung wryly noted, developed later into a psychological technique by Rorschach (*Letters I*, p.323).

The idea of psychic projection was a central one for Jung, and is, according to him, 'one of the commonest facts of psychology' (MM, p.163). Under the influence of the Enlightenment and of positivism we have come to think of projection as a feature of primitive mentality. The argument may be expressed in this way: at one time people saw the cosmos in personal terms, they saw the elements, the features of the landscape, natural occurrences of all sorts, as being the work of quasi-human beings with thoughts, feelings and intentions; with the rise of scientific rationalism in the seventeenth century all this was unmasked and exposed as projection of human qualities onto nature; we were now in a position to strip away these 'idols' (Francis Bacon's term) and to see nature as it really is. Karl Marx, following the inspiration of Ludwig Feuerbach, offered what is perhaps the most famous example of this unmasking in his contention that religion is an illusory solution to the real problems of human existence, a projection onto a fantastic transcendent realm of issues whose true but disguised nature lies closer to hand.

Now, according to Jung projection is not some sort of primitive or prescientific aberration which can one day be superseded, but is an essential feature of the human mind. The types and objects of projection may change over time, but the process is inescapable for human beings as such. Thus while in earlier times we might see the world as teeming with demons or with witches, which are in effect nothing more than projections of our inner fears and obsessions, in more 'enlightened' times our world is filled with scapegoats, enemies and malignant foreigners. Such projections as these spring from the unconscious and are little affected by rational argument.

Furthermore, according to Jung metaphysical systems are projections as well: 'The whole metaphysical world is understood as a psychic structure projected into the sphere of the unknown' (CW18.1658). This is fairly evident in the case of astrology, for '[the] starry vault of heaven is in truth the open book of cosmic projection' (CW8.392), a kind of grand Rorschach test in which we perceive writ large on the heavens features of our own psychic lives. Alchemical and magical practices, likewise, 'are nothing but projections of psychic events, which then exert a counter-influence on the psyche' (CW13.36).

There is no reason to suppose that empirical science itself is anything less of a projection than myth or metaphysics. According to the Enlightenment 'myth', science is a product of pure reason and hence transcends local and personal prejudice. Jung saw things differently. Following Nietzsche's lead, and ultimately influenced by Kant, he viewed science, as indeed all knowledge, as an interpretation or perspective on the world, involving the process of reading-into the world concepts and categories which are the unconscious product of mind. Naturally, like the astrologers, alchemists and magicians of old, we think we are making discoveries and discerning features of the real world 'out there', whereas what we are actually doing is seeing reflections of our own psyches. In no sense was Jung 'against' science, as has sometimes been suggested, but like many thinkers from Nietzsche onwards he was at pains to show that science is a form of human discourse, not a species of disembodied logic.

In the final analysis, however, can Jung's work be described as 'scientific'? He certainly claimed that it was, and even asserted that analytical psychology 'is fundamentally a natural science' (MDR, p.226), and that the psyche, as a natural phenomenon, could be studied scientifically in the same way as any other. In a letter written in 1960 he argued that 'psychic events are observable and can be dealt with in a scientific way', and went on to claim that his method conformed to the standards of scientific procedure, for 'I observe, I classify, I establish relations and sequences between the observed data, and I even show the possibility of prediction' (*Letters II*, p.567).

At the same time he frequently sought to distance his own work from that of the other natural sciences. Two chief considerations bore on him in this regard. The first was the fact, as he saw it, that the activity of the psyche, unlike other natural phenomena, could not be quantified; his phenomenological approach meant that he was concerned with *meanings*, not with events that could be measured and studied statistically. The second, following from the first, was the belief that persons are unique and hence their activities cannot be subsumed under general laws in the way that physical events can, a view with loud Kantian echoes. The third consideration we have already noted: the study of the human psyche is peculiarly subject to distortion and bias in view of the identity between the subject and the object of investigation.

In his approach to the scientific study of the psyche Jung was much influenced by a number of nineteenth century pioneers in this field, such as Galton in England and Fechner and Wundt in Germany. But the path he followed was much closer to the one which had been laid down by Wilhelm Dilthey (1833–1911). A brief account of the ideas of this great and increasingly admired Neo-Kantian philosopher will help to cast light on Jung's method.

Dilthey's central concern was not specifically with psychology but human sciences in general and history in particular. He was himself part of the Neo-Kantian revival that took place in Germany in the latter half of the nineteenth century, and which was seeking to build philosophy, not on grand metaphysical foundations such as had been characteristic of Hegelianism, but on a critical awareness of the assumptions underlying our claims to various forms of knowledge. While Kant's central concern in his *Critique of Pure Reason* had been with the assumptions underlying the physical sciences, with *Naturwissenschaft*, the new movement was concerned with understanding what was involved in the human sciences, with *Geisteswissenschaft*. Dilthey was himself a pupil of Leopold von Ranke (1795–1886), a leader of the new historicist school which sought to align the study of history with the methods of the natural sciences. For Dilthey, however, this approach, and that of positivists such as Comte and Mill, was inadequate in that it failed to distinguish between methods appropriate for the study of nature on the one hand and mind on the other. In the case of nature our knowledge is based on the process of placing particular instances or events within general causal laws; Newton's law of gravity and laws of motion are classical cases of this. The human sciences, on the other hand, are grounded on what Dilthey called 'understanding' (*Verstehen*). Since this concept is crucial for grasping Jung's method, we will examine it further.

Understanding human beings implies communication. Knowing another person involves, not just observing their movements, as we might observe particles in a physics laboratory, but grasping the meaning and significance of their words and actions. This requires what Dilthey called 'lived experience' (*Erleben*), which means that I am able, through my own experience of willing, feeling, imagining and acting in the world, to make sense of the actions of other people. It is only to the extent that I, as a whole living person, have experienced the world that I am able to intepret the actions of my fellow humans. To do this requires not the application of abstract concepts so much as the reproducing (*Nachbilden*) or reliving (*Nacherleben*) in ourselves the experiences of others. There is nothing mysterious about this, no leap is required whereby I penetrate the innermost secrets of another's mind, for understanding is based on the empirical observation of 'expression' (*Ausdruck*). Human beings, according to Dilthey, are essentially expressive in that their inner experiences and thoughts naturally come to present themselves to the outside world through a system of marks, signs, and gestures. We can know what people think, feel and want by the sounds they utter and movements they make, by messages conveyed by a rich variety of means from grunts through language and gesture to the whole gamut of cultural artifacts and institutions that go to make up the fabric of human life and history. Furthermore this method leads us, not to general laws by way of induction (*nomothetic* as he called it), but to the understanding of *individuals* (*idiographic*). This indeed is the hallmark of the human sciences and the essence of historical understanding, for here, in contrast with the physical sciences, our concern is with the particular person, action or event set within its unique historical or cultural context.

This attempt by Dilthey to base the human sciences on lived experience and the understanding of expression is closely linked with the notion of understanding and interpreting a written text, in other words with what has traditonally been called *hermeneutics*. Hermeneutics as the art of interpretation is essentially the process of disentangling the meaning of something that is not obviously clear. It originated in the need for theology to clarify the meaning of sacred texts, but in the hands of the German theologian Schleiermacher (1768–1834) it was extended to embrace not only written texts in general but the whole sphere of human symbolic expression. This, according to Dilthey, was essentially the method of the human sciences – of history, sociology, anthropology, comparative religion, and psychology – the method of *Verstehen*. Human actions, whether on the stage of history or in face-to-face interaction, are like texts which can be read and variously interpreted; as one commentator on Dilthey has put it: 'studying a person's character, the culture of a community, or the activities of a trade union is more like interpreting a poem or a law than like explaining the acceleration of falling bodies or the properties of magnetic fields' (Rickman, 1988, p.57).

Dilthey's conception of the human sciences as a form of hermeneutics has had a considerable influence on certain twentieth century thinkers, most notably on Heidegger, the central figure of modern phenomenological and existential philosophy, and on his follower, Gadamer. It is not clear what influence, if any, his thought had on that of Jung, who made no direct reference to him in his writings. But there is a remarkable similarity in their approach to the scientific study of human action, so close indeed as to suggest that in his wide reading Jung may have absorbed some of Dilthey's ideas, and indeed so strong was the Neo-Kantian influence in late nineteenth century German thought that he is unlikely to have escaped its influence. He showed awareness of the nineteenth century hermeneutical tradition (see CW7.493), and referred to Schleiermacher as 'one of my spiritual ancestors' (*Letters II*, p.115. In fact Jung's grandfather was converted to Protestantism by Schleiermacher!). He also used the term with reference to his own clinical method, on several occasions likening the understanding of a patient, and in particular of a patient's dream, to that of textual interpretation, and also in the course of studying the symbolic traditions of other cultures. Reflecting on his own method in 1944, he pointed out, in terms reminiscent of Dilthey, that the psyche becomes known to the conscious mind through its outward *expressions*, in other words through dreams, fantasies and public symbols, and went on to argue that

> [we] are obliged to adopt the method we would use in deciphering a fragmentary text or one containing unknown words: we examine the context. The meaning of the unknown word may become evident when we compare a series of passages in which it occurs.
>
> (CW12.48)

And speaking specifically of dream interpretation, he wrote that 'I handle the dream as if it were a text which I do not understand properly. . . . I merely apply the ordinary method any philologist would apply in reading such a text' (CW18.172).

Several further points of contact with Dilthey emerge. In the passage just quoted Jung spoke of the need to examine a particular dream within its context rather than in isolation, a requirement repeatedly emphasized by him. This closely parallels Dilthey's idea of the *hermeneutic circle*. He saw that in understanding a text (the same considerations apply to an historical event or cultural artefact) we need to go beyond the actual words, and even beyond the author's intentions, and try to make sense of it within the whole linguistic and cultural context. Such a procedure is not carried out once and for all in a simple step-by-step fashion, but involves a continual oscillation between text and context, comparing the one with the other, indeed more like a spiral than a circle, a process which has no definitive beginning and no definitive end.

Jung too believed that the hermeneutical endeavour involved a circling, rather than a linear, movement, and that our attempts to understand the human psyche cannot rest on absolutely secure foundations or be guaranteed to reach finally satisfactory and inescapable conclusions. For him the hermeneutical method 'does not follow straight lines', does not yield 'general principles or universally accepted ideals, but points of view and attitudes that have a provisional value' (CW7.501). This is in fact nothing other than his process of amplification, which we discussed in the last chapter, a process whereby our understanding of a symbolic process, whether individual or cultural, involves a to-and-fro exploration, which can at first sight seem random and directionless, but which actually enables us to view things as a whole in terms of a network of analogies and meaningful relationships. The use of analogies is especially important, a point which is stressed in the following passage:

> The essence of hermeneutics, an art widely practised in former times, consists in adding further analogies to the one already supplied by the symbol: in the first place subjective analogies produced at random by the patient, then objective analogies provided by the analyst out of his general knowledge. This procedure widens and enriches the initial symbol.
>
> (CW7.493)

A further point of contact concerns Jung's exploration of other cultures. Dilthey, as we have noted, was concerned not so much with psychology – though he recognized the fundamental importance of this within the field of human studies – as with history. The proper method for the historian is not that of the physicist but rather that of the philologist – the interpreter of texts. History itself is a kind of text in which our understanding must be directed, not towards the formulation of general laws, but towards the understanding of the meaning of events and of the actions of individuals, as expressed through overt activity, and within their historical context. This method differs from that of the physicist, not only in terms of general laws, but also in that the historian must approach his or her material as one human being attempting to understand another. Historical understanding is therefore in effect a kind of *dialogue*. It involves the overlapping of what Dilthey called the 'horizons' of the present and the past, of one conceptual domain with another. Historians can no more escape from the attitudes and presuppositions of their own culture than can one person engaged in conversation with another. We have to recognize, in other words, that when we engage with a person or a person from another culture we are enmeshed with a network of beliefs, indeed with a whole way of seeing the world, which is not identical with our own.

Jung fully recognized this. Not only did he view the relationship between therapist and patient as 'a dialogue or discussion between two persons' (CW16.1), but in his own endeavours to draw the cultures of the East or of the Christian Middle Ages, or indeed of individual thinkers, into the orbit of his psychological speculations, he was aware that here also he was engaged in a dialogue, drawing analogies and meaningful parallels between his work with patients on the one hand and the strange symbolisms and practices of yogis or alchemists, or the long-forgotten world-views of philosophers, on the other, yet always recognizing the inescapable 'otherness' of cultures and philosophies different from his own. And just as the doctor is 'as much part of the psychic process of the treatment as is the patient, and is equally exposed to the transforming influences' (MM, p.58), so too the historian is changed and transformed through dialogue with the past.

We can now see in what sense Jung's work can be described as scientific. His science was that of hermeneutics, the kind which Dilthey perceived to be the method of the human and historical sciences. He himself claimed it to be one of the '*Geisteswissenschaften*' (CW17.165), and referred to the unconscious as a 'language' (CW16.253), a notion later developed by the Neo-Freudian, Lacan. In one of his later works he drew a sharp contrast between 'knowledge' and 'understanding', seeing the former as the province of the physical sciences with their need to generalize, and the latter pertaining to the unique individual and to the unique products of individual cultures (US, p.7). It is, Jung accepted, possible to group individuals and the symbolic products of individuals into categories for the sake of making comparisons and analogies – a factor in historical studies fully recognized by Dilthey also – but without implying that this can lead to general laws from which predictions can be made.

Again it must be emphasized that there is nothing mysterious or esoteric about this method. Whether in the hands of Dilthey the historian or Jung the psychologist it is strictly empirical, requiring as we have seen not insight into another's mind but a careful examination of what the former called 'expressions', namely the manifestations of human thinking, imagining and intending. This is what some of Dilthey's followers have called the 'life-world', the domain of human action and interaction. It is in this domain that we can locate Jung as both empiricist and scientist.[2]

# 4

# HISTORICAL PERSPECTIVES

> Without history there can be no psychology.
>
> (C.G. Jung)

We are now in a position to understand another characteristic feature of Jung's thinking, namely its profoundly *historical* orientation. Dilthey, as we have seen, was a key figure in a movement which sought to rethink the nature of the human sciences in general and of the historical sciences in particular. In Germany during the second half of the nineteenth century a new historical awareness emerged which became for a time a leading cultural force. It went under the name of *historicism*, and was associated with the names of Droyson and Rickert as well as Dilthey. According to these historicists, the study of history was no longer to be seen as a record of past events, leading perhaps to the formulation of general laws, but, in Droyson's words, as a study of 'the way in which humanity becomes and is conscious of itself' (Schnädelbach, 1984, p.34), a study which was concerned with the unique intentional acts of human persons with inner conscious lives, rather than with repeatable external events. It was also concerned with the whole interconnected range of human cultural experience, with art, religion and ideas, as well as with the more narrowly defined political history, and in this sense could be described as 'holistic', though not in any Hegelian sense for the historicist school rejected the idea that history could be explained in terms of any overarching metaphysical concept such as *Geist* (spirit or mind).

The term 'historicism' has several related meanings, and refers to no single universally accepted theory, but for Dilthey it carried the important sense of *relativism*. This can be broken down into two contentions: first, that all persons and events are rooted in and shaped by history; and secondly, that historical knowledge itself is dependent on the position of historians relative to their place in the historical world. Thus, human nature, contrary to the earlier Enlightenment view, is not something that can be grasped in a universal and timeless way, and the study of history does not reveal its changeless essence beneath the flux of events, but rather it has to be understood as embedded in a long process of diversified cultural development. And on this view reason, and even consciousness itself, becomes relative to history. The human mind, therefore, does not stand above history, able to judge it in a detached and objective way, but must be seen as part of the historical reality it is attempting to comprehend.

This historicist attitude was one which, in certain important respects at least, Jung shared. He saw the need to view his own psychological studies within as wide a cultural context as possible, and though he was a psychiatrist, and was concerned centrally with problems concerning the nature and development of human personality, his interests ranged over the whole spectrum of human experience, and in formulating his ideas he drew inspiration from a dauntingly wide variety of cultural and historical contexts. Ira Progoff points out that Jung's work is one of the leading instances of a holistic point of view applied to the study of man, for he realized at an early point in his work 'that he would not be able to understand his material unless he studied man on a canvas large enough to include the history of the human race as a whole, particularly its varieties of mythology, religon and culture' (1953, p.4).

Jung had a strong sense of history, both as a person and as a thinker. In his youth he acquired a great love for antiquity and for the Renaissance, developed a strong sense of identity with the culture of the eighteenth century, and throughout his life read widely in the fields of history and mythology. His first major 'Jungian' work, *Symbols of Transformation*, is almost embarrassingly replete with allusions both to classical history and to the world's intellectual traditions. The contrast with Freud here is illuminating. While Freud certainly made use of historical material, and in the case of the Oedipus complex showed a recognition of the archaic roots of the psyche, his thinking was cast in essentially biological terms. In contrast with Freud's 'bias against the past', as Philip Rieff put it, Jung's whole way of thinking was suffused with history. He was very conscious of his own personal and cultural roots, and was always aware of the way in which his own thinking had evolved from that of his predecessors, and in all his writings he displayed great sensitivity, backed by painstaking scholarship, towards historical precedents, influences and provenance with respect to his own ideas.

Furthermore, as we shall see in a later chapter, Jung viewed the psyche itself as essentially historical in the sense that its development can only be understood in the context of its personal and collective past; our being stretches out and embraces, not only contemporary humanity, but the whole cultural and even biological past of the human race: '[Man]) carries his whole history with him', he wrote, 'in his very structure is written the history of mankind' (CW6.570). For this reason we can only hope to understand ourselves and to come to terms with our present condition if we relate this to the past whence we spring. His interest in history, therefore, was not simply a scholarly concern, but stemmed from his need to understand the present condition of the human psyche.

A major influence on Jung's historical outlook was undoubtedly his fellow Baseler, the cultural historian Jakob Burckhardt (1818–98), who has played an important role in shaping the development of cultural history as an integral component of traditional historical studies. Burckhardt was a renowned professor of history at the University of Basel in Jung's early years there as a student. There is no evidence that they ever met, but it is clear that his influence was felt by Jung who remarked many years later that 'Burckhardt was our daily bread' (JS, p.204), and it is most probably from Burckhardt that he acquired his enthusiasm for the Renaissance. It was indeed to the works Burckhardt, amongst others, that he turned in his more mature years when, still a close friend of Freud, he began his research into the historical and pre-historical origins of the psyche, and much later he was to speak of his 'spiritual affinity or at least sympathy with Jakob Burckhardt' (*Letters II*, p.80).

The importance of the latter for the shaping of modern historical attitudes lay in his attempt to see an historical epoch, such as the Renaissance, as a whole. He rejected the approach of his teacher, Leopold von Ranke, who placed politics, diplomacy and the functions of the state at the centre of historical concern, and sought instead to understand history as a field of human, even of psychological concern. In his study of the Renaissance, for example, he sought to show that the rise of the Italian city states was linked to the rise of a new post-mediaeval individualism, which in turn was expressed in the personalities and works of the great artists and humanists of the period; the conception of the state as a work of art could only be understood in terms of the typical Renaissance idea, voiced by the great scholar and architect Alberti, that 'Man can do anything that he wills'. In effect Burckhardt was employing psychological categories in attempting to understand an historical epoch. This fell short, as Jung himself noted, of a psychological explanation of historical phenomena, but the linking together of the historical study of society and culture on the one hand and psychological analysis on the other is clearly a significant point of convergence between the two thinkers.

Another fellow Baseler who had a great influence on Jung's historical outlook, and indeed on the whole direction of his mature thought, was J.J. Bachoven (1815–87). Little-known nowadays in the English-speaking world, Bachoven was an important and widely discussed thinker in his day who influenced not only Jung but Marx and Freud as well. His work grew out of the Romantic interest in mythology, an interest initiated in the eighteenth century by Herder, but transformed by Bachoven into a systematic scholarly study. He claimed to be able to discern two wholly distinct cultural patterns in primitive societies, the one depending on the rule of men and the other on the rule of women, and saw these patterns manifested in the myths and symbols of particular societies. The symbolic material culled from such societies can, he believed, only be understood with reference to its historical meaning, and hence with the aid of this material it should be possible to reconstruct the history of pre-historical societies. It is difficult to be precise about the nature of Bachoven's influence on Jung. Undoubtedly the latter's inclination to interpret the contemporary dream material of his patients in mythological terms owes much to Bachoven's psychological and symbolic understanding of primitive myth and his belief that there is a continuity of psychic development in each society. And Bachoven's distinction between patriarchal and matriarchal societies may well have stimulated Jung's interest in gender issues. But perhaps most important was the sense of the relevance of history and its importance in gaining an all-round conception of human nature.

In order to understand the mind of the present, therefore, Jung believed it necessary to study the mind of the past. Unlike many twentieth century thinkers who, under the influence of scientism and positivism, have simply rejected as childish nonsense the thought-systems which predate the scientific revolution of the seventeenth century, Jung studied them, as Bachoven had, with utmost seriousness and commitment. Like Arnold Toynbee, on whom he exercised some fascination and influence, Jung believed that despite the bewildering range of the cultural and social products of history, and the diversity of beliefs and practices evinced by different societies, there must be some underlying bond, at however deep a level, which binds humanity, and hence history, together. Thus while on the one hand he was well aware of the strangeness of belief systems other than one's own, he nevertheless insisted that amidst the diversity there lay an underlying psychic unity which united mankind and which made historical, and indeed human, understanding possible.

It must be evident from this that Jung's concern with history was different in several important respects from that of the typical historian. The first obvious difference lies in his implicit conception of what constitutes the 'context' of belief systems. He displayed little interest in the broad social framework within which ideas arise and flourish, in the complex interweaving of ideas, economic power and political control, but concentrated wholly on their symbolic meaning in relation to the process of psychic transformation, the process which he called 'individuation'. He would certainly have had little sympathy with the sociology of knowledge approach of such thinkers as Scheler and Mannheim who have sought to explain ideas in sociological terms. His study of alchemy is a conspicuous case in point. His scholarship was exemplary; as one authority, Walter Pagel, puts it, 'There is hardly an alchemical treatise or manuscript which he left unturned. . . . Consequently his representation is extremely well documented, impressive by the breadth of its scholarship' (see Holt, 1987–8, p.43). Nevertheless he avoided any attempt to explain this phenomenon in terms of the social or economic conditions of the Middle Ages, but concentrated on deciphering its mysterious texts and practices in terms of psychological symbolism and underlying universal archetypal patterns.

It is hardly surprising that Jung's approach has not always endeared him to orthodox historians. Robert A. Westman, for example, complains that despite his enormous erudition, Jung had 'failed to capture the sympathy of . . . historians, because he sought to use his studies as evidence for his theory of archetypes, rather than in an open-ended scholarly way – to deepen the hermeneutics of the self rather than historical knowledge for its own sake' (Vickers, 1984, p.209).

It was in this 'hermeneutics of the self' that Jung drew together history and psychology. He was fully aware of the parallel between his historical activity and his analytical work with patients, and indeed it was precisely this parallel that propelled and motivated his work. He viewed the processes of chemical transformation, which was the characteristic mark of alchemical practice, as symbolizing an inner psychic or spiritual transformation of the kind which his own patients were undergoing, and interpreted the laboratory techniques as unconscious *projections* by the alchemist of the need for inner transformation and growth. From this we can see that Jung tended to view the realm of the psyche, and hence of ideas, as having a kind of life of its own. He found no difficulty in linking together ideas from different times and cultures, and in viewing these ideas as arising, not from any specific historical conditions, but rather from underlying universal dispositions within the psyche iteself.

This point is seized upon by John-Raphael Staude who argues that for Jung the great events of history were unimportant except in so far as they reveal and are explained by the inner life of the individual, and that for this reason Jung was fundamentally anti-historical. He writes that 'Behind the panorama of historical events and the melodrama of personal history, Jung looked for the eternal play and transformation of archetypal images, patterns and structures'. The same is true, he argues, of his followers, for 'most Jungians have a very undeveloped historical consciousness' (1981, pp.xvi–xvii).

There is some justification in this, for Jung certainly took little account of the external forces of history, and to this extent it would be true to say that his historical sense was limited. But in my view it does not imply that Jung was anti-historical. It would be more correct to say that he sought to offer an alternative *psychological* view of history, supplementing rather than competing with the approach typical of more traditionally minded historians. Here, as in so much of his thinking, he avoided anything like a reductive theory. In speaking about the situation in Europe in the 1930s, for example, he pointed to the complexity of events, and to the need for a multi-valent approach which would include explanations in political and economic, as well as psychological, terms. Modestly he suggested merely that it was 'within the reach of contemporary psychology to produce a certain point of view at least' (CW18.1307). One might see his work therefore as a challenge to those who, in Robert Solomon's words, 'insist that history can be understood only in terms of economics and disasters, endless catalogues of treaties, tariffs, taxes, Tories and tithes, the means of production, the promise of profit, and of course battles' (1980, p.xvi). His study of alchemy is indeed an important correction to one of the standard interpretations, namely that it is a rather muddled precursor to modern chemistry, and from the point of view of the history of science can help to rectify a rather simplistic construal of scientific 'progress'; and as Pagel argues, Jung's work is 'a monumental reminder of the part played by non-scientific motives in the History of Science' (Holt, 1987–8, p.43).

The second significant difference between Jung's approach to history and that of the typical historian lies in the use to which he put his scholarship. He did not aim at disinterested understanding, but rather at an understanding which is quite consciously and explicitly *interested*, namely from the point of view of his concern with the psyche of the contemporary human being. This, again, is clearly evident in his treatment of alchemy which as we have seen he studied, not for its own sake, but for the ultimate purpose of casting light on the nature of the human mind, and in particular on the notion of individuation. As Gerhard Wehr puts it: 'he was guided by his need to document, by means of "historical prefigurations", what he had experienced for himself and explored psychologically, to place the productions of the unconscious of modern people in a larger historical context' (G. Wehr, 1987, p.245). The same is true of his studies of Oriental thought. Here too his considerable erudition on the subject was pursued, not in the service of disinterested scholarship, but in order to understand the nature of spiritual liberation. In investigating the correspondences between his own psychological theories and pre-scientific ways of thinking, therefore, he was seeking to set up a dialogue which would, he hoped, lead not just to an expansion of knowledge for its own sake but a deepening of self-awareness.

This search for parallels, and the setting up of dialogues between present and past concerns and between East and West, goes deeper, however, for it represents, not just a scavenging of history to find parallels with his own viewpoint, but a recognition of the purely *relative* status of cultures in general and of modern Western culture in particular, and it is here that we can begin to draw Jung close once again to the thinking of Dilthey in particular and the historicist school in general. We can also draw some parallels with twentieth century hermeneuticists such as Gadamer (1975) and Rorty (1980).

The flavour of Jung's relativistic outlook is captured in remarks such as the following: 'If I call something true, it does not mean that it is absolutely true. It merely seems to be true to myself and/or to other people' (CW18.1584). Concerning his own views he wrote: 'I hold the truth of my own views to be equally relative [to those of Freud and Adler], and regard myself as the exponent of a certain predisposition. . . . We should be modest and grant validity to a number of apparently contradictory opinions' (MM, p.65).

The thrust of his relativistic philosophy was aimed with special force against any attempt to give Western culture a privileged status. In Jung's writings we find the persistent claim that Western civilization in general, and Western scientific rationalism in particular, does not represent any kind of pinnacle or apotheosis of human progress. His travels in India, Africa and America enabled him to put European culture into perspective, and reinforced his belief that 'Western consciousness is by no means the only kind of consciousness there is: it is historically conditioned and geographically limited, and representative of only one part of mankind' (CW13.84). He was contemptuous of 'that megalomania of ours which leads us to suppose . . . that Christianity is the only truth, and the white Christ the only Redeemer' (MM, p.246), and referred rather dismissively to Europe as 'only a tiny fraction of humanity, living mainly on that thickly populated peninsular of Asia which juts out into the Atlantic Ocean, and calling themselves "cultured"' (CW7.326). He stood firmly against any racist attitudes in such remarks as 'somewhere you are the same as the Negro or the Chinese . . . you are all just human beings' (CW18.93), a comment that was made in public in his Tavistock Lectures in 1935 at a time when, according to Masson (1989), he was offering encouragement to the Nazis in their racist ideology. The whole tenor of Jung's thinking, here as elsewhere, was in fact totally at variance with that of the Nazis, a point that we will return to in Chapter 10.

It is true that Jung often expressed a great personal admiration for modern Western culture, as well as for science and for Christianity, and emphasized his own inescapable historical bond therewith. I indicated above the strong sense he felt of his own historical roots, and his recognition that his own ideas were profoundly influenced by the traditions from which he sprang. In spite of this, he displayed a remarkable ability to stand back from his own culture and to see it as only one possible manifestation of the human spirit, standing alongside, and of equal status with, many others, whether past or present, East or West.

He had a global perspective, and believed it was 'absolutely necessary that one treats the problem of the human psyche from many standpoints' (Evans, 1979, p.151). The different philosophies and world-views which he encountered on his travels, literary as well as geographical, though often strange and alien to his modern Western mind, were not to be seen as false or illogical but simply as different ways of interpreting the world. Thus, in opposition to the once popular views of the French anthropologist Lévy-Bruhl, he consistently denied that primitive mentality was less logical than our own, it was merely based on different assumptions: 'Primitive man is no more logical or illogical than we are. His presuppositions are not the same as ours. His thinking and his conduct are based on assumptions other than our own' (MM, p.146).

Here too he moved conspicuously away from Freud. It is true that the latter made use of anthropological data and sought to place his psychological findings within a wide cultural context, but in the end Freud remained Eurocentric, a child of the Enlightenment who viewed the culture of science and rationalism as the only possible way forward for mankind – as for example in his book *The Future of an Illusion*. Jung, on the contrary, rejected the Enlightenment as the exclusive expression of truth, and with it the view that history represents some sort of progression, that science is the only source of truth, and that Western rationalism represents the summit of human achievement. '[The] rationalist attitude of the West' he wrote 'is not the only or possible one and is not all-embracing, but is in many ways a prejudice and a bias' (SY, p.95).[1]

For Jung, then, there was no single correct view of the world, and even if there was we would have no way of knowing that we were in possession of it. 'There is no one single philosophy but many' (MM, p.207) is a typical remark which sums up his viewpoint. This attitude inevitably led him to the sort of eclecticism which we noted in an earlier chapter, a habit which, as we saw there, has drawn on him the wrath of his critics. 'My empirical material' he remarked 'seems to include a bit of everything – it is an assortment of primitive, Western and Oriental ideas. There is scarcely any myth whose echoes are not heard, nor any heresy that has not contributed an occasional oddity' (CW18.1512). In constructing his view of the world and of the human psyche he did indeed draw on a great variety of sources. But it will by now be clear that this was not carried out in the random spirit of an intellectual beachcomber, but rather arose from his conviction that there is an element of truth in all philosophies since they all represent a way of interpreting the world from a particular unique viewpoint. A hostile commentator such as Glover has seen in this eclecticism a mere indisciplined 'mishmash', an objection which fails to understand that for Jung human thought is essentially historical and cannot be encapsulated into a single timeless logically watertight system. The historically relative nature of human thinking inevitably leads to variety and paradox, a feature of human experience which most Western philosophers have strenuously attempted to ignore.

Jung's relativistic approach and his neutral stance with regard to cultural differences, and indeed his whole historicist outlook, were not, as is often the case, a negative form of scepticism, a wearied denial of the possibility of any objective knowledge, and an acceptance of the growing nihilism of his age. For him the opposing and mutually contradictory philosophies and idealogies that history reveals to us were not to be viewed as, in Matthew Arnold's phrase, 'ignorant armies that clash by night', but rather as a variety of perspectives which, in the never-ended attempt to comprehend the world, complement each other by their very opposition. Thus, just as the psyche, in ways that we will examine more fully in Part II, is characterized by elements and tendencies which are in tension with each other, yet which seek some kind of balance and harmony, so too Jung believed that similar sense could be made of the intellectual history of mankind. He therefore viewed the great cultural and doctrinal diversity of the world's religions, not as a hopeless cackle of discordant voices, but as so many different manifestations of underlying unconscious impulses that were common to mankind and pointed towards an underlying unity. His journey through history was undertaken with this as its guiding principle.

His attitude here shows some important affinities with the Renaissance of the fifteenth and sixteenth centuries. He frequently spoke of his admiration for the great Renaissance thinkers, such as Paracelsus, Ficino, Kepler, Agrippa of Nettesheim, and Angelus Silesius, and was in sympathy with their search for a concordance between opposing authorities and their impulse towards the unity and reconciliation of seemingly opposed beliefs. For the Renaissance thinkers this meant seeing beneath the diversity of creeds a single truth towards which all were pointing, an ideal expressed by one of its most eloquent spokesmen, Pico Della Mirandola (1463–94), in his *Oration on the Dignity of Man* where he spoke of his desire to 'bring into view the things taught not merely according to one doctrine . . . but things taught according to every sort of doctrine, that by this comparison of very many sects and by the discussion of manifold philosophy, that radiance of truth which Plato mentions in his *Letters* might shine more clearly in our minds, like the sun rising from the deep' (1965, p.23). Jung did not travel all the way down this road. Unlike Pico he did not envisage the possibility of any sort of ultimate reconciliation of all opposing creeds in a single synthesis, and, of course, consistently denied that he possessed any insight into the 'truth'. His spiritual affinity with the Renaissance lay in his conviction that the various conceptual systems devised in the course of mankind's history, which seem on the face of it to be implacably hostile to one another, were traceable to symbolic paradigms that were the common inheritance of humanity. And like the great humanists of the earlier period he believed that the education of the human spirit necessarily involves an ever-widening circle of cultural and philosophical sympathies.

In the final analysis, then, his relativistic, historicist outlook moved beyond that of Dilthey and his colleagues, for whereas they, in their zeal to reject the Enlightenment assumptions of historiography, claimed to discern no abiding unity beneath the flux of history, Jung made use of their methods to come to a somewhat different conclusion, namely that the unconscious can be traced to symbolic universals which represent a common psychic inheritance. He believed that human history is not merely the account of unique cultures each pursuing its goals independently of the rest. It is also the key to the fundamental unity of mankind – a form of 'self-knowledge', though in a somewhat richer sense than that intended by Droyson. In his historical investigations, in his dialogue with history, he was constantly made aware of the ties which bind the human race together, an awareness which formed the basis of his theory of universal archetypes. This theory argues that the experience of mankind is not entirely contingent upon local and historical circumstances, but is also built around certain themes, expressed symbolically, which are common to all cultures; here as in so many respects Jung sought to steer a middle course between two extremes, namely between on the one hand an historical outlook which sees nothing but contingencies and differences, and on the other one which claims to identify a single meaning beneath the flux of events. We will return to this in Part II in our examination of his theory of archetypes and the collective unconscious.

In the meantime, having discussed in broad terms the historical orientation of Jung's thinking, we now need to look more closely at some of the major ideas and systems of thought which preoccupied him and which had the most influence on the shape and direction of his philosophy.

# 5

# ROMANTICS AND IDEALISTS

> So far as psychology takes its own premises into account, its relevance to philosophy and the history of ideas is self-evident . . . certain of those premises are a restatement of ideas dating back to the time of the Romantics.
>
> (C.G. Jung)

Jung was concerned to set his psychological theories within the widest possible intellectual context, and to underline their 'relevance to philosophy and the history of ideas' (CW18.1739). He felt the need to 'bring the experiences of a medical specialist out of their narrow specialist setting into a more general context', and justified the 'amplification' of his ideas on the grounds of their 'wide significance and application' (CW6 p.xi). For this reason it is important to locate Jung's thought within the history of ideas, in particular within the intellectual history of the nineteenth century. He frequently drew attention to the fact that his own conception of the psyche was rooted in nineteenth century philosophy, and while in the previous chapter we have discussed his relation to the historicist tradition in an attempt to illuminate his methodology, in this chapter we will focus on the influences of nineteenth century philosophy on the development of his psychological theories.

In the light of Jung's eclectic historicist outlook, combined with his non-linear thinking style, it is not surprising that he showed a great affinity with Romanticism, that great sprawling cultural and intellectual phenomenon that gripped the heart and mind of Europe in the late-eighteenth and early-nineteenth centuries, and which had such a profound influence on the subsequent development of Western culture. Despite the affinity he felt from early days with the writers of the Romantic period, it was only in 1935 when he was sixty that, in a foreword to a book by Rose Mehlich on the German Romantic philosopher Fichte, he explicitly acknowledged this affinity. He admitted that the 'parallelism [between Romanticism and his own psychology] is sufficient justification for calling

[it] Romantic' (CW18.1740), and saw his task of exploring the unconscious mind as having been anticipated by the Romantic poets.

Jung's affinity with the Romantics can be seen in almost every aspect of his work: in his commitment to the exploration and rehabilitation of instinct, intuition and imagination, in his concern with symbols, with archetypes and the world of dreams and fantasy, in his belief that art is created from the unconscious depths of the soul, in his understanding of the human need for roots and a symbiotic relationship with nature. Like them he challenged the hegemony of scientific rationalism with its mechanist conception of mind and nature, and sought to formulate a wider cosmology which could do justice to the role of spirit and integrate it within a non-dualistic philosophy. Like them he recognized that we are essentially historical beings and for this reason felt compelled, like Herder before him, to take seriously the various manifestations of human culture and to treat each one as an individual to be judged in its own, rather than in universal, terms. Above all we can see between Jung and the Romantics a continuity of concern with the exploration of the human self in all its dimensions, but most especially in its unconscious depths, and a commitment to a deeper understanding of mind and the role of imagination than was possible within the framework of earlier Enlightenment thinking.

References to the poets and writers of the Romantic epoch, other than the strictly philosophical figures, abound in Jung's writings, but two in particular received special attention from him: Goethe and Schiller. A few words must be said about each.

Johann Wolfgang von Goethe (1749–1832) is a pivotal figure in German culture, and though not in his own estimation a Romantic, he had an enormous influence on the shaping of the culture of that period. His dramatic poem *Faust* was in many ways the central literary work of the epoch, summing up its spirit and aspirations, and providing an archetypal symbol of the unrequited striving which was such a characteristic feature of Romantic sensibility. Jung himself, while still a schoolboy, was drawn to this work at the instigation of his mother and, as he later admitted, the character of Faust came to mean more to him than that of the Jesus of the Gospels (see MDR, p.107). In *Faust* he discovered a kindred awareness of the duality of life, of the painful cleavages within one's personality, and the need to confront and integrate the shadow within. Goethe himself appears to have experienced a strong need to bring into some kind of balance the opposing elements within himself, and arrived at an organic, holistic conception of nature which sought to reintegrate the living and spiritual dimensions of the natural world which had been increasingly marginalized by mechanistic philosophy. His rejection of Newtonianism, especially Newton's theory of colour with its attempt to reduce white light to its component elements, was not so much a rejection of science, for Goethe was deeply committed to the empirical study of nature and carried out important biological investigations, but rather a rejection of what he saw as a one-sided mechanistic model. Like Jung after him, he was wary of the seductions of abstract *a priori* thought – 'grey is all theory, but green grows the tree of life' – and believed in the value and validity of unmediated experience, whether directed to the outer world of nature or the inner world of emotions and imagination.

Jung's attachment to the idea of the tension between opposing principles was also influenced by Goethe's contemporary, the German poet and dramatist, Friedrich Schiller (1759–1805). Like Goethe and other contemporaries such as Schelling and Hegel, Schiller was concerned with what he saw as the deep cultural divisions of his time which resulted, he believed, in one-sided development of the human spirit. Following the lead of Rousseau, he saw the contemporary European as being torn between the extremes of nature and civilization, and in the French Revolution he discerned a similar split between wild bestiality on the one hand and lofty reason on the other. Like Kant and Fichte, Schiller was passionately committed to the cause of freedom and human emancipation, but it was in the realm of art and beauty rather than in politics, that he found the potential solution to the divisions within mankind. In an essay entitled *Letters on the Aesthetic Education of Man* he offered an image of the ideal life of harmony and wholeness based on the release of the powers of artistic creation and the appreciation of beauty, and advocated aesthetic education as a way of restoring mankind's state of oneness with nature and with itself.

Jung was clearly inspired by these ideas and devoted a long chapter to the study of Schiller in his book *Psychological Types*. Jung rejected what he described as the 'all too constricting mantle of aestheticism' which in his opinion is 'not fitted to solve the exceedingly serious and difficult task of educating man', since it emphasized the beautiful and the happy at the expense of ugliness and evil (CW6.194). But he recognized in Schiller a deep understanding of the drama taking place within the psyche with its tensions between opposing energies and its drive towards a reconciling harmony. The aesthetic impulse, according to Schiller, arose from the need to mediate between what he called the 'superior' and the 'inferior' functions of man, which could roughly be identified with the rational and the irrational forces within the psyche. Schiller believed that it was in the playful activity of art, in the self-expressive activity of fantasy and imagination that this mediation becomes possible, a seed of an idea which came to full flower in Jung's psychology, and which he explicitly attributed to Schiller when he commented that 'man is completely human only when he is playing' (MM, p.76). Schiller also drew a distinction between 'naïve' and 'sentimental' attitudes, a distinction which Jung employed in the development of his own theory of psychological types, and which corresponded roughly to the latter's 'extraverted' and 'introverted' types respectively.

The Romantic movement marked a major turning point in European thought and sensibility, a 'counter-Enlightenment', as Isaiah Berlin called it, which had the effect of challenging, if not quite overthrowing, the mechanical concept of mind which had dominated European thought from the time of Hobbes and Locke. This revolution was initially the work of poets and artists, often inspired by the introspective explorations of Rousseau, and propelled by a renewal of interest in the ancient Neoplatonic and Hermetic traditions. But by the end of the eighteenth century it had acquired the status of a major intellectual movement in which philosophers and theologians elaborated and systematized the insights of poets.

There were two features of this movement that were to be of central importance for the subsequent development of German philosophy and hence for the shaping of Jung's own thought, both of them traceable to the influence of Kant. The first was that the subject or self was brought back onto centre stage. The mind–body dualism that resulted from both the rationalist and the empiricist streams of post-Renaissance thought had, as I suggested above, tended to marginalize the world of mind and to give centre-stage to the material world. Kant's revolution changed this by demonstrating that the mental and the physical were mutually dependent, and that no conception of the world of nature was possible without the active participation of the subject.

The second feature of importance was the opening up of the possibility of a unified philosophy of nature which was inclusive of both the world of matter and the world of spirit. This possibility had been rigidly excluded by both Cartesian and Newtonian thinking which viewed nature as exclusively material, all vestiges of spirit having been parcelled off into the totally distinct world of mind. The Kantian philosophy pointed the way back to the *unus mundus*, the one world of the Renaissance in which the physical and the spiritual realms constituted parts of a single unified cosmos.

Now, despite the great advance achieved by Kant in demonstrating the contribution that our minds make to our knowledge of the world, he bequeathed to his successors a philosophy which retained a fundamental split at its core, one which we discussed in Chapter 3 above, namely between the world as we perceive it on the one hand and the world as it is in itself on the other. Furthermore this split seemed to strike right at the heart of human nature itself, for just as we have no knowledge of the world in itself, so too the self or subject is known, not in itself, but only in its manifest activites. This situation seems to leave the human world still unhappily divided against itself, with the inner world of freedom and moral responsibility apparently unconnected with the physical world of nature. Nature and mind, necessity and freedom, seemed as estranged from each other as ever, and as a consequence man in his essential being seemed condemned to be a perpetual alien in the world of nature. Here we have the philosophical equivalent of Schiller's divided culture and Goethe's split psyche.

It was the aim of Kant's philosophical successors, aided and abetted by the Romantic poets, to heal this rift and to forge a unified conception of human nature, one which would enable us to feel at home in the world. Whatever their strictly philosophical merits, and however unwieldy and even fantastic the methods which they employed, there can be no question that they succeeded in redefining the issue of human nature and began a far-reaching exploration of the inner structures of the psyche, opening up whole areas of the inner world of mind that had been quite opaque to their predecessors in the seventeenth and eighteenth centuries. Their perception of nature as a living organic whole in which consciousness was an integral, indeed a crucial, part, placed them firmly in an older tradition which had flourished in the mediaeval and Renaissance worlds but which had been marginalized in the period of the Enlightenment. But at the same time their use of Kant's critical method, plus their commitment to a developmental evolutionary model, and their conception of mind as a dynamic self-expressive agent, enabled them to make spectacular advances in the understanding of the processes of the psyche, advances upon which Jung himself was later to capitalize in the development of his psychological theories.

The first of these great successors to Kant was Johann Gotlieb Fichte (1762–1814). Fichte was at the outset of his philosophical career a zealous supporter of Kant, particularly of the latter's belief in the inherent moral worth of the human person. But he soon parted company from his master on the crucial question of Kant's distinction between the phenomenal and noumenal worlds. He developed a philosophy which sought to unify these two principles by showing that the world could be derived from the idea of the absolute ego alone without recourse to a mysterious thing-in-itself, and that from the ego itself it was possible to derive the variety and complexity of reality, physical as well as mental. In propounding this new philosophy, Fichte drew on Kant's conception of the central role of the self in our knowledge of the world. He argued that the ego is the supreme principle, independent and sovereign, the creative fount and origin not only of all human action but of the very world in which that action takes place. The world beyond the self is no more than an obstacle posited by the ego in order that it may have something to overcome, the self thereby being elevated into a cosmic principle, a creator of the world, and not merely a passive observer of it.

This does not mean that each individual person creates their own private world. Fichte was no solipsist, but conceived the ego, not in individual but in absolute terms, the individual self being merely an expression of the wider activity of absolute or cosmic mind. The ultimate achievement of this absolute mind is consciousness and the free activity of individual moral agents acting in moral communities or societies. But the activity of mind is not fully to be understood in terms of rational consciousness. Indeed rational consciousness is only the surface and end-product, for the mind is driven, not by reason, but by an inner unconscious striving which, through the tension of opposing forces, seeks to attain a higher kind of unity. Thus for Fichte the human spirit is fundamentally an active principle, working out its destiny through the reconciliation of opposing forces which arise from within itself. Its theoretical activity is therefore secondary and derivative. From this he inferred that the highest aspiration of the human spirit is moral autonomy, the independence of the self from any kind of external constraint other than those of a rational nature, and hence the idea that self-unfolding and self-expression represent the supreme goals of the moral life. Self-cultivation is therefore man's highest moral aspiration, a view which became a hallmark of German Romanticism.

Many intimations of Jung's thinking are evident in Fichte's philosophy, and though he himself denied having read the latter's work, he came to recognize late in his career the 'strange but undeniable analogy' that prevailed between their respective points of view (CW18.1732). Not only do we find the common endeavour to overcome the dualism of mind and matter, and to establish the cosmic eminence of the psyche, but also the understanding that mind unfolds itself through an inner-directed activity whose source lies below the level of consciousness, and whose driving force is not to be understood in terms of the linear progression of logic but rather of the dialectical conflict of opposing energies. Although Jung never went so far as Fichte in reducing the whole of being to the self-expressive activity of the ego, he nevertheless adopted Fichte's phenomenological standpoint and was clearly fascinated with the idea that the world, if not quite the product of mind, could only be illuminated and find meaning through the mind's activity. Both thinkers were convinced that mind is not a simple object amongst other objects, but rather a self-creative agent whose sole purpose is to express what lies potentially within itself, and thereby to carry out the god-like function of world-creation.

One of the drawbacks of Fichte's view was that it overcomes the dualism between matter and spirit, a dualism still present in Kant's thought, by absorbing the former into the latter: nature simply becomes part of the self-expressive activity of mind, which in turn is unfettered by any external limitation. Thus, while it brings into focus the notion of mind as dynamic and self-creative, rather than merely another, passive, substance alongside physical substances, it does not do justice to the fact that the mind is *embodied* and *en-natured*, and that its expressive activity takes place in the domain of, and in interaction with, nature. Fichte did indeed attempt to derive nature from his conception of the self-conscious ego, but the deduction is unconvincing and leaves one with the uncomfortable sense of the world as a figment of the mind's imagination rather than as in any sense a reality confronting it.

This shortcoming became the starting point for the speculations of Fichte's great successor in the line of German Idealist philosophers, Friedrich Wilhelm Joseph von Schelling (1775–1854). Schelling recognized that what was missing in Fichte's account was any true dialectical opposition between mind and nature, since for Fichte the human spirit unfolded purely in relation to itself. What Schelling attempted to do was to show that mind and nature, though not radically distinct substances, had to be seen as engaged in a mutually interdependent process of creative interaction. Thus while, like many other Romantics, he sought unity and integration between self and not-self, he believed that such unity is essentially the unity of opposites. Whether or not Jung read Fichte, he certainly as a young man read Schelling, and frequently in his writings acknowledged his debt to him as a major formative influence, so we will need to take a close look at his philosophy.

Nature for Schelling was a teleological system which displays a tendency to growth, such growth being the result, not of an externally imposed force or intelligence, but of an inner creative potential. According to the mechanistic system of Descartes and Newton, nature is a static system of matter governed by eternal and unchanging laws, with its order imposed from without by a transcendent architect-deity. In marked contrast with this, Schelling viewed nature in dynamic, evolutionary terms, as a system in the process of self-formation, with spirit emerging from the womb of nature as its highest manifestation. Nature has an unlimited tendency to expand and proliferate, to give rise to new and more complex phenomena. It begins with the world of physical objects in which the spirit acts in an unconscious way, rising through living beings which begin to manifest consciousness, and culminating in self-consciousness. It is in this last stage that the ego reflectively differentiates itself from the non-ego and becomes transparent to itself. The various stages of development are marked by strife and conflict, by a polarity of forces, by a creative tension between higher and lower – between matter and spirit, good and evil – tensions which are necessary for the creation of new forms. Schelling conceived God, not as an absolute being who stands outside of and directs this whole process, but rather as the very process itself. Just as the individual person becomes what they are through their life's activity, so God is fully realized only in the self-expressive act of world-creation. In a sense, the history of nature/spirit is the history of God's self-creation. In the light of this it is not surprising that Schelling gives a high place to the role of art, for the work of the artist represents, in human terms, the unity of the unconscious and the conscious, and the fullest expression of the self-creative activity of spirit.

The work of Schelling can at one level be seen as a rather grandiose metaphysical system which seeks to understand everything in terms of the development of Absolute Spirit. At another level it is a phenomenological investigation of the structure and growth of human consciousness, an account of the mind's inner process of development and its relationship to the world of nature and of other selves. It is at this latter level that we can discern the powerful influence of Schelling's thought on Jung. We can see in Jung's work an elaboration of the idea of the evolution of self-consciousness from the womb of the unconscious, and the teleological tendency of the spirit for some higher kind of unity. Furthermore, according to both Schelling and Jung, in contrast with the mechanistic tradition, we do not as conscious human beings enter a world that has already been created and perfected, but we actually co-operate with nature in the activity of world-creation, a view which revives the older Hermetic philosophy that was forced underground after the Renaissance.

We also find in both thinkers (again in concert with the Hermetic tradition) an emphasis on the dynamic force of opposites, the recognition of the essential role of darker, negative aspects of experience, the central role of intuition, and above all an organic outlook which seeks to unify spirit and nature in a single whole. This organic outlook represented, in Schelling's case, a radical shift away from the mechanistic model that prevailed in the physical sciences of his day, but it was one which in the latter half of the twentieth century has begun to emerge from within the physical sciences themselves. A holistic, evolutionary approach to nature, along with attempts to transcend the traditional division between mind and matter, has emerged under the impact of relativity and quantum theory, and while Schelling's metaphysical system-building is as little to the taste of modern science as it was to Jung's way of thinking, it is interesting to witness here a convergence of views between two hitherto embattled world-outlooks, with Jung playing what can only be described as an intermediary role. For what Jung did was to bring Schelling's inspired speculations down to earth and to anchor them firmly in the ground of empirical investigation; to adapt Marx's metaphor, deployed to express his relationship to Hegel, Jung turned Schelling upside-down and stood him back on his feet.

The whole question of the nature of mind and the process whereby it achieves some kind of self-fulfilment in relation to nature was taken up and developed further by Hegel (1770–1831). In his younger days Hegel had been a friend and admirer of Schelling, but with the publication of his *Phenomenology of Mind* in 1807 he established his own independent position, albeit one that still owed much to Schelling, Fichte and Kant. He criticized Schelling for the unspecificity of his account of the emergence of spirit and its dialectical relationship with nature, comparing the latter's concept of Absolute Spirit as 'the night in which all cows are black'. He then proceeded to develop his own account of the emergence of mind by elaborating in detail the process whereby mind, through progressive interaction with 'the other' by means of the dialectical process of opposition succeeded by reconciliation, achieves its fullest development in what he called the Absolute Spirit.

Hegel, like Schelling, viewed the mind as emerging gradually through the conflict of opposites from a state of natural oneness and simplicity to a higher state of spiritual fulfilment, in which the actualizing of possibilities and the painful striving towards self-consciousness set the direction and purpose of the whole enterprise. This view was essentially an elaboration of the ideas of Schelling, and while it is from the latter rather than from Hegel that Jung derived his inspiration, it will be useful, in view of Hegel's overwhelming importance in the history of modern thought, to draw attention to some of the links between the thinking of Hegel and Jung.

The latter, like Hegel, conceived the psyche, not as some static substance, but rather as a continually evolving process which arises from unconscious roots in nature, and, while retaining all the marks of its origins in unconscious nature, is nevertheless engaged in a struggle to rise to a higher state of fulfilment and self-expression. Further, like Hegel he believed that this struggle is essentially dialectical in nature, that is to say it depends on the creative conflict between opposite tendencies which, through their very opposition, provide the energy whereby the psyche is sublimated in a higher state. There is also an important theological comparison to be made here, for Jung, again like Hegel, tended to reject the idea of a transcendent God standing outside and beyond creation, but saw the Divine Spirit as a reality that can be discovered within the psyche itself.

The convergence of the two thinkers over theological questions is reflected in the problem of evil and the broad issue of the meaningfulness of existence in the context of a world beset with pain and suffering. Thus both were concerned with the age-old question: what sense can we make of a world which contains suffering? Hegel, in his writings on the philosophy of history, spoke movingly of the 'slaughter-bench of history' on which countless individuals and nations had been sacrificed, and argued that the perfection of the spirit was only possible at the cost of pain, negation and destruction. Jung, in his book *Answer to Job*, argued that evil must counterbalance good in our conception of God, and that theologians had been profoundly mistaken in their attempt to show that evil is merely an absence of good rather than a reality. Orthodox Christian theology had responded to the problem of evil by placing the focus of man's life outside and beyond this world in the eternal and inscrutable purposes of God. This was unsatisfactory to Hegel who endeavoured to show that human reason was capable of making sense of life without going beyond the bounds of history and human experience. The meaning of life was contained within history, in the unfolding of the human spirit, and ultimately in the complete self-consciousness of Absolute Spirit. 'The goal is this,' he wrote, 'that spirit come to consciousness of itself'. Providence rules the world and endows it with purpose and meaning, not through externally imposed law, but through the ever-growing awareness of the spirit of itself, mediated through the cultural, religious and philosophical activities of mankind.

Jung likewise attempted to construct an image of human life bounded by the limits of intra-worldly existence, and while he did not rule out the possibility of an afterlife – in this he demonstrated his underlying empiricist leanings in comparison with the more rationalistic-minded Hegel – his conception of individuation as the goal of life did not call upon the support of any trancendent beliefs.

It is worth elaborating in a little more detail the relationship between the two thinkers on this issue. Hegel offered a systematically developed answer to the problem of life's purpose, an answer which encompassed the whole of thought and of human history. For him, the 'real', in all its evolutionary unfolding in nature and in history, is the 'rational'; as philosophy reflects on the course of this grand process it can plot its inner logic and discern the inevitability of both its process and its outcome. Jung's answer was at once less systematic and more personal. He rejected not only Hegel's rationalist dialectic which viewed history as an inevitable procession of stages, but also the assumption that history is pointing towards an ultimate apotheosis, the final overcoming of all contradictions. Hegel's notion of Absolute Spirit as the ultimate fulfilment of all possibilities, containing and reconciling all opposites, was anathema to Jung's way of thinking. He was much more of a pragmatist and a realist who, as a result of his wide clinical experience, was acutely aware of the inescapable presence of evil in the world, a presence too massively obvious to be conjured away by clever philosophical arguments.

Nevertheless, despite these differences there remain some striking parallels to be drawn between the two thinkers in this regard. For like Hegel Jung believed that the only thing that can give meaning to life is the development of the potential that lies inherent in the human spirit. His language is that of the psychologist rather than that of the metaphysician, but the essential point remains the same. 'The ultimate aim and strongest desire of all mankind', he wrote, 'is to develop that fullness of life which is called personality' (CW17.284), such a development meaning 'nothing less than the optimum development of the whole human being . . . in all its biological, social and spiritual aspects' (CW17.289). Crucial to this development, for Jung as for Hegel, was the emergence of consciousness and ultimately of self-consciousness: 'As far as we can discern,' Jung wrote 'the sole purpose of human existence is to kindle a light in the darkness of mere being' (MDR, p.358). It is therefore in 'the miracle of reflecting consciousness' that the meaning, 'concealed somewhere within all the monstrous, apparently senseless biological turmoil' is revealed (p.371). If there is any meaning in life at all – and Jung is careful to avoid making any claims for the cosmos as a whole – then it must lie in, or rather in the unending quest for, what he called individuation, namely the wholeness and harmony of the total personality.

In view of the evident parallels between the two thinkers, it is surprising that Jung frequently went out of his way to distance himself from Hegel. This is undoubtedly due in part to the obscure and high-flown nature of Hegel's philosophical language: 'He seemed to me like a man who was caged in the edifice of his own words and was pompously gesticulating in his prison', he complained (MDR, p,87). This was not just a matter of style, for Jung adopted an explicitly nominalist view of language, seeing words as conventional man-made symbols rather than as conveying the true essence of things. Hence he was suspicious of Hegel's tendency to hypostatize concepts, to concretize words like 'spirit' and 'state' such as to make them seem like real, even super-real, entities, or even personalities (see US, p.75f).

A further more substantial objection lay in his claim that Hegel was a 'psychologist in philosopher's garb' (CW18.1734), that his great philosophical system was in reality nothing other than psychology projected onto the cosmos, that it was 'misfired psychology', couched in language reminiscent of schizophrenics. This objection seems surprising at first glance, for in a sense his characterization of Hegel's thought appears to sum up the central core in his own thinking, namely that much that we have hitherto taken for external reality, from gods to flying saucers, is in fact a projection of the mind, and refers, strictly speaking, to features of the inner rather than the outer cosmos. But while for him the projection factor was central to his analysis of metaphysical systems, in Hegel he discerned an unconscious inflation of his own subjective psychology into a fantastic metaphysical system whose 'objectivity' he never doubted. Hegel's bombastic language hid, in effect, his projection 'of great truths out of the subjective sphere into a cosmos he himself had created' (CW8.358), a projection of which he was entirely unaware. In this respect Jung's psychologizing of metaphysics could be seen as an early form of deconstruction, aimed at humbling the hubris of human reason of the sort most conspicuously represented by Hegel.[1]

Another factor separating the two thinkers lay in their opposite approaches to the relationship between the individual and the universal. In his study of the biography of the spirit Hegel saw the individual person as ultimately subsumed into the universal world-spirit. Jung by contrast was an uncompromising individualist who, like Hegel's nineteenth-century critic Kierkegaard, was convinced that the individual cannot be encompassed within an abstract philosophical system.

In spite of these differences, there can be little doubt that Hegelian thinking played a role in the formation of Jung's central ideas. There are great psychological insights embedded in the philosopher's 'megalomanic language', especially in his view that mind or consciousness develops through a process of alienation and return. And even if he had never read a word of Hegel, the ideas of the latter were so pervasive in the German-speaking intellectual world of the nineteenth century that he could hardly have failed to imbibe them.

It is a different story, though, with Hegel's arch-rival, Schopenhauer, for here the relationship and influence was fully recognized and documented. Arthur Schopenhauer (1788–1860) had set himself up to rival and even overthrow the Hegelian hegemony at the University of Berlin in the early nineteenth century. He failed, somewhat ignominiously, in this aim, but after some decades of obscurity, his great work, *The World as Will and Idea*, first published in 1818, achieved wide acclaim and had a great influence on a number of figures, including Wagner and Nietzsche in the nineteenth century, and Thomas Mann and Wittgenstein in the twentieth. By the turn of the century his influence on European culture as a whole was, as Bryan Magee puts it, 'all-pervasive' and 'inescapably strong' (1983, p.264).

Like Schelling and Hegel, Schopenhauer believed in the evolution of mind. But he went much further in identifying its roots as planted firmly in the ground of nature and the biological kingdom, and saw the whole process as driven by a blind and pointless energy which he called 'will'. Whereas Hegel had identified the real with the rational, and had adopted an optimistic view of the final outcome of history, Schopenhauer took no comfort at all from the evolution of consciousness, and saw the emergence of higher manifestations of mind as the source of human suffering.

He saw reality as an unbroken chain, rather like the old Great Chain of Being, extending from the most primal and undifferentiated aspects of nature at one extreme to the most differentiated and highly developed forms of consciousness at the other, impelled forward towards greater differentiation in accordance with what Schopenhauer called the 'principle of individuation'. This latter term was later to be employed by Jung as a way of characterizing what he saw as the final goal and ideal of human development. His use of the term differs in some important respects from that of Jung, but there is much common ground between them in the idea that there is a natural compulsion in nature towards the production and refinement of individual consciousness.

The most important link between them lay in the belief that rational self-consciousness emerges from some deeper unconscious level of reality. Schopenhauer spoke of consciousness as being like the Earth's surface which, while seeming to be a separate and independent phenomenon, both hides and reveals the forces at work beneath. And just as a full understanding of the Earth's topography must lead in the direction of geological investigation, so our understanding of human consciousness must lead us to consider the dynamic forces that lie beneath its surface. Jung's theory of the psyche was clearly modelled on this, though it must be stressed that he never went as far as Schopenhauer in suggesting that rational consciousness was *merely* a manifestation of, and therefore wholly determined by, the unconscious, for he was always concerned to leave room for free will and some measure of individual autonomy.

Schopenhauer's belief in the emergence of self-consciousness from pre-conscious origins in the natural world is connected with his rejection of Cartesian dualism. He saw that it was impossible to mark any absolute boundary between mind and matter, between subject and object, for 'just as there can be no object without a subject, so there can be no subject without an object' (Schopenhauer, 1883, ii. para 202). We cannot conceive or make sense of an ego distinct from world, nor of world distinct from mind, for in all our cognitive acts we presuppose both a subject and an object of awareness. In the final analysis, then, we must conceive the world as one and undivided. Yet at the same time we experience it under two distinct aspect or modes, either internally as subjective mind or externally as things in space and time – as 'will' or as 'idea' respectively in Schopenhauer's terminology. From a purely phenomenological standpoint, then, there are two quite distinct ways of grasping the world, even if ontologically it must be thought of as an undivided whole. Following Spinoza, he held that mind and body are not two distinct substances, but rather different attributes of a single reality. This means that there can be no causal interaction between mind and body, for there are not two distinct sets of events – the mental and the physcial – which can properly be said to interact, there is only one set of events which can be viewed or described in two alternative ways (see Magee, 1983, Ch.5).

Jung devoted to this issue nothing like the sophistication of Schopenhauer, but like his great mentor he sought to avoid on the one side the objectivism and empiricism of Locke, and on the other the subjectivism of Fichte, as well as the dualism of Descartes. His arguments were cursory and impressionistic by comparison, but he clung to the view that a monistic world-view can be reconciled with the belief that the mental world is distinct from, and need not be reduced to, the world of matter. He too realized that the key to this lay in the analysis of the nature of experience itself which points to the indissoluble unity of subject and object, an attitude which is expressed in Jung's constantly reiterated assertion of the primacy of experience over theory. He also realized that Schopenhauer's total rejection of the old idea of substance, whether mental or material, and his prescient adoption of an energic standpoint was another key to the refutation of dualism. For both men the world is to be understood as a dynamic continuum, an undivided web of events, though segmented by our structuring minds into convenient pieces and categories. We will return to these matters in Chapter 14 below.

Among the many figures in the latter half of the century to be influenced by Schopenhauer, two require special mention. The first is Eduard von Hartmann (1842–1906), who was frequently mentioned by Jung as someone who helped shape his conception of the unconscious. Von Hartmann's book, *Philosophy of the Unconscious*, published in 1869, did much to formulate and popularize the notion of the unconscious. It was largely based on Schopenhauer's philosophy of will and offered little that was new of a philosophical nature, but its accumulation of empirical data concerning instincts, personality traits, emotions, etc., and its attempt to understand the unconscious in cultural as well as personal terms, anticipated in many respects the approach and method of Jung.

The second is the more substantial, and historically more important, figure of Nietzsche (1844–1900). Like Jung he acknowledged his profound indebtedness to Schopenhauer, and, while rejecting the latter's moral and aesthetic theories, and fundamentally transforming his theory of the will, he developed many of his predecessor's psychological insights, and reaffirmed in general terms his view of the relationship between the higher and lower realms of the psyche. What is common to all three is a heightened awareness, in many respects novel in Western thought, of the irrational forces that lie beneath the rational surface of consciousness.

Jung's indebtedness to Nietzsche was frequently expressed in his writings. As a young man he was very familiar with the latter's works, and spoke of the air at Basel University as being 'full of talk about Nietzsche', the latter having resigned his chair at the university in 1879, sixteen years before Jung embarked on his medical studies there. More than any other thinker, Nietzsche seems to have stood behind Jung's shoulder, sometimes like a shadow disturbing and haunting him, sometimes as a source of vision and inspiration.

Nothing attests more eloquently to this than the series of seminars which Jung gave between 1934 and 1939 on Nietzsche's most compelling and most difficult creation, *Thus Spake Zarathustra*, a work which ranks alongside Goethe's *Faust* as a key influence on Jung as a man and as a psychologist. He commented that

> When I read *Zarathustra* for the first time as a student of twenty-three, of course I did not understand it at all, but I got a tremendous impression. I could not say it was this or that, though the poetical beauty of some of the chapters impressed me, but particularly the strange *thought* got hold of me. He helped me in many respects.
>
> (NZ, p.544)

The seminars have now been published, based on the notes of a professional secretary, and those of a faithful band of colleagues and students with whose aid he struggled through the text line by line (in fact only two-thirds of the text were completed by the time the seminars were terminated by the onset of war).

It is difficult to sum up the content of two massive volumes, but it is important to record that Jung's interpretation of Nietzsche's work is entirely psychological, and is based on his method of amplification whereby pieces of text are filled out by means of a whole network of psychological, mythological and historical associations. Thus, he argued that 'Nietzsche is really a modern psychologist. In our days, he would have made a famous analyst, for he had an ingenious flare for the dark background and the secret motivations; he has anticipated a great deal of Freud and Adler' (NZ, p.120). This view of Nietzsche is now widely held, but at the time was nothing less than revolutionary.

It hardly needs recalling that these seminars took place at a time of great political crisis in Europe. Nietzsche's ideas had supposedly given some support to the Nazi ideology, and Jung himself has sometimes been accused of Nazi sympathies. I deal later in Part II with this charge against Jung, and point out that Nietzsche's association with the Nazi philosophy has now been dismissed as a gross distortion and misinterpretation. Reading the seminars, one is struck, however, by the surprising lack of political interest displayed by the professor and his students. Had Jung harboured any Nazi sympathies, here was the golden opportunity to develop these and to share them with his admiring and attentive audience. But references to current events in general and to Hitler in particular are sparse and arise only incidentally. Jung appeared reluctant to be 'sidetracked' into political questions, and when these did arise displayed considerable apprehension concerning current events in Germany. On the question of German nationalism, for example, he dismissed the idea of the Germans as a chosen people as 'damned nonsense', and exonerated Nietzsche from any such imputed sympathies (see NZ, p.827).

The psychological interest in these seminars focuses on the *Übermensch*, or 'overman', a central idea in Nietzsche's mature thought, which finds its first full, if elusively poetic, treatment in *Zarathustra*. This concept has notoriously been pressed into perverted political service, but for Jung it was clearly a precursor of his own idea of *individuation*. In this, as in other matters, he was not uncritical of Nietzsche; he was wary of the latter's self-inflationary tendency towards identification with Zarathustra, and frequently noted that Nietzsche came dangerously close to being invaded and overtaken by an archetypal force, one which led to a puffed up and illusory attitude to himself. But at the core of the idea of the overman Jung claimed to discover a deep psychological wisdom. This is the belief, which he believed is to be found in all the world's great religions, that the essence of human life consists in its capacity for growth, that 'we have not yet discovered man in his totality' (NZ, p.822). Overman (*Übermensch*) is, he claimed, 'the becoming of the self', it is 'the idea of rebirth in the self or to the self' (p.839). The 'death of God', which according to Nietzsche presages the coming of overman, and which allows the divinity to become incarnated in man, is, Jung surmised, nothing other than 'a sort of intuition of an individuation process in man' (p.1527).

The common ground between the two thinkers becomes even more evident when we broaden out our view to take in the whole of Nietzsche's teaching concerning the human psyche. Like Jung, he explicitly rejected the view of the self as some kind of simple substance, sovereign in its own domain, that revealed itself in the immediacy of self-awareness. Such a view, most celebrated in the work of Descartes, was typical of philosophers' propensity to reduce complex processes to simple entities. In the first place, human consciousness is not some disembodied unmoved mover that can stand above and even rule the forces of nature. In this respect, as in most others, philosophers have got things the wrong way round, according to Nietzsche, for 'that which is last, thinnest and emptiest is put first as a cause in itself' whereas in truth consciousness is 'the last smoke of an evaporating reality' (1968, 'Reason in Philosophy', para.4). Secondly, human consciousness, in so far as one can speak of it in substantive terms at all, is part of the total dynamic process of human life, not strictly a thing but a complex of activities, of contradictory and opposing tendencies which, while manifesting itself on the surface as rational consciousness, at the same time is the outward expression to some of the most fundamental irrational forces of nature.

There are many other intriguing points of contact and comparison between them which require at least a brief mention: their ambivalent attitude to Christianity and Western culture; their sense of an epochal crisis in which modern man is at a turning point, and in relation to which they both saw themselves as having some important role; their investigation of the dark and scary side of human nature, which Nietzsche called the Dionysian, and Jung the shadow; their recognition of the relative and perspectival nature of all human cognition which they saw as intepretation, even myth-making, rather than the pure pursuit of truth; their recognition of the importance of dream and fantasy, and of the role of creativity and spontaneity in the life of the human psyche; and their celebration of the body and the earth in contrast with what they both perceived as their neglect or denigration in Western philosophy. Many of these points will be touched upon and further elaborated in the course of this present work.

In the mean time one final influence must be noted, namely that of Carl Gustav Carus (1789–1869). He was an heir to the ideas of the nature philosophers, especially those of Schelling, and played an important part in broadening the concept of the mind. In his book *Psyche*, published in 1846, Carus put forward the view that the conscious life rests on the foundations of the unconscious, and that the psyche must be viewed as the total interacting field that embraces both conscious and unconscious realms. His work was in effect the first attempt to give a complete systematic account of the life of the psyche, an endeavour which he described as a 'science of the soul'. His view was an essentially dynamic one which saw the psyche, not as some kind of ready-made entity, but rather as a continually evolving process in which consciousness emerges slowly out of unconsciousness, which in turn arises from the womb of nature herself. He paid particular attention to dream-life which he saw as having a restorative function for conscious life, and viewed consciousness and unconsciousness as having mutually compensatory functions. The connections between these views and those of Jung are very evident, and Jung himself was clearly a great admirer of Carus whom he saw as an important influence on his understanding of pre-modern thought systems.

Jung's role in the history of thought may be seen as carrying the speculations of the thinkers discussed in this chapter one stage further, and especially in transposing their metaphysical concepts into more familiar keys. The common concern of these thinkers was not just with the exploration of the psychic world, but with the attempt to formulate a unified world-view, one in which matter and spirit, the physical and the mental not only have a place but are seen to occupy places on a continuum in which there are no unbridgeable gaps. Their efforts, often weighed down with obscure metaphysical encumbrances, have not always found favour in the twentieth century, particularly in the English-speaking intellectual world with its suspicion of philosophical speculation. Now as the twentieth century draws to a close something of a rapprochement has taken place and these once outmoded ideas and traditions are again being taken seriously and being reintegrated into the common discourse of our culture, a process in which Jung can be seen to have played an important early role.

# 6

# SPIRITUAL TRADITIONS, EAST AND WEST

Religions are psychotherapeutic systems.

(C.G. Jung)

So far we have explored Jung's thought within the context of the cultural and intellectual traditions of modern post-Renaissance Europe. But his interests ranged much more widely than this, both in space and in time, taking him through and beyond the more familiar lands of traditional Christian theology into the strange seas of Eastern thought and the remote, forgotten lands of alchemy and Gnosticism. His fascination with the world's religious and spiritual traditions, and the central role they played in his thinking, have caused confusion amongst his critics. On the one hand Erich Fromm contemptuously dismissed 'his blend of outmoded superstition, indeterminate heathen idol-worship, and vague talk about God' as representing 'exactly the right mix in an age which possesses but little faith and judgement' (quoted in G. Wehr, 1987, p.475). By contrast Murray Stein sees Jung as attempting nothing less than a reconstruction of Christian theology (1985). And Colin Wilson, standing somewhere between these two extremes, believed that Jung was never actually the scientist he claimed to be, but was an occultist in disguise, and a 'guru of the Western world' (1984, p.9). Jung himself was painfully aware of the confusion thus caused, and ruefully commented in 1952 that in his time he had been regarded 'not only as a Gnostic and its opposite, but also as a theist and an atheist, a mystic and a materialist', adding that he approved by contrast the opinion of the *British Medical Journal* that he was, as he had always claimed, 'an empiricist first and last' (CW18.1502).

By contrast with Freud, Jung saw a positive role for religion and for the pursuit of spiritual goals, and consistently maintained that 'a religious attitude is an element in psychic life whose importance can hardly be overrated' (MM, p.77). Religious beliefs and practices he saw not as superstitions or as whimsical fantasies but as expressions of basic psychological needs, in particular the need for meaning and purpose, and in religious doctrines he saw, not regression to the childish play of the pre-adult mind of the human race, but the manifestation of universal unconscious archetypal forces. Where Freud had understood religious experience in terms of the pathology of repression and sublimation, as the 'obsessional neurosis of mankind', Jung viewed it as 'man's greatest and most significant achievement, giving him the security and inner strength not to be crushed by the monstrousness of the universe' (CW5.343).

Jung himself, as the son of a Lutheran pastor, had been reared in a Christian atmosphere, and despite personal scepticism about the truth of orthodox doctrine, remained emotionally and intellectually close throughout his life to the religion of his childhood. But was he a man of faith? At the age of seventy he wrote that 'the charisma of belief has never arisen within me' (CW18.1407), yet a few years later in a famous interview with John Freeman he was able to say 'I don't need to believe [in God]. I know' (JS, p.383). Fortunately we are not required to pursue this question here since Jung was always careful to separate his subjective and personal beliefs from his 'official' scientific convictions, namely those subject to public rational debate. 'As a responsible scientist', he affirmed, 'I am not going to preach my personal and subjective convictions which I cannot prove' (CW18.1589), and in 1958 he wrote that he could 'find access to religion only through the psychological understanding of inner experiences, whereas traditional religious interpretations left me high and dry' (CW18.1643). There was no place in empirical psychology, he claimed, for matters of faith or of doctrine, and hence he could never allow himself 'to make statements about the divine entity, since that would be a transgression beyond the limits of science' (*Letters I*, p.384). True to his Kantian convictions, he argued that religious truths must of their very nature transcend our rational understanding, and wondered 'why should we be so immodest as to suppose that we could catch a universal being in the narrow confines of our language' (CW18.1589). Yet at the same time the psychological fact of religious experience was of immense importance since it constituted, he believed, the core process whereby the individual psyche develops and grows towards its goal of wholeness and integration. In an argument worthy of the Pragmatist philosopher William James, he stated that there was 'a strong empirical reason why we should hold beliefs we know can never be proved. It is that they are known to be useful. Man positively needs general ideas and convictions that will give a meaning to his life and enable him to find a place in the universe' (CW18.566).

According to Jung the importance of religious belief and spiritual practice lay, therefore, in their inner psychological importance, not in their claimed objective truth about which he remained agnostic. He defined religion as a certain kind of *experience*, which he described as 'numinous', creeds being merely codified, dogmatized, and organized forms of a special sort of inner experience. The outer expressions of these inner experiences are symbols whose meanings must not be taken literally but rather in terms of their significance for the individual psyche. Thus, for example, the doctrine of the Resurrection represented for him not an historical or metaphysical 'fact', but rather a symbolic meaning, 'the projection of an indirect realization of the self', an image pointing towards psychological wholeness and perfection (CW18.1567). In his most extensive work on Christian thought, *Aion*, he sought to draw a detailed parallel between the image of Christ on the one hand and the self on the other, but he was careful to stress that the parallel 'is not to be taken as anything more than a psychological one', and that there is 'no question of any intrusion into the sphere of metaphysics, i.e. of faith' (CW9ii.122). The Christ he spoke of in this work was not the Christ of theology or of pious religious practice, but was rather a symbol of the psychological process of individuation. He spoke of religious doctrines as 'psychological truths' rather than as 'external truths', meaning that their 'truth' lay in their therapeutic value for psychic health rather than in any claims they might seem to make about the world at large. Jung's thinking on this question was in effect a contribution to that long tradition of theological speculation, stretching as far back as Hegel, which has sought to 'dymythologize' Christian theology by treating its claims in symbolic rather than in literal terms, retaining thereby its power to shape our lives while discarding its metaphysical scaffolding.

Jung has often been accused of *psychologism*, namely in this context of reducing religious beliefs to psychological statements. However, none of the above considerations *precludes* the possibility of a faith based on transcendent realities. It merely places these considerations into parentheses and refuses to make a judgement as to their 'external truth'. Thus in his discussion of the symbolism of the Mass Jung was careful to note that 'to treat a metaphysical statement as a psychic process is not to say that it is "merely psychic"' (CW11.448), for 'metaphysical and psychological statements do not contradict one another'. It would therefore be a mistake to regard the limits of science as the limits of reality, for 'no science can consider its hypotheses to be the final truth' (CW11.376). Concern with the psychological significance of religious symbols leaves the question of 'external truth' on one side, and hence, for example, while the image of God in the human psyche may express an archetypal need, this need is quite independent of the question whether there is something 'objective' corresponding to that need. In much the same way, the existence in a child of an archetypal mother-image is in itself no guarantee of the existence of an actual mother.

In the light of this it is hardly surprising that he displayed an ambivalent attitude towards Christianity. On the one hand he saw it, and indeed all religions, as a psychotherapeutic system: Christianity, he exclaimed, 'is a beautiful system of psychotherapy. It heals the suffering soul' (JS, p.86). This positive attitude was directed in particular towards Catholicism which, in contrast with Protestantism, offered through its sacraments and its rich symbolic life 'a wealth of possibilities for expression [which] act as an incomparable diet for the psyche' (JS, p.57).

Nevertheless in the final analysis for Jung orthodox Christianity had failed to satisfy mankind's deepest psychological needs. In the modern world its symbols and rituals had become ossified, emptied of spiritual meaning, and had 'lost their root connection with natural experience . . . and their capacity to recall and evoke the original [religious] experience' (CW9ii.65). Echoing the criticisms of Kierkegaard a hundred or so years earlier, he lamented that the church and its doctrines had become 'a fortress whose purpose is to protect us from God and his Spirit' (CW18.1534). But the problem has a much longer history for right from its early days orthodox Christianity preached a partial and one-sided doctrine which emphasized the spirit over body, the higher over the lower, and thereby failed to engage adequately with man's need for wholeness. The Church had consistently taken the side of the good and the perfect, projecting these onto the godhead, thereby failing to come to terms with what he called the 'divine darkness', and leaving mankind with a sense of its own alienation both from itself and from God.

It was this one-sidedness, and Jung's deepseated unease with the religion of Pastor Jung, which led him to engage in a lifelong dialogue with other faiths and religions, seeking thereby not an alternative faith but a revivification of the inner life of the psyche which he believed had atrophied in the West. It must be said, however, his deep interest in the philosophies of the East, in alchemy and in Gnosticism have, even more than his identification with Christianity, fed the suspicions of those who have sought to marginalize Jung and to dismiss him as a mystic. The problem lies not only with his critics. Even some of his closest colleagues, such as Antonia Wolff, have found his concern with alchemy unduly protracted, and most general discussions of his work devote only cursory attention to his Oriental preoccupations. But if we are to understand Jung in the perspective of the history of ideas, it is important that we look more closely at these exotic interests, and try to understand why he engaged in an intimate and protracted discussion with these 'alternative' traditions.

Jung had a lifelong interest in Eastern thought, and in his autobiography expressed his deep conviction of 'the value of Oriental wisdom' (MDR, p.304). References to the thought of ancient India and China appear quite early on in his writings, and indicate a more than superficial acquaintance with both primary and secondary sources. He recalled that even at the age of six he was fascinated with stories about the religions of India, and two of his early major works, *Symbols of Transformation* and *Psychological Types*, both contain extensive and carefully documented comparative studies of Vedic, Buddhist, and Taoist ideas. During the 1920s his interest in these matters was further stimulated by acquaintance with two men, Hermann Keyserling and Richard Wilhelm. Keyserling was a German social philosopher who wrote a number of popular works after World War I on the theme of spiritual regeneration, and his writings were much admired by Jung who wrote reviews of several of his books. He travelled widely and endeavoured to propagate an internationalist viewpoint in an epoch increasingly dominated by narrow nationalisms. His travels and writings spanned several continents, but he had a special interest in the Orient, and in the early twenties he founded a 'School of Wisdom' in Darmstadt devoted to bringing about a reconciliation of the ideas of East and West.

It was while attending a meeting there that Jung first met Richard Wilhelm, a missionary and sinologist who was to have a great impact on his thinking. He wrote that Wilhelm's life-work was of 'immense importance to me because it clarified and confirmed so much that I had been seeking, striving for, thinking', and he felt himself 'so very much enriched by him that it seems to me as if I had received more from him than from any other man' (CW15.96).

The particular textual source of this enrichment lay in two Chinese classics, the *I Ching* or *Book of Changes* (i.e. of life transformations), and *The Secret of the Golden Flower*, the one a book of divination, the other of alchemy. Even prior to his meeting with Wilhelm Jung had read and made use of the *I Ching*, attempting to see if this ancient book, with its hexagrams and Delphic utterances, which seemed to depart so completely from our ways of thinking, had any significance for the modern European reader (see MDR, p.405, and CW11.964f). But it was Wilhelm's translations of these texts, along with their conversations about them, that moved his thinking a stage further by enabling him to find some corroboration for his recently formulated ideas about the collective unconscious. It must be remembered that this was a period when he was still emerging from the trauma of his break with Freud, a period in which he suffered an acute sense of isolation and had not yet fully established his own independent position in the intellectual world. The support of the great sinologist, and corroboration of his ideas from a totally different cutural milieu, were therefore matters of considerable psychological significance to him.

What in fact both men discovered was that each in his own apparently distinct discipline had been moving imperceptibly towards the other; in their work East and West had met. Many years after Wilhelm's death Jung wrote of him that 'what I had to tell him about the results of my investigations of the unconscious caused him no little surprise; for he recognized in them things he had considered to be the exclusive possession of the Chinese philosophical tradition' (MDR, p.406).

Wilhelm had asked Jung to contribute a commentary to his edition of *The Secret of the Golden Flower*, and in it he wrote of the parallel he had discovered between the contents of that ancient text and the psychic development of his own patients:

> Observations made in my practical work have opened out to me a quite new and unexpected approach to Eastern wisdom . . . when I began my career as a psychiatrist, I was completely ignorant of Chinese philosophy, and only later did my professional experience show me that in my technique I had been unconsciously following that secret way which for centuries had been the preoccupation of the best minds of the East.
>
> (CW13.10)

What then was this 'secret way', and how did it come to converge with Jung's own way? The answer to this question is in several parts, and in each we will see that he was engaged in a dialogue with the past, not for its own sake, but for the sake of the present, in order, as he put it, 'to alleviate the psychic sufferings of Europeans' (CW15.96).

The first is to do with what he called the 'spiritual crisis of modern man'. Jung's ideas concerning this spiritual crisis will be discussed more fully in Chapter 12 below. There we will see that for Jung this 'crisis' involved a number of interconnected factors, centring on the progressive loss of religious belief in the West since the Age of Enlightenment, and the resultant shrinking of our roots in our traditions with their rich store of archetypal myths, images, and rituals. As a result we are set adrift, having lost touch with the sources of individual and cultural meaning and are thereby made prey to all sorts of impersonal social and political forces which threaten to take over and absorb the individual. We have, by way of compensation, turned our attention towards the physical and social worlds to the neglect of our inner sources of psychic and spiritual life which are, according to Jung, essential for the well-being of the individual human being. Hitherto in the West the Christian religion has provided a framework of meaning, symbol, and ritual, but it can no longer give us what we need. 'For [modern man] the various forms of religion no longer appear to come from within, from the psyche; they seem more like items from the inventory of the outside world . . . he tries on a variety of religious beliefs as if they were Sunday attire, only to lay them aside again like worn-out clothes' (CW10.168).

Out of this crisis has emerged not only a renewed interest in the inner world, 'an indication that modern man expects something from the psyche which the outer world has not given him' (CW10.168), but also a fascination with the ideas of the East. The history of this fascination dates back to the Enlightenment period when leading figures such as Leibniz and Voltaire turned eagerly to the ideas emerging from Confucian China *via* the Jesuit missionaries, and used them as the basis for a critique of what they saw as a decadent Western culture.

The focus of attention switched during the Romantic period from China to the more metaphysical and religiously coloured ideas of India. Many of the Romantics, such as Herder, Novalis and Friedrich Schlegel, seized upon these newly discovered ideas with enthusiasm, and as the nineteenth century progressed the spiritual riches of the Vedic and Buddhist traditions were studied with increasing interest in the West. The period saw, not only a rapid growth in scholarship directed to the Orient, and the translation of many of its classical texts, but also a proliferation of cults and societies, most conspicuous of all being the Theosophical Society which sought to build a new universal spiritual movement founded on a synthesis of ideas from both East and West. In addition to this burgeoning popular movement, which expressed a deep and widely felt spiritual need which was not being fulfilled by traditional Western belief systems, there were several important nineteenth century intellectual figures who were influenced by these newly discovered currents of thought, the most significant being Schopenhauer and Nietzsche.

Jung's interest in the Orient, therefore, was not something odd or idiosyncratic. Anyone educated within the German cultural ambience of the late nineteenth century would have been aware of the flood of new ideas coming from that direction, and would have recognized their significance for a European culture that was evidently passing into a period of grave self-doubt. The end of the century witnessed a kind of world-weariness, an echo of the *Weltschmerz* (world pain) of the earlier Romantic period, and for many these newly imported ideas, especially those of Buddhism, represented an alternative outlook. Jung himself was fully aware of the historical importance for the West of this invasion of Eastern ideas and, in a letter dated 1932, spoke of 'the long history' of the 'intrusion' of Eastern thought, especially in the writings of Eckhart, Leibniz, Voltaire, Kant, Hegel, Schopenhauer, and von Hartmann (*Letters I*, p.87).

In some ways, then, Jung was riding the crest of a wave of popular and scholarly enthusiasm for Oriental ideas. But before we jump to the conclusion that he was merely carried away by this wave, indulging in escapist delusions and, like some Theosophists, encouraging a wholesale defection from orthodox Western values and traditions, let us look more closely at precisely what Jung believed the East had to teach us.

In the first place, in the spirit of Voltaire, he saw it as offering us a platform on which to build a critique of our own cultural values. These values have ceased to bring us satisfaction because of their increasingly one-sided emphasis on non-spiritual goals. In order to balance the excessive emphasis in our culture on the external world of matter, and on the need to understand and dominate that world, we must learn something of the inwardness and non-dogmatic spirituality which, he believed, was characteristic of the thought and culture of the Orient. This demands a radical switch of attention from the outer physical world to the inner world of consciousness, and beyond that to the unconscious world that lies beneath. He saw that Indian and Chinese philosophers have long been engaged in a systematic exploration of this inner world and have devised a range of techniques and disciplines for its understanding and direction, techniques which we in the West have only very recently begun to explore in our own terms. He pointed out that we are

> just a peninsula of Asia, and on that continent there are old civilizations where people have trained their minds in introspective psychology for thousands of years, whereas we began our psychology not even yesterday but only this morning. These people have an insight that is simply fabulous, and I had to study Eastern things to understand certain facts of the unconscious.
>
> (CW18.139)

In spite of the waves of enthusiasm for the East mentioned above, we have over the past few centuries developed a tendency to denigrate the achievements of the East and to dismiss their cultures as being backward in comparison with our own. But just as Joseph Needham, in his great work *Science and Civilization in China*, has shown that the East had until the eighteenth century produced a science and a technology at least as sophisticated as that of the West, often anticipating many 'discoveries' made in the West, so too Jung was at pains to show that in his own sphere, psychology, recent advances in the exploration of the psyche had long been foreshadowed in the philosophical and religious systems of the East. Thus psychoanalysis, 'a development which we consider specifically Western', is actually 'only a beginner's attempt compared with what is an immemorial art in the East' (CW10.188), and the insights into the human psyche of the Indian *Upanishads*, frequently dismissed by us as barbarian or childish, are of 'extraordinary depth and astonishing psychological accuracy', and show a far deeper understanding of the human unconscious than anything so far produced in the West (CW6.357).

Despite the idealist trend in German Romantic thought, which was in some ways a reaction against the mainstream, and has much in common with Indian metaphysical thinking, the tendency in Western thought since the Renaissance has been towards increasing emphasis on the secondary, or even illusory, nature of mind. In the East, on the other hand, the situation is reversed, especially in the religious thought of India where primacy is given to mind and consciousness, with the material world taking second, even derivative, place. In Hindu thought the world as it appears to our senses is seen as an illusion, or at any rate as a construct of our modes of perception and of conception, and which therefore depends to some extent on our own consciousness. As Jung put it: 'For us the essence of that which works is the world of appearance; for the Indian it is the soul. The world for him is a mere show or facade, and his reality comes close to being what we would call a dream' (CW11.910).

This does not mean that Jung advocated a complete denial of our traditional ways of looking at things. The East was in many ways just as one-sided as the West. But he saw the East's emphasis on inwardness and self-awareness as offering us a chance to reassess the relative importance of the world of mind and consciousness, and to discover a greater balance between the spiritual and the material. As Coward puts it: 'The truth of the East [for Jung] is not in the Eastern way itself, but in the demonstrated need for a balance between intellect and intuition, between thinking and feeling' (1985, p.8). In our culture, Jung declared, 'No one has time for self-knowledge or believes that it could serve any sensible purpose. . . . We believe exclusively in doing and do not ask about the doer' (CW14.709). Furthermore the idea of the balance between opposites is itself one which is central to Hindu thinking, and though Jung rejected the notion of *moksa* in which opposition is completely transcended, he found this idea very congenial to his own way of thinking, and important as a tool for grasping, not only the psyche, but also the spiritual predicament of Western culture.

Of special importance to Jung was the fact that the East had discovered, in its own terms, the world of the *unconscious* well before the West. He believed that Eastern cultures had developed ways of tapping into and assimilating material from the deeper levels of the psyche which modern Western man has blocked off through an excessive development of rational consciousness. Here again it is a matter of the limitations of one-sided development. Rational consciousness – or directed thinking as Jung called it – is well and good in its own sphere, but the need for psychic wholeness means that we must come to terms with the irrational part of our natures. Eastern methods of meditation and yoga, Jung believed, constituted techniques which have been developed and used over the millennia throughout the East to achieve this end.

Contact with the East has, furthermore, enabled us to realize the importance of *symbols* in the life of the psyche, and in particular those universal symbols called archetypes which represent, Jung believed, the underlying common structure of the human mind. This has an important connection with the increasing loss of meaning experienced in Western cultures today. Every culture has its stock of symbols which emerge from what Jung called the collective unconscious. But in the West our store of collective symbols has become progressively impoverished due in large part to the growth of scientific rationalism and the loss of traditional religious faiths, and for this reason we turn to other cultures which, unlike ours, have retained and kept alive a rich variety of symbolic resources. Thus, while 'the Christian view of the world has paled for many people, the symbolic treasure rooms of the East are still full of marvels that can nourish for a long time' (CW9i.11). Western Christian symbols, such as the trinity and the virgin birth, which provided the spiritual nourishment of the West for many centuries, have in the modern world begun to ossify, 'to stiffen into mere objects of belief', and so to lose the sort of vitality which is able to find a response in the individual soul. In such circumstances, therefore, it is not surprising that Europeans have been attracted to the symbols of other seemingly more vital spiritual traditions.

But in case we should jump to the conclusion that Jung, in his attempt to find healing for our stricken civilization, was ready to adopt a collection of beliefs with entirely different cultural roots from our own – an assumption that has frequently reinforced the accusation of mysticism – we must now enter two important caveats.

The first is that he was as sceptical of the metaphysical content of Eastern religions as he was of Christianity, and claimed to treat both from an exclusively phenomenological standpoint. It is not so much that he rejected the beliefs involved, but rather that he placed the question of their truth into agnostic parentheses, and set himself the task of dealing solely with their psychological significance.

> I quite deliberately bring everything that purports to be metaphysical into the daylight of psychological understanding. . . . One cannot grasp anything metaphysically, one can only do so psychologically. Therefore I strip things of their metaphysical wrappings in order to make them objects of psychology. . . . My admiration for the great philosophers of the East is as genuine as my attitude towards their metaphysics is irreverent.
>
> (CW13.73-4)

Indeed he went even further and suggested that the metaphysical teachings of the East, along with their exotic symbolism, were really at bottom nothing but psychology in metaphysical clothing: 'I suspect them of being symbolical psychologists, to whom no greater wrong can be done than to take them literally' (CW13.74). Thus while he maintained a great respect for the spiritual teachings of the East he did not use them as a way of refuting or modifying the teachings of Christianity, or of supplanting the symbols of the latter with those of the Buddhist or the Hindu. Their importance lay, not in furnishing our culture with new symbols, or in providing us with a new belief system, but rather in giving us new insights into our own psyches, and a better understanding of our own culture and its spiritual disorders.

The second caveat is that Jung's approach to the East must be understood in the light of his conviction that cultures, such as that of

Western Christendom, are as it were organic entities which cannot simply be cut up, transported from their original home, and reassembled elsewhere. All cultures are historically conditioned, and their psychological identities are firmly rooted in their own peculiar traditions with their distinctive array of symbols, practices, beliefs and assumptions. Here he sided with the Romantics against the Enlightenment, the one affirming the unique identity of cultures, the other tending to see the classical traditions of Western Europe as representing some kind of universal standard. He frequently underlined his conviction that human consciousness is like an organism which is adapted to and grows within a unique environment, and hence it makes no sense to imagine that the Western mind can by an act of will disengage itself from its own historical roots and graft itself onto another. Jung's own continued attachment to Christianity, in spite of grave doubts about the literal truth of its doctrines, is in part explained by a sense of his own organic attachment to his indigenous culture.

Some in their enthusiasm for things Oriental have been seduced by what he called the 'allurements of the odorous East' (CW9i.29), and have fallen victims to its magic and novelty. He was highly critical of what he described as the attempt 'to put on, like a new suit of clothes, ready-made symbols grown on foreign soil' (CW9i.27–28), and in an ironic twist to the standardly perceived relationship between East and West, he commented that 'The spiritual beggars of our time are too inclined to accept the alms of the East in bulk and to imitate its ways unthinkingly' (CW15.88). We only make profitable use of these ideas if we remain firmly rooted in our own traditions. Of what use to us, he asked, 'is the wisdom of the *Upanishads* or the insight of Chinese yoga if we desert our own foundations. . . . We need to have a firmly based, three-dimensional life of our own before we can experience the wisdom of the East as a living thing' (CW15.88–9). Our task

> is not to imitate what is foreign to our organism [but] to build up Western civilization, which sickens with a thousand ills. This has to be done on the spot, and by the European as he is, with all his Western ordinariness, his marriage problems, his neuroses, his social and political delusions.
>
> (CW13.5)

Jung's attitude towards the East, therefore, was far from one of enthusiastic emulation, and despite his evident fascination for the philosophies of India and China he remained firmly and consciously rooted in the Western Christian traditions in which he had been reared. Indeed he urged considerable caution over what he called 'the imitative urge', the growing fashion of people in the West to 'possess themselves of outlandish feathers and deck themselves out in this exotic plumage'

(CW12.126). At one level such a tendency may be merely superficial, applying, as he put it, magical ideas like an ointment, and failing therefore to address the fundamental problems of loss of direction and meaning that beset our culture. At another level the adoption of Eastern practices such as yoga may be positively harmful since, without the protective disciplines of the total culture from which they derive, they may release unconscious forces which cannot be controlled and precipitate psychotic episodes (see CW11.847).

Jung's caution here may very well be exaggerated. The adoption in modern times of yoga and meditation techniques in a piecemeal fashion without any attempt at total immersion in a foreign culture, has undoubtedly been highly beneficial for many individuals. At a deeper level, furthermore, the exploration in recent decades of spiritual bonds between Christian and non-Christian religions points to the opening up of intercultural links which can surely only be salutary. His tendency to set up East and West as psychological opposites could very well mask a deepseated Western prejudice about the distinctness of its own culture in contrast with the 'mysterious Orient', a prejudice which has all sorts of social and political implications for the history of the twentieth century. His organic view of cultures, each with its own unique and separate identity, may well fail to do justice to the universal bonds which tie quite disparate cultures together, bonds which, as we shall see in Part II, formed the very basis of his own theory of the collective unconscious. Nevertheless his attitude here should help to silence those critics who have accused Jung precisely of those unbounded enthusiasms of whose supposed dangers he so conscientiously warned us.

Rather than capitulation to the East's allurements, therefore, Jung was seeking nothing more ambitious than a *dialogue*, 'a bridge of psychological understanding between East and West' (CW13.83), the purpose of which was not to supplant or even rival our own culture, but to restore it to a state of healthy balance and spiritual effectiveness. The one-sided emphasis in the West on the 'breathless drive for power and aggrandisement in the political, social, and intellectual sphere' (CW11.962) needs to be balanced in favour of those functions of feeling and intuition about which the East has so much to teach us. The East represented, in Jung's own words, 'a different point of view which would compensate the one-sidedness of the European outlook', and hence '[the] wisdom and mysticism of the East have . . . very much to say to us. . . . They serve to remind us that we in our culture possess something similar, which we have already forgotten, and to direct our attention to the fate of the inner man, which we set aside as trifling' (CW11.963).

Jung's constant attempt to anchor our explorations of other exotic cultures in the familiar waters of our own culture and concerns has other more practical implications. However far he wandered in the strange seas of Oriental thought, he was always aware of his role as healer and therapist, and of the fascinating links between modern psychotherapy and the ancient spiritual practices of the East. The key to Jung's therapeutic work lay, as we shall see in a later chapter, in the process of self-transformation, or 'individuation', and while his commitment to the process was well established by the time he came to be fully acquainted with Eastern thought, he nevertheless found some important and encouraging links between his own work and certain aspects of these ancient Oriental traditions. The first explicit statement of this appeared in his commentary on the Chinese alchemical text, *The Secret of the Golden Flower*, published in 1929. The central message of that work, he believed, lay in the concept of psychic integration, the reconciliation of the conscious and unconscious elements in psychic life into a balanced and harmonious whole, a process of self-realization in which fractured components of the psyche, in particular those shadowy elements that are feared and ignored, are acknowledged and brought into play within the psychic life. This goal, furthermore, can be achieved, not through action in the external world, but only by way of an inner journey of self-discovery. The aim of this process, then, 'is to detach consciousness from the object so that the individual no longer places the guarantee of his happiness . . . in factors outside himself . . . but comes to realize that everything depends on whether he holds the treasure or not' (CW18.377).

This Chinese text is only one of the many places where Jung saw a close parallel between the ancient pursuit of wisdom in the East and the modern practice of psychotherapy. The disciplines of self-transformation, conveniently brought together under the term 'yoga' (meaning 'yoke' or 'discipline'), have for millennia been central to the cultures of India, China, Tibet and Japan. The cult of yoga, which has become so popular in the West in recent years and which is often associated with little more than the pursuit of physical well-being, is in its indigenous form nothing less than the pursuit of psychic wholeness, embracing the mental and the spiritual as well as the physical. Many beliefs, practices and techniques are associated with the term yoga, including various forms of active and passive meditation, but in essence it may be summed up as a way of release from suffering, and as a training method for seeking enlightenment.

Some forms of Indian yoga have been associated in Western eyes with the development of trance-like states, leading to detachment from the world, and no doubt versions corresponding to this description may be found amongst the myriad forms of Eastern cults. But Jung recognized in yoga not a way out of the world but a way of coming to terms with it. This is especially evident, he believed, in the case of Buddhism, an offshoot of the Indian yogic tradition. Buddhism, he pointed out, is not a religion in the Western sense of that term, but is a method of psychic healing, for its task is not the worship of God or the pursuit of eternal salvation, but the understanding and amelioration of states of mental suffering. He spoke of 'the immense help and stimulation' he had received from Buddhist teachings, and, dispensing with some of his usual caution, argued that these teachings offered 'Western man ways and means of disciplining his inner psychic life . . . [that] can give him a helpful training when either Christian ritual has lost its meaning or the authority of religious ideas has collapsed' (CW18.1577).

It must be emphasized again that it was far from Jung's mind that we should actually adopt Oriental methods, unmodified, as techniques of mental healing. Such a strategy would, he believed, have disastrous consequences, and he frequently used strong words to discourage those who unthinkingly adopted the methods of yoga in their search for enlightenment: 'I wish particularly to warn against the oft attempted imitation of Indian practices and sentiments. As a rule nothing comes of it except an artifical stultification of our Western intelligence.' To make proper and fruitful use of the therapeutic practices of the East we must remain firmly rooted in our own culture, for we 'cannot and should not give up [our] Western understanding' (CW11.933). Such an understanding, whether of yoga or of Zen or of Buddhist techniques of meditation should, he argued, only be carried out as part of a bridging operation between Eastern and Western ideas – 'let us build a bridge which may lead to a European understanding of yoga' – rather than through the total absorption into an alien tradition. We need to foster the growth of our own yoga, cultivated in the soil of our own traditions. Though inspired by the East we must in the final analysis 'build on our own ground with our own methods' (CW11.773).

Following his visit to India in 1938, the focus of Jung's interest shifted from India and the East to alchemy and to the needs, as he saw them, of his own culture. Towards the end of his visit there he had a powerful dream which led him to see that 'India was not my task', but only a part of the way, and that he needed to turn his attention to the perilous state of Western Christendom (MDR, pp.310–13). He soon became absorbed in the study of alchemy, and through the remaining years of his life he expended considerable scholarly energy on it. In contrast with his studies of the East, which were spasmodic and rather amateurish, his work in the field of alchemy was systematic and highly original, involving the discovery and analysis of many hitherto unknown manuscripts, and bore fruit in a sizeable body of writings amounting to three volumes of his collected works.

Here, as with Eastern thought, he found significant analogies with his own ideas which brought him the confirmation he needed of the wider applicability of his theories. Clearly in the case of alchemy there was no question of imitating or reviving the methods and techniques of its mediaeval practioners. No modern cult of alchemy has appeared to match that of yoga, and indeed until Jung decided to investigate it from a psychological standpoint, it had remained as an historical curiosity, viewed as little more than a quaint and muddled precursor to modern chemistry. But as with the theories and practices of the East, his investigations into alchemy were conducted in the spirit of a dialogue, aimed at illuminating the present as much as the past.

The earliest known practice of alchemy dates back to eighth century BC China where it was essentially a medical phenomenon, connected with what we now know as the Taoist tradition of nature philosophy, and concerned with the search for the elixir of life and cures of various sorts. It stressed the idea of self-transformation and of giving birth to a new man inside oneself, and was based on the energic principle of the dynamic interplay of the opposing forces of *yin* and *yang*. It entered India and then the Hellenic world in about the third century BC, was preserved and developed by the Arabs, and re-entered Western culture in the twelfth century. It reached its full flowering in the West during the Renaissance period, achieving widespread adherence amongst the learned, and was still practised by early modern scientists such as Newton. It all but perished in the eighteenth century for, as Jung put it: '[its] method of explanation – *obscurium per obscurius, ignotum per ignotius* (the obscure by means of the more obscure, the unknown by means of the more unknown) – was incompatible with the spirit of the Enlightenment and particularly with the dawning of science and chemistry towards the end of the century' (CW12.332).

In its late mediaeval form alchemy became associated almost exclusively with the transmutation of base metals into gold. An extraordinary array of techniques was devised to achieve this, some of which have survived into modern chemistry, aimed at refining and purifying gross matter – *prima materia* – through a series of stages, and producing therefrom a perfected substance. The principle of opposites still prevailed in this Western tradition, with its typical use of antagonistic pairs such as fire and water, blackening and whitening, separation and unification, growth and putrefaction, and summed up in the symbolism of the 'sacred marriage' or 'chemical wedding' of male and female elements. Although in many respects alchemy stood outside the mediaeval intellectual tradition, and indeed hovered on the brink of heresy, it shared the prevailing view of nature in which the world was seen in terms of symbols, as a text whose meaning required interpretation. It shared too the belief that nature is a living thing, and hence that the transformation of matter is in principle the same as the process of organic growth.

Jung, as I pointed out earlier, was clearly not interested in the historical phenomenon of alchemy for its own sake, far less for the sake of reviving it as either a belief system or set of techniques. As with Eastern philosophy his attitude was one of strict agnosticism with regard to its objective validity. In fact his early acquaintance with it led him to regard alchemy as 'something off the beaten track and rather silly' (MDR, p.230). But after reading *The Secret of the Golden Flower*, and stimulated by the ideas of the psychologist Herbert Silberer, he came to the realization that alchemy represented an analogue of his own psychotherapeutic endeavour, and that it was 'a projected psychology of the collective unconscious' (CW18.1619).

At one level the alchemical *opus* can be viewed as a purely physical endeavour, and perhaps as the tentative beginnings of modern chemistry. But according to Jung it can at a deeper level be interpreted in a spiritual way, as unconsciously symbolizing 'the transformation of personality through the blending and fusion of the noble with the base components, of the differentiated with the inferior functions, of the conscious with the unconscious' (CW7.360). At this level, therefore, the work of alchemy 'portrays the process of individuation but in a projected form because the alchemists were unconscious of this psychic process' (CW18.1704). Historical research, he claimed, confirms this double meaning, making it more than just a projection of his own psychological interests, permitting him to conclude that 'the alchemical *opus* deals in the main not just with chemical experiments as such, but with something resembling psychic processes expressed in pseudo-chemical language' (CW12.342).

Moreover the alchemist achieves through direct experience something that the believer struggles to attain through faith; it is a form of *gnosis* (knowledge) in which the individual seeks wisdom through personal endeavour unmediated by the Church. As with Buddhism, salvation is reached, not through the redemptive activity of another, but through one's own works. Here too is a prefigurement of psychotherapy in which the patient, though guided by the therapist, is actually engaged in a quest for self-knowledge and self-healing. By contrast, in the orthodox Christian tradition the work of salvation has already been carried out, the function of the Church and its ministers being to act as mediators for Christ's everlasting redemptive act. The alchemists 'ran counter to the Church in preferring to seek through knowledge rather than to find through Faith' (CW12.41), and in effect, therefore, alchemy was 'rather like an undercurrent to the Christianity that ruled on the surface' (CW12.26).

But why seek self-knowledge in such a seemingly cumbersome and roundabout way? If the alchemists were unconsciously seeking, not chemical, but spiritual ends, why did they not pursue them within the orthodox framework of the sacraments of the Church?

The answer lies in the concept of 'projection'. We have already noted the importance for Jung of this idea. From a psychological angle it points to the fact that the contents of the unconscious are not directly observed but are to be found projected onto the world at large. The mediaeval church provided a whole constellation of archetypal symbols which manifested and expressed the needs of the unconscious, and which allowed the faithful to project their innermost need for wholeness and fulfilment. But with its emphasis on the spirit and on other-worldly values it failed to provide a vehicle adequately to express the need to redeem, or make sense of, *matter*.

It was this need, Jung believed, that alchemy served. With its emphasis on the transformation of material substances, in its employment of physically manipulable processes, with its vessels, retorts, and furnaces, with its imagery of sexual conjunction, it was able to provide a means for the psyche to get in touch with its earthy 'chthonic' side, an aspect which was inadequately served by orthodox Christian theology. Along with astrology and magic, which had also experienced a revival in the late mediaeval period, alchemy represented a 'bridge to nature', a recognition of the darker forces in human nature that the Church had banished as remnants of paganism. Thus, along with the other occult arts whose origins lay beyond those of Christianity, alchemy afforded, in Jung's words, 'numerous "hooks" for the projection of those archetypes which could not be fitted smoothly into the Christian process' (CW12.40). Murray Stein, in arguing that Jung's self-appointed task in his later years was the reconstruction of Christian theology, confirms that for Jung alchemy 'was doing the work that Christianity avoided, redeeming that part of human nature rejected by the Christian builders', and that 'the images of alchemy [such as the "chthonic feminine"] reveal the compensatory reaction of the unconscious toward the dominant attitude of Christian consciousness' (1985, pp.143–4).

But this still leaves us with the following question: why was it necessary for Jung to go to such lengths, and to expend such scholarly efforts, in order to find parallels for his own psychological *opus*. Would it not have been enough to have pointed to the parallel with alchemy and to have left it at that? The interpretation of mediaeval alchemy as a system of psychic growth with goals and methods similar to those of analytical psychology is a hermeneutical *tour de force*, involving the drawing of many striking analogies between alchemical symbols on the one hand and on the other the symbols produced by himself and his patients in dreams and in active imagination. This in its own terms may appear convincing enough, but how does it give real support to the central claims of Jung's philosophy other than by merely offering it company?

The answer to this has already been suggested and lies in Jung's belief that a dialogue with other cultures reveals universal psychological qualities lying underneath the superficial differences. It reveals what Coward has called the 'underside of human experience' through which we may attain insight into the 'interior landscape' of the human psyche (1985, p.12). Our discussions in this chapter have pointed to his awareness of the psychological gulfs that divided nations, both historically and contemporaneously, and of the strangeness and alien character that the investigation of the belief systems of other cultures revealed. But he also believed that beneath the superficial forms of alchemy, in its Eastern as well as its Western forms, he had discovered a 'text' that was common to mankind, a level of meaning in the psyche that suggested a universally shared inheritance, the collective unconscious. This serves to underline once again Jung's purpose, which was not to revive long-discarded belief systems, even less to engage in scholarly pyrotechnics, but to illuminate the psyche of our own age, as revealed in the dreams and fantasies of his patients, but placed, as figure to ground, in the wider context of a variety of cultural forms that can still speak to us across the barriers of place and time.

A similar point can be made concerning Jung's investigations into *Gnosticism*. Originally this was an early Christian 'heresy', but it has persisted in various forms and has taken many guises over the past two thousand years, always standing as a spectre on the fringes of Western thought. Its presence can be detected in Renaissance Humanism and amongst some of the great figures of the Romantic period such as Goethe and Blake. It is difficult to define this strange and diffuse historical phenomenon, but its characteristic teachings may conveniently be summarized: (1) The cosmos is the result of a divine accident or fall, the world as we know it – the phenomenal world – being the product of an inferior deity, the 'demiurge', not of the supreme Godhead who is beyond rational comprehension. (2) The Gnostic seeks to overcome this fallen state and to return to the original state of oneness with the Godhead. (3) The path to wisdom lies not through faith in the sacramental powers of the Church but through direct insight – *gnosis*. There are evident links between Gnosticism and Eastern thought, suggesting historical influence, and indeed the early Christian Gnostic, Origen, is known to have been acquainted with Oriental philosophy.

Jung discovered in Gnosticism an early intimation of his emphasis on the primacy of experience over faith, and of some of his own psychological insights, such as the distinction between basic types of psychological functioning, the emphasis on polarity, and the idea of inner exploration and individual development. They were also concerned, he believed, with the question of archetypes, and recognized the presence in the psyche of personified psychic components, not unlike his own autonomous psychic complexes. The Gnostic philosophy undoubtedly played an important role in Jung's thinking throughout his life, though its remoteness, along with the sparseness of historical material, led him to pay greater attention to alchemy which he considered to be its mediaeval manifestation. As with the other so-called esoteric traditions which he investigated, it represented, not just a fascinating alternative cultural tradition, in competition with the more orthodox traditions, but a phenomenon which represented the neglected world of the unconscious.

Martin Buber, amongst others, has made the mistake of supposing that Jung's interest in these doctrines implied that he was in some sense a Gnostic, offering to mankind a divine truth revealed through a personal revelation (see CW18.1499f, also Hoeller, 1982, who argues that 'we may consider Carl Jung a Gnostic'). Jung was indeed a Gnostic in the sense that he saw the necessity of following the path which led out of one's own individual experience, rather than a road laid down by some external authority for all to follow. But his interest in the Gnostics lay, not in their specific doctrines, but in the fact that they revealed themselves to be engaged in a work which in modern terms can be viewed as psychotherapy. He spoke of 'the astonishing parallelism between Gnostic symbolism and the findings of the psychology of the unconscious', claiming that 'it is clear beyond doubt that the Gnostics were nothing other than psychologists' (CW9ii.347), and in his reply to Buber he recalled that his enthusiasm for the Gnostics 'arose from the discovery that they were apparently the first thinkers to concern themselves (after their fashion) with the contents of the collective unconscious' (CW18.1501).

It must be mentioned, however, that whilst agnostic in regard to their doctrines taken in a metaphysical sense, Jung acknowledged that the Gnostics had a much fuller awareness of the reality of evil than the more orthodox Church fathers, a point which he also made with regard to alchemy. Whereas Christianity in its central traditions has sought to neutralize evil by giving it a purely negative status – the so-called *privatio boni* or 'privation of good' doctrine – the Gnostics gave both good and evil equal status in the divine reality. Jung perceived in this a profound truth, not about the cosmos but about the human psyche; in Hoeller's words: 'his recognition of the importance of evil runs like a fiery thread through his work' (1982, p.82). He saw in Gnosticism, with its image of a cosmic struggle between the powers of light and darkness, an expression of the struggle taking place within the human psyche for a totality which embraces both the acceptable and the unacceptable aspects of our being. This, for Jung, was a universal theme representing the fundamental need of the human psyche for growth, integration, and wholeness.[1]

Though in these few brief paragraphs alchemy and Gnosticism may appear to the reader as somewhat isolated and spasmodic episodes in the history of Western ideas, it must be emphasized in summing up this chapter that Jung believed they represented the manifestation of a much broader and more pervasive tradition of spiritual endeavour in the West, which he saw as a corrective to the one-sidedness of its more orthodox religious traditions. It is one which has been marginalized, first by Christianity and later by scientific rationalism, and has not until recently been given anything like adequate treatment by historians of ideas. This alternative tradition, as we might call it, reaches back into the ancient past through the long thread of Hermeticism, Neoplatonism and the Jewish Kabbala, is clearly evident in the Renaissance revival of magic, alchemy and astrology, and is associated especially with such names as Agrippa, Paracelsus, Thomas Fludd, Kepler and Boehme. It re-emerged in the Romantic period, and has found expression in recent times in a myriad of new spiritual enthusiasms.

We have come to assume since the eighteenth century Enlightenment, not only that the Western intellectual and cultural tradition represents the pinnacle of human history, with the East seen as locked into the stage of childhood, but that in the West first Christianity and then empirical science have constituted the historical core of our traditions, and the touchstone of our 'official' cultural identity. This has led in the one case to an arrogant contempt for the ideas and philosophies of the East, and in the other to a conspiracy of silence and neglect, amounting at times to fear and paranoia, for those alternative traditions of which alchemy and Gnosticism are singular examples.

None of Jung's enthusiasm for the alternative traditions represented a rejection of the Christian spiritual tradition with which he felt such a strong historical and psychological bond, but rather an attempt to cast new light on it and to revivify it. The importance of Jung in this context lies in the fact that he took the alternative traditions seriously, studied them in depth, and forced us to recognize in them a mirror of a part of *ourselves* which has been consistently neglected. It was for him a way of forcing us out of our accepted modes of thought, and his dialogue with them was nothing less than a dialogue with the hidden and repressed aspects of our own psyches. As such it was an essential part of his exploration of the self and its discontents, and it is to this exploration that we turn in the second half of the book.[2]

# Part II

# THE REDISCOVERED SELF

# 7

# PSYCHE AND ITS PLACE IN NATURE

The 'reality of the psyche' is my working hypothesis.

(C.G. Jung)

Jung's chief contribution to modern thought, I have suggested, lay in his revival and reformulation of the unfashionable idea that man is a kind of cosmos – a microcosmos – and that mind or psyche is as real, as complex and as full of wonders, as the world at large – the macrocosmos. In his picture of the world 'there is a vast outer realm and an equally vast inner realm; between these two stands man, facing now one way now the other' (CW4.777), and hence the human psyche, far from being just a dim reflection of the material world, is 'of unimaginable complexity and diversity', an internal, 'non-spatial universe [which is] the only equivalent of the universe without' (CW4.764).

We have in modern times become habituated to a materialistic world picture in which matter is seen as the real stuff of the world, and in which we rather grudgingly find a place on its fringes for mind, perhaps as no more than an epiphenomenon, a shadow with no substance of its own. It is true that some thinkers, such as the philosophers of the Romantic period whom we discussed in Part I, have rejected this world picture, and indeed science itself has, in the shape of quantum physics, begun to call into question its basic assumptions. Yet by and large the materialistic outlook has prevailed throughout this century.

It was against this world-view that Jung, consistently and throughout his life, took his stand. He reminded us that materialism, as a dominant ideology, was of relatively recent origin, and that other radically different world pictures have taken hold of people's minds at different times and in different places. For instance primitive man tended to see the world as if it were full of spirits and of influences and forces which, though closely tied to matter, nevertheless had an independent reality whose effects were pervasive. Primitive man, he wrote, 'lives in two worlds. Physical reality is at the same time spiritual reality. The physical world is undeniable, and for him the world of spirits has an equally real existence' (CW8.572).

Moreover, the primitive does not merely *believe* in a spiritual or psychic world but *experiences* it directly. It is not just a theory for which there is evidence but a fact which is inescapably present. The most important source of this belief Jung considered to be dreams which for the primitive are of 'an incomparably higher value [than for] civilized man' (CW8.574). A similar sense of the reality of the spiritual or psychic world pervaded the Graeco-Christian civilization of the West. For the Greeks the world was 'full of gods', to use a phrase attributed to Thales, the first philosopher. In reading the works of Homer, who was the chief cultural authority for the Greeks, one is constantly struck by the narrowness of the divide which separates the physical from the spirit world. This is even more true, of course, of the world of mediaeval Christianity in which people, at all levels of intellectual and spiritual sophistication, lived with an acute sense of the immediacy and importance of the realm of souls and spirits. As Jung put it: 'The mediaeval man had not yet fallen such a helpless victim to worldliness as contemporary mass man . . . he still acknowledged the equally influential metaphysical potencies which demanded to be taken into account' (CW8.426).

A feature of our own times, Jung noted, is a renewed popular interest in the spirit world, largely in reaction against orthodox materialism; modern man 'turns his attention to the psyche with very great expectations' (MM, p.239). But whereas in earlier times this interest expressed itself in terms of a spirit world projected *outwards* onto the cosmos at large, more recent investigation has focused on the *inner* world of the psyche, and in particular on the world of the unconscious. It is in this context that Jung saw the significance of his own contribution. Despite his constant reference to earlier beliefs, his aim was not to reconstruct, much less merely to recapitulate, these earlier views, but to use them as a stepping stone and inspiration towards the articulation of a new and more scientific account of the psychic world. What in earlier times had been discovered and experienced in the form of projected symbols was now being rediscovered and repossessed at its source in the subjective world of the mind.

The first stage in this voyage of exploration is the realization that we ourselves, far from being mere appendages to the material world, are in a sense at its centre, and indeed may be said to be the very condition of its existence. In Chapter 5 I argued that Jung followed the German philosophers of the nineteenth century in believing that the mind is not a passive onlooker upon the world but participates in the creation of knowledge, and is in a sense a world-maker. He referred to the psyche as 'that infinitesimal unit on whom a world depends' (US, p.113), and argued that 'without consciousness there would, practically speaking, be no world, for the world exists as such only in so far as it is consciously reflected and consciously expressed by the psyche. Consciousness is a precondition of being' (p.46). Man, he argued, is 'indispensable for the completion of creation', he is 'the second creator of the world, who alone has given the world objective existence (MDR, p.285), a view which intriguingly anticipates some recent speculations growing out of quantum physics, in particular the so-called 'anthropic principle' which argues that the way the world is can only be understood if we take into account our own presence in it as conscious participant observers (see Davies, 1982, pp.142–61).

However, in spite of the renewed interest in the world of mind and spirit, and in spite of the efforts of the German Idealist philosophers to place consciousness back into the centre of our thinking about nature, the prevailing and dominant world-outlook of the modern age is undoubtedly a *materialist* one. How did this come about? Was it not the product of the inevitable advance of science, and hence the triumph of reason over superstition?

Jung suggested an interesting answer to this question, one which is worth elaborating in a little detail. He believed that this great historical change was not the result of sustained rational argument, but due to what Thomas Kuhn has more recently called a 'paradigm shift', a radical change of outlook more akin to a religious conversion than to a reasoned change of mind. The supplanting of the mediaeval by the modern view, according to Jung, was the result, not of the overwhelming strength of argument in its favour, but rather of what amounts to a change of fashion.

At the beginning of the modern period, he argued, roughly at the time of the Reformation and the Scientific Revolution in the sixteenth and seventeenth centuries, a 'spiritual catastrophe', 'an unexampled revolution in man's outlook on the world', occurred in which 'a metaphysics of the mind was supplanted by a metaphysics of matter'. The result of this was that 'Other-worldiness is converted into matter-of-factness, empirical boundaries are set to man's discussion of every problem, to his choice of purposes, and even to what he calls "meaning". Intangible, inner happenings have to yield place to things in the external, tangible world, and no value exists if it is not founded on a so-called fact'. However, he continued, 'it is futile . . . to attempt to treat this unreasoned change of opinion as a question of philosophy', for many philosophers have insisted on rejecting it. Rather it appears to constitute a non-rational change of opinion. The modern view is no more rational than the old, '[it] is a religion, or – even more – a creed that has absolutely no connection with reason'. It is a matter of '[the] spirit of the age [which] cannot be compassed by the processes of human reason. It is an inclination, an emotional tendency', and therefore '[to] grant the substantiality of the soul or psyche is repugnant to the spirit of the age, for to do so would be heresy' (MM, pp.200–3).

This view clearly flies in the face of one of the great 'myths' of our time, namely that scientific rationalism has succeeded in dispelling, through reasoned argument and empirical evidence, the superstitious beliefs of an age of faith. This is one of the central tenets of the Enlightenment which saw itself as progressing with the aid of logic and science from the childish fantasies of the Middle Ages towards a more mature and realistic outlook. This view has acquired a powerful grip on the mind of the modern world and is to be found as an assumption underlying many aspects of the thinking and culture of our age, not only in the field of psychology, but in the sciences, in philosophy, ethics, and politics.

For Jung the pre-scientific world-view, which gave an important, perhaps even a primary, place to mind and spirit, was no less rational than our own. Neither world-view can be established on logical or empirical grounds. Both rest on what R.G. Collingwood called 'absolute presuppositions' which are either accepted or rejected, but cannot be proved. Jung's basic assumption is that of an 'autonomous psyche'; the reality of the psyche was his 'working hypothesis'. This procedure, he claimed, 'is no more fantastic than to postulate matter' (MM, p.208), and indeed either extreme view – whether materialism or idealism – involves unwarranted metaphysical assumptions, for '[as] to the ultimate we can know nothing' (p.205).

Jung's attitude to this question anticipated a strong methodological tendency in recent years to understand the major changes in the history of ideas in terms which point to the irrational underpinnings of thought. I have already mentioned Thomas Kuhn's highly influential idea of a 'paradigm shift'. This idea, put forward in his book *The Structure of Scientific Revolutions*, is linked to his belief that the major developments in scientific thought cannot be understood wholly in terms of explicit rational argumentation, or in terms of a steadily progressive accumulation of well established knowledge. The great scientific revolutions, such as those associated with the names of Newton and Darwin, were thus not models of rational argument but total transformations in which the whole way of looking at the world became radically altered.

But the rejection of the Enlightenment myth does not imply the rejection of rational considerations as such. Leaving aside the whole question of changes in intellectual fashion, there are to be found in Jung's writings a number of important *arguments* in support of a belief in an independent psychic reality. Central to these arguments was the belief that the mind or psyche has certain characteristics which clearly differentiate it from physical reality, and there are differences in kind between the two which prevent any attempt to reduce the one to the other. The question of whether matter can have or produce mental properties has been at issue amongst philosophers since the time of

Descartes and Locke, and while Jung did not profess to have any definitive solution to the question, he was insistent that it is a problem that cannot be simply swept away by any kind of materialist-reductionist argument. 'To postulate mind', he argued, 'is no more fantastic than to postulate matter', and though we have 'literally no idea of the way in which what is psychic can arise from physical elements . . . yet [we] cannot deny the reality of psychic events' (MM p.208).

He accepted, even at his most idealist, that the psyche clearly depends in some sense on the brain, and consistently maintained that there is a fundamental ontological unity between mind and matter, even if phenomenologically they might appear under two different aspects. But at the same time he argued that the 'structure and the physiology of the brain furnish no explanation of the psychic process. The psyche has a peculiar nature which cannot be reduced to anything else' (US, p.46). Thus, whereas physical objects occupy space and have objectively measurable properties, mental contents possess none of these, and we cannot ascribe to them any specific location in space or any physical dimensions such as bulk or weight. Of course we do ascribe certain bodily locations to thoughts and feelings, but as Jung pointed out, different cultures at different times have offered a variety of competing views on this question, and it is difficult to see how one might adjudicate between them by means of objective testing. Indeed '[if] we wished to form a vivid picture of a non-spatial being of the fourth dimension, we should do well to take thought, as a being, for our model' (MM, p.213).

Furthermore, he held that the psyche, at least in its conscious aspects, is present to us in an immediate and undeniable way, and that the immediate world of experience is not. as might commonly be supposed in our age, the world of matter, but rather that of mental images and sensations:

> All that I experience is psychic. Even physical pain is a psychic event which belongs to my experience. My sense-impressions – for all that they force upon me a world of impenetrable objects occupying space – are psychic images, and these alone are my immediate experience, for they alone are the immediate objects of my consciousness.
>
> (MM, p.219)

Even my illusory fears are real, despite the fact that they may have no corresponding object in the physical world. The absence of an object may make no difference to the intensity of my feelings or the range of possible consequences. If we look at the history of mankind it is clear that fears of 'unreal' dangers from within the psyche – such as dreams or fantasies, or of imagined dangers from without such as of the dark or of ghosts – can exercise an effect equal to those which arise from more obvious and 'real' dangers in the physical world; such psychological phenomena can indeed be 'just as pitiless and inexorable as the outer world, and just as useful and helpful, provided one knows how to circumvent its dangers and discover its hidden treasures' (CW5.221).

Jung frequently expressed astonishment at our persistent refusal to take the power of the psyche seriously, of the 'curious underestimation of anything psychic', and of our dismissal of the unconscious as 'nothing but fantasy'. He observed that:

> The gigantic catastrophes that threaten us today [1932/4] are not elemental happenings of a physical or biological order, but psychic events. To a quite terrifying degree we are threatened by wars and revolutions which are nothing other than psychic epidemics. At any moment several millions of human beings may be smitten with a new madness, and then we shall have another world war or devastating revolution. Instead of being at the mercy of wild beasts, earthquakes, landslides and inundations, modern man is battered by the elemental forces of his own psyche. This is the world power which vastly exceeds all other powers on earth. The Age of Enlightenment, which stripped nature and human nature of the gods, overlooked the God of Terror who dwells in the human soul.
> (CW17.302)

Hence, we should not imagine that for Jung the psyche represented an inner world hermetically sealed off from the outer physical world. He did not see it in that way. Of course, there are whole areas of the unconscious which, by definition, are in a sense hidden from view, and he always maintained that the psyche was in its innermost nature a mystery which would never yield all its secrets. Nevertheless the psyche, however deeply its roots reach down into the unconscious, expresses and projects itself within and upon the external world. Jung was clearly not in any sense a behaviourist, for he certainly did not identify psyche with overt behaviour, nor reduce it to the sum of its publicly observable manifestations. But he believed that the psyche presupposes an external environment within which to express itself and through which to achieve its goal of self-realization.

In this respect he was close to Hegel who, in his *Phenomenology of Mind*, argued that the mind can only come into being through interplay with the world of nature and of other people; in itself the mind remains merely in a state of perpetual possibility. He was also in tune with certain existentialist thinkers such as Merleau-Ponty who maintained that human consciousness necessarily operates through the medium of the body. It is true that in his later years Jung contemplated the possibility of a disembodied psyche, but up to about 1945 he continued to express the view that incarnation is essential to the psyche, that 'The body is . . . the visibility of the soul, the psyche; and the soul is the psychological experience of the body' (NZ, pp. 350, 355). Indeed consciousness itself would be impossible without the body, he argued, for consciousness implies discrimination, and it is only through the body's organs that distinctions and differentiations can be made (p.349).

The psyche, then, is an actor on the world's stage, not a recluse confined within some sealed-off spiritual realm of its own. Furthermore, it not merely operates within and through the world of nature, it is itself a natural phenomenon, 'a living psychic organism', with characteristics of life and growth which are analogous to those of the organic world. The psyche is, Jung claimed,

> among the elementary manifestations of organic nature, which in turn forms one half of the world, the other half being the inorganic. Like all natural formations the psyche is an irrational datum. It appears to be a special manifestation of life and to have this much in common with living organisms that, like them, it produces meaningful and purposeful structures with the help of which it propagates and continually develops itself. And just as life fills the whole earth with plant and animal forms, so the psyche creates an even vaster world, namely consciousness, which is the self-cognition of the universe.
>
> (CW17.165)

One of the chief consequences of this view is that, like an organism, the psyche has a *life*, that is to say it grows and matures, and suffers vicissitudes analogous to those of organic beings. The traditional idea of consciousness, which takes its philosophical origin from Descartes, but can be traced back to Christian teaching on the soul, views the conscious mind as a kind of miracle which, like the breath of God infused into Adam's body, comes into existence and perpetuates itself without any prior development or any continuing means of support. For Jung the psyche, however different it may be from a physical organism, has deep roots which lead back beyond the conscious existence of the individual and eventually to the non-psychic living world. It is a natural growth whose origins can be traced back into the natural world but which, like the lotus flower – to use a classic Buddhist image – rises above and transcends its purely natural origins. This picture is summed up in the following words: 'The psychic process does not start from scratch with the individual consciousness, but is rather a repetition of functions which have been ages in the making and which are inherited with the brain structure' (CW8.227).

How does this come about? By what process does the psyche, or more particularly human consciousness, emerge from the living world of nature? The answer is through *evolution*.[1] In *The Descent of Man* Darwin had suggested that some of the apparently unique features of the human mind, such as its capacity for language, its possession of a moral sense, and its appreciation of beauty, could be seen to be foreshadowed in the behaviour of some of the animal species. From this it was only a short step to the conjecture that even the 'higher' functions of the human species might have evolved from animal functions through a process of natural selection. Now, Jung did not embrace the full Darwinian theory; indeed his rejection of any form of reductionism would seem to distance him from some of the more radical materialist forms of Darwinism. Nevertheless in certain crucial respects his ideas on the evolution of human consciousness have a distinct Darwinian flavour.

This is evident in Jung's belief that the contemporary psyche displays marks, not only of an individual past, but of the history of the human race. Speaking of his clinical experience, he once remarked that 'Together the patient and I address ourselves to the 2,000,000 year old man who is in all of us' (JS, p.100), for what he observed there was not merely the evidence of a single life's vicissitudes, but the experience of the human race. He argued that

> every human being, whatever his conscious development, is still an archaic man at the deeper levels of his psyche. Just as the human body connects us with the mammals and displays numerous relics of earlier evolutionary stages . . . so the human psyche is likewise the product of evolution which, when followed up to its origins, shows countless archaic traits.
>
> (MM, p.144)

It seemed reasonable to suppose, therefore, that in some sense or other the mind evolved in much the same way as the body. But the question can still be asked: Why did consciousness emerge at all? Why should this peculiar and often rather painful phenomenon have made its appearance in the long process of evolution?

Jung approached this question from two quite distinct viewpoints, the first of which was explicitly Darwinian. He recognized that conscious psychic functions could equally well take place at an unconscious level: 'There is in my opinion', he wrote, 'no tenable argument against the hypothesis that all the psychic functions which today seem conscious to us were once unconscious and worked as if they *were* conscious' (CW8.412). The reason that such functions emerged into the light of consciousness, he speculated, must lie in the fact that consciousness confers some kind of *advantage* in the struggle for survival, that the animal which possesses consciousness has an adaptive advantage over the animal that lacks it. Furthermore, by implication an *increasing* level of consciousness would also confer adaptive advantage, so that the highly individuated consciousness observable in civilized societies has an advantage from the point of view of survival over the less differentiated consciousness of primitive people. Unconscious functioning has the automatic or blind character of an instinct, and because of this its constituent tendencies can come dangerously into collision with one another. The advantage that consciousness confers is that it enables us 'to adapt in an orderly way and to check the instincts' (CW8.412). Thus consciousness is to be seen as 'an emancipation of function from its instinctual form, from the compulsiveness which . . . causes it to harden into a mechanism', and hence 'becomes capable of more extensive and freer application' (CW8.377). In brief: 'The reason why consciousness exists, and why there is an urge to widen and to deepen it, is very simple: without consciousness things go less well. This is obviously the reason why Mother Nature has deigned to produce consciousness, that most remarkable of all nature's curiosities' (CW8.695).[2]

But this Darwinian answer to the question of the origin of consciousness was only part of the story. Jung constantly reiterated his belief that consciousness is something special and wonderful, an attribute which places man immeasurably beyond the animals. It is 'the greatest of all cosmic wonders' (CW8.357), 'the world's pivot', 'the disturber of the natural laws of the cosmos' (CW8.422–3), and just as in its lower reaches in the unconscious 'the psyche loses itself in the organic-material substrate, so in its upper reaches it resolves itself into a "spiritual" form' (CW8.93). Even more portentously he described consciousness as that 'tremendous experiment . . . which nature has laid upon mankind' (CW13.83), and assigned to the development of consciousness a role as the very purpose of existence itself, for it is only through the meaning-creating power of human consciousness that 'man found his inescapable place in the great process of being' (MDR.285). As far as we can discern 'the sole purpose of human existence is to kindle a light in the darkness of mere being' (MDR, p.358), and hence we are in a sense the self-consciousness of the universe.

This takes Jung well beyond Darwin, and beyond the bounds of empirical science. As Edinger suggests, this view constitutes nothing less than a new myth for our time, a new paradigm for modern man in which 'the purpose of human life is the creation of consciousness' (1984, p.17). It is a view which has obvious links with Schelling. As we saw in Part I, Schelling constructed a philosophy which sought to integrate the worlds of spirit and nature, seeing them as two sides of the same living, developing force. He taught that the whole system of nature is impelled by its own inner logic towards an end or goal, evolving from an original state of undifferentiated unity into all the differentiated and variegated forms of nature, and ultimately to the emergence of consciousness and then of self-consciousness. The Absolute is the state in which the universe achieves complete self-knowledge and in which all opposites are reconciled in ultimate unity. We have in Schelling's philosophy of nature, then, an evolutionary theory which, unlike Darwin's, postulates a goal or ideal towards which nature is striving.

There are clearly a number of points of contact between Jung and Schelling. Most significant of these lies in the idea that the conscious psyche is but a late emergent from the womb of nature, and that rational consciousness represents some special outcome of the long process of cosmic evolution. In addition to this they both took a teleological view of mind, seeing in it an emancipation from the forces of brute mechanical nature, and hence an expression of self-directed autonomy. For both thinkers, as indeed for all the spiritual descendants of Kant, the dignity of human freedom was in some form or other a central tenet.

Jung's affinity with Schelling, however, fell far short of embracing the full implications of the latter's philosophy. Schelling saw human consciousness as a means towards a higher goal, namely the Absolute, the ultimate unity of all things in an all-embracing totality, whereas for Jung the goal lay in the full development of the individual consciousness and the individual self. The pilgrimage of Schelling's cosmic self towards its apotheosis in the Absolute has, in Jung's philosophy, become the quest for the individual self and for personal fulfilment, thereby transposing the lofty speculations of German Romantic thought into a key more familiar to twentieth century ears.

Any notion that the evolution of human consciousness might be conceived as part of some wider cosmic goal was foreign to Jung's way of thinking. This point must be emphasized in view of the fact that his name has sometimes been associated with a certain kind of philosophical evolutionism according to which the present state of human consciousness is seen as only a stage on the road towards some higher fulfilment, and that the whole evolutionary process points towards a preformed transcendent goal. A philosophy of this sort has been formulated with persuasive force by Pierre Teilhard de Chardin. In his book, *The Phenomenon of Man*, he argues that human consciousness is evolving towards a final spiritual unity – the Omega point – in which a higher integration of individual consciousnesses is attained. In contrast with this sort of cosmic evolutionism, Jung took the view that the conscious self is essentially irreducible, and any attempt to absorb it into some higher category is a mistake. For him, the goal of human consciousness lay in the fullest actualization of what is potential within the individual, not in some purpose that lies beyond. His talk of the 'cosmogonic dignity of human consciousness' must, therefore, be seen as an allegory for self-actualization, not an invitation to metaphysical speculation of a pre-Kantian kind.

Neither did he espouse any form of cosmic optimism according to which the world is moving inevitably towards some higher state of *perfection*. While, as we have seen, he recognized that consciousness confers clear advantages in the struggle for survival, he also observed that its possession is often a doubtful privilege. Like Kierkegaard and Dostoyevsky before him, and Sartre after him, he often wondered whether consciousness, which carries with it such a train of sorrows and anxieties, probably unknown to our animal cousins, is really such a benefit. It is the growth of consciousness, he lamented, which 'we must thank for the existence of problems; they are the dubious gift of civilization' (MM, p.110). It is for this reason that we sometimes rebel against 'this greatest of cosmic wonders', and seek to return to the state of *participation mystique*, the supposed state of childhood and primitive man in which we have not yet gained our full self-conscious identity. And as we shall see more clearly in Chapter 12 below it is for the same reason that the problems of life are never fully resolved, for the aim of life lies not in the solution of its problems, but rather 'in our working at [them] incessantly' (p.119).

The life of the psyche, then, while rising out of organic life, transcends it, though, through the power of self-creation. For Jung the psyche has this special quality, perhaps unique in the universe, that it creates itself through its own activity. This is not just a matter of conscious will, as Sartre would have it, since for Jung consciousness is only a small part of the whole psyche. Even less is it just a matter of conscious rational decision. For while both will and reason have their parts to play, creative imagination arises out of the whole being of the psyche, both conscious and unconscious.

Here in outline, then, we have a picture of Jung's unique conception of the psyche. In the following chapters we will elaborate this picture in greater detail, beginning with the germination of the psyche in the womb of nature, the realm of instincts and the unconscious, moving up through the symbolic world of the archetypes to the emergence of the self and its fulfilment in the process of individuation, and finally returning to the image of unity in Jung's speculations concerning the reconciliation of body and spirit. This procedure will provide the opportunity to place Jung's theory of the psyche into the context of the philosophical and historical considerations introduced in Part I, and at the same time will enable us to examine some of his more controversial ideas and some of the criticisms they have provoked.

# 8

# THE UNCONSCIOUS AND THE IRRATIONAL

> The unconscious is neither tricky nor evil – it is nature, both beautiful and terrible.
>
> (C.G. Jung)

We begin our exploration of the life of the psyche where it is closest to its natural roots – the region of the unconscious. From his earliest days as an assistant in the Burghölzli mental hospital, several years before he met Freud, Jung was convinced of the existence and importance of the unconscious mind. The germ of this idea had been sown even prior to his university days when, as we have already seen, he avidly read the works of Schopenhauer and von Hartmann, along with the other major German philosophers from Kant onwards. Indeed one can trace its origin even further back to his early teens when he recognized the existence, both in his mother and in himself, of a shadowy alter ego which he described later as 'personality number 2', in contrast with his conscious everyday self, 'personality number 1'.

The influence of Schopenhauer was crucial. In *The World as Will and Idea* Schopenhauer spoke of the sufferings of the world, of passion, of evil and of many other things which other philosophers seemed to ignore. But most important of all he spoke of a world driven by a blind, amoral and purposeless force, which he called the *will*. This concept of the will is in effect the basis of Jung's notion of psychic energy or *libido*:

> we see only a continuous life-urge, a will to live which seeks to ensure the continuance of the whole species through the preservation of the individual. Thus far our conception of libido coincides with Schopenhauer's Will, inasmuch as a movement perceived from outside can only be grasped as the manifestation of an inner will or desire.
>
> (CW5.195)

The influence of Schopenhauer is especially important in enabling us clearly to separate Jung's conception of the unconscious from that of Freud. Jung's own fully developed model of the unconscious dates from about 1911, with the publication of his *Symbols of Transformation*, and was in many ways the exact opposite to that of Freud, for whereas the latter saw the unconscious as a product of the conscious mind, Jung saw it the other way round. For him consciousness is 'a late-born descendant of the unconscious psyche', and just as it would 'show perversity if we tried to explain the lives of our ancestors in terms of their late descendants . . . it is just as wrong . . . to regard the unconscious as a derivative of consciousness. We are nearer the truth if we put it the other way round' (MM, pp.216–7). To Freud, Jung noted, the unconscious is 'chiefly a receptacle for things repressed. He looks at it from the corner of the nursery. To me it is a vast historical storehouse. I acknowledge I have a nursery too, but it is small in comparison with the vast expanses of history' (CW18.280). Moreover, like Schopenhauer Jung conceived the relationship between conscious and unconscious, not as one of embattled opposition, but as somehow embedded in the natural order of things, as inseparable phases in a process of organic development, in which 'the unconscious is the matrix out of which consciousness grows' (CW17.103).

Let us now look in a little more detail at what is distinctive in Jung's conception of the unconscious, both as it emerged in this early work and as it grew and matured in his later writings.

The groundwork, as I have indicated, was laid in *Symbols of Transformation*. Most of this book is occupied with a study of the fantasies of an American woman called Miss Miller who was not known personally to Jung, but rather through the work of his colleague, Theodore Flournoy. No attempt was made in the book to offer any analysis of Miss Miller herself, but rather her fantasies were used to weave an elaborate hermeneutical web of interpretation. An essential feature of the hermeneutical method, as I described it earlier, involves the oscillatory movement from the text to a wider context and back again, a movement known as the 'hermeneutical circle'. It was a method such as this that Jung adopted. Moving back and forth from the woman's fantasies to the world's mythologies, he attempted to convince us that the mental world of a modern woman has its roots in the archaic world of myth-making, and therefore that contemporary consciousness is historically embedded in the whole of the past of the human race, and not merely in the past of the individual herself. In other words the true meaning of our modern symbols and fantasies can only be elicited by reference to the cultural history of the race. He called on Freud to support his claim that, especially in dreams, the psyche 'regresses back to the raw material of memory', and that they are essentially archaic in character. 'These considerations', he went on to conclude, 'tempt us to draw a parallel between the mythological thinking of ancient man and the similar thinking found in children, primitives, and in dreams' (CW5.25–6).

This view was, in one respect, not at all original for, as Jung himself pointed out, it tallied with the belief, widely held since Darwin, and indeed almost a dogma in the early decades of this century, that the biological history of the individual is parallel to, and in some sense explicable in terms of, the biological history of the species. This view had been formulated in the late nineteenth century by the German biologist Ernst Haeckel who is perhaps best known for his highly popular and much-translated book, *The Riddles of the Universe*. The basis of this belief lay in the perception – since shown to be mistaken – that the stages of growth of the human embryo recapitulate the stages of evolution of the species itself. The idea was usually summed up in the phrase 'ontogenesis recapitulates phylogenesis', in other words the development of the individual is a kind of speeded-up verson of the process of evolution.

Jung's original contribution to this idea, which is sketched out in the work of 1911 but developed more fully later, was to argue that this principle applies to the mind as well, namely '[the] supposition that there may also be in psychology a correspondence between ontogenesis and phylogenesis', and that therefore 'infantile thinking and dream-thinking [including fantasy thinking such as Miss Miller's] are simply a recapitulation of earlier evolutionary stages' (CW5.26). And where this view went beyond Freud was in the claim that, without the need for any repressive mechanism, the mind of the child, and thereby of the modern adult, is already 'seeded' as it were with the full potential for the creation of fantasies which are, in essence, identical with the mythological products of the human race. For,

> [just] as our bodies still retain vestiges of obsolete functions and conditions in many of their organs, so our minds, which have apparently outgrown those archaic impulses, still bear the marks of the evolutionary stages we have traversed, and re-echo the dim bygone in dreams and fantasies.
>
> (CW5.36)

This positive appreciation of the role of the primitive and the infantile, of fantasy and dream, in the mature psyche has inevitably led to the accusation of irrationalism. This is unfounded, in my view, for what he sought was, not to replace reason with unreason, the mature rational consciousness with the primitive and infantile, but to re-establish a balance between them, for 'the rational is counterbalanced by the irrational, and what is planned and proposed by what is' (CW9i.174).

The model of the human psyche which has dominated thinking in modern times derives most immediately from Descartes, but has its roots in Aristotle and Plato: it is the view that man is essentially and uniquely *rational*. He may of course be characterized by other factors, such as feelings and passions, and possess other faculties such as the will, but in the end the human essence – that which makes us human and not animals – lies in the fact that we possess the power of reason. Plato wove a myth around this view. He imagined that the soul, or psyche, was divided into a hierarchy of levels, with the passions and the will placed in the lower levels, and with reason sitting on top, governing, or at any rate attempting to govern, all below.

Jung did not reject this model entirely, for he had a great regard for intellect, and in his ideas of individuation and self-development he saw the need for the cultivation of the conscious, rational mind; indeed he sometimes spoke of the conscious rational ego as the highest product and goal of psychic evolution. The problem, rather, is one of balance again, for while recognizing the high value of the rational function, he feared that it had been elevated to such a position of pre-eminence that we tended to underrate the other, irrational, side of the psyche. This, he thought, was especially a problem for modern Western civilization which had put a high premium on intellect, and had correspondingly neglected or undervalued the opposite functions of sensation, feeling, intuition, and imagination. In 1916 he wrote:

> Civilized life today demands concentrated, directed conscious functioning, and this entails the risk of a considerable dissociation from the unconscious. The further we are able to remove ourselves from the unconscious through directed functioning, the more readily a powerful counter-position can build up in the unconscious, and when it breaks out it may have disagreeable consequences.
>
> (CW8.139)

In the final chapter of *Symbols of Transformation*, entitled 'The Sacrifice', Jung recognized that in some sense the affirmation and domination of rational consciousness is a 'lofty' ideal (CW5.674). But this goal, if pursued single-mindedly, inevitably leads to the sacrifice of the natural man, which has ever been the aim of Christian moral teaching. The danger, on the one hand, of being the victim of the irrational forces of one's unconscious is compensated, on the other, by 'the opposite danger of consciousness being separated from its instinctual foundations and of setting up the conscious will in the place of natural impulse' (CW5.673). The deep fear of being taken over and overwhelmed by irrational, perhaps diabolical, forces is at the heart of Christian theology with its one-sided affirmation of the Good and the Virtuous. But this is echoed in the apparently opposing tradition of scientific rationalism which is guilty of a parallel over-estimation of the intellect and of an undervaluation of the shadow side of the human person.

To obtain a more balanced view of the psyche it is necessary, Jung believed, to draw a distinction between two kinds of thinking: *directed* thinking on the one hand and *non-directed* or *fantasy* thinking on the other. Directed thinking is the kind which has some form of logical progression, is shaped by conscious intention, and normally takes the form of *words* which are aimed outwards towards external reality. It is characteristic of directed thinking that it is a tool of communication – an instrument of culture, as Jung called it – which serves to orientate us towards the physical and social world, and is therefore the very basis of community and civilized life. Language on this view is simply a set of articulated and socially agreed signs which, though arising from within the psyche, are directed outwards towards others.

In contrast to this is non-directed or fantasy thinking in which trains of images and thoughts follow one another spontaneously and without conscious direction. It may take the form of words or of images, or even of feelings, and its characteristic feature is an effortless welling-up of psychic contents. From an historical and evolutionary standpoint the one kind of thinking has developed from the other: the thinking of primitive societies tended to be of the latter type, whereas modern civilizations have increasingly developed and perfected thinking techniques of the former type. On this view of history, modern scientific rationalism is the most fully developed, albeit one-sided, expression of directed thinking.

Now, it is important to note that for Jung this did not mean that primitive people were less intelligent than ourselves; as we saw in Chapter 4 there is no room in his thought for the privileging of one segment or age of mankind over another. Fantasy thinking may be just as sensible and effective as the more obviously rational kind; it would, he insists, 'be a ridiculous and unwarranted presumption on our part if we imagined that we were more . . . intelligent than the men of the past – our material knowledge has increased, but not our intelligence' (CW5.23). All that has happened is that there has been, to use Thomas Kuhn's phrase, a 'paradigm shift' in which the balance of our thinking has moved from one pole to another: 'The centre of gravity of our interest has switched over to the materialistic side, whereas the ancients preferred a mode of thought nearer to the fantastic type' (CW5.23). The increasingly common use of the term 'subconscious', with its implicit elevation of consciousness to a superior position, typifies this attitude (CW5.670). Jung's reply to the charge of irrationalism was in effect to argue that the concept of reason has been too narrowly defined in modern thought, and that it has come to coincide with only a segment of the whole spectrum of human intelligence.

This view of the unconscious and its relation to consciousness is in many ways an elaboration of Nietzsche's insights. He too has been accused of irrationalism, but like Jung his concern was not to demolish reason but to comprehend it as a function of the wider totality of the human psyche. Both thinkers saw the need to make space for the darker side of human nature as a counterbalance to prevailing idealizations, to acknowledge the role within the human psyche of the 'shadow', a term first used by Nietzsche in 1879 in his essay *The Wanderer and his Shadow*. Both were at pains to point to the roots of mind in nature, even in its apparently most lofty activities. Both feared the human and social consequences of failing to recognize and to give voice to the 'beast within'.

The pursuit of a greater balance between the various aspects of one's nature was not, for Jung, a purely intellectual process. It was not just a matter of rational understanding but also an emotive, even a cathartic, process. Self-observation and intellectual analysis, though useful as auxiliaries, are 'entirely inadequate as a means to establishing contact with the unconscious' (CW8.165). 'Getting in touch with one's emotions' is an idea with a contemporary ring about it, but one can spot its origins in Jung's claim that the goal of psychotherapy is 'no mere intellectual acknowledgement of the facts, but their confirmation by the heart and the actual release of the suppressed emotions' (MM p.41), a view shared, of course, by Freud who placed great emphasis on the process of 'transference' whereby a patient projects emotional traumas onto the therapist. The variety of practical techniques which Jung developed in his clinical work, such as active imagination and art therapy, is a witness to his belief that the unconscious must be allowed to speak in its own language – and that is not necessarily the language of articulated speech. Thus, for example, the dark side of our natures, including those things we are too ashamed even to recognize in ourselves, will only yield their secrets if we allow them to use the vocabulary of images and of feelings such as emerge in dreams and fantasies.

We need to look a little more closely at Jung's views about this darker side of human nature, the 'shadow'. We have a tendency, he thought, to underrate or ignore that side of our personality which is disagreeable to us, those characteristics which do not fit with the image we have of our better selves, and which show us often to be mean, petty, even violent and sadistic. But we need to recognize that 'the shadow is indispensable for the making of the whole personality' (NZ, p.123). Just as nature is capable of extremes of beauty and of horror, so we inherit these opposing possibilities *via* the unconscious depths of our psyche. Within these depths, often deceptively calm on the surface, there lie the hidden stirrings of violent storms which, if not recognized and accounted for in our personal development, will wreak havoc on us. We are, Jung was fond of remarking, living on the edge of a volcano. The price of repression, of refusing to recognize the volcano and its dangers, is a high one, not only for the individual, who from being a gentle and reasonable being may be 'transformed into a maniac or a savage beast' (CW11.25), but also for society which can destroy itself if it fails to acknowledge and give expression to the powerful unconscious forces within it.

In making this point Jung frequently referred to those twin Northern and Mediterranean gods of nature, Wotan and Dionysus respectively, who represent all those pagan forces of nature – a distillation of sex, wine and primal instinct – which both our Christian and our scientific heritages have conspired to tame or even, if possible, to destroy. 'But though we may throw out nature with a pitchfork', he was fond of remarking, 'she will return to have her revenge on us'.

Speaking of the shadow side of human nature should not lead us to imagine that Jung saw the unconscious in wholly negative or threatening terms. Despite Jung's admiration of Schopenhauer, the latter's pessimistic attitude to nature and to the blind striving of 'will' was one which he did not share. He never espoused the bland optimism of the Enlightenment, or concurred with its rejection of the myth of original sin, but neither on the other hand did he give way to the unbridled, even self-indulgent, *Weltschmerz* and disillusionment which was a feature of many post-Romantic intellectuals in the nineteenth century. Nor was he influenced, as was Freud, by the *fin-de-siècle* gloom encouraged by many of Darwin's admirers who viewed nature in terms of a harsh and uncompromising battle for survival, a domain in which man, like his fellow animals, could only hope to survive and prosper by superior cunning and more advanced savagery. Moreover, despite his affinity with Nietzsche on many points, his conception of nature never carried with it the uncompromisingly masculine connotations associated with Nietzsche's idea of the 'will-to-power', but sought to balance the power and violence of nature with the image of maternal sustenance and nurturing.

Freud's teaching, which in many ways represented a perpetuation of the spirit of Darwinism – at any rate in its more pessimistic, 'nature red in tooth and claw', form – was depreciatory both of the unconscious and of nature itself, and has helped to foster an attitude towards the unconscious which sees it as a 'dangerous monster', and to view it almost as an unhealthy and malignant growth. By contrast, for Jung the unconscious 'is neither tricky nor evil – it is Nature, both beautiful and terrible' (*Letters I*, pp.108–9), it is 'not a demonic monster, but a thing of nature that is perfectly neutral as far as moral sense, aesthetic taste and intellectual judgement go' (MM, p.19). Freud saw the higher things of cultural life – art, religion, philosophy – only as sublimations or transformations of something dark and troublesome, whereas Jung saw them as the natural expression of the human mind which, nurtured on both good and evil impulses alike, grows from and gives expression to its roots in nature. The aim of human existence, therefore, is not the life and death struggle with nature, but the full expression of all the rich variety of opposing and complementary tendencies that lie within it.

We have seen in this chapter that Jung spoke of the unconscious, not just as some force lying beneath the surface of consciousness, nor as the repository of unacceptable thoughts and feelings, but as 'a vast historical storehouse', and as an 'eternally living, creative, germinal layer in each of us', that must be understood in terms that go beyond the individual human being. In his later writings he elaborated this insight into one of his most characteristic and controversial theories, namely that of the *archetypes* and the *collective unconscious*. This theory will occupy our attention in the next chapter.

# 9

# ARCHETYPES AND THE COLLECTIVE UNCONSCIOUS

Our mind has a history just as our body has a history.

(C.G. Jung)

Jung's view of the collective unconscious is something of a scandal. While the idea that there is such a thing as an *individual* unconscious has, since Freud popularized this notion, become widely accepted, Jung's belief that there is another layer beneath the unconscious which in some way binds us to the whole of mankind seems to fly in the face of both common sense and conventional wisdom, to be 'mystically conceived', as Wilhelm Reich dismissively put it.

Since John Locke supposedly demolished the concept of innate ideas in the seventeenth century, it has become virtually a dogma of Western thought that the mind is furnished only with ideas which come through the senses during the lifetime of the individual. Even the mediaeval theologians had followed the Aristotelian dictum: *nihil in intellectu quod nisi prius in sensu* – anything in the intellect must first come from the senses. Any idea that the mind already has at birth a stock of knowledge, or that we inherit from our parents anything other than our physical constitution, smacks of metaphysics or, worse, of mysticism. This is linked with the widespread assumption amongst modern psychologists that all distinctively human behaviour is acquired through learning, and a parallel assumption of ethologists that human qualities are based on culture rather than genetic transmission.

In this chapter I want to show that Jung's views on the collective unconscious are neither metaphysical nor mystical and that, whether or not we accept them as true, they do represent a plausible hypothesis, and make an important contribution to contemporary debates on human behaviour and its evolution.

Let us begin by clarifying terms. According to Jung 'the collective unconscious means that individual consciousness is anything but a *tabula rasa* ['blank sheet' – an expression used by Locke] . . . [but] is in the highest degree influenced by inherited presuppositions. [It] comprises in itself the psychic life of our ancestors right back to the earliest beginnings' (CW8.230). As such it constitutes what Jung described as 'the matrix of all conscious psychic occurrences', a kind of framework which determines the overall shape and boundaries of conscious life, for just as the body inherits a structure that determines our bodily outlines, so too the mind is structured by inherited factors. Thus, 'in so far as the child is born with a differentiated brain that is pre-determined by heredity . . . it meets sensory stimuli coming from outside not with *any* aptitudes, but with *specific* ones', such aptitudes being 'inherited instincts and preformed patterns' (CW9i.136). The term 'collective unconscious' is indeed misleading since it suggests some kind of supra-individual psyche, perhaps a world-soul, into which individual identities are dissolved, an interpretation which supports the common accusation of mysticism. But this was far from what Jung had in mind, for he meant it, not in any substantive sense, but rather as a *potential* for certain kinds of typically human psychic activity, not so much a thing, therefore, as a disposition. The notion that the individual mind is merely a manifestation of some larger group, or even cosmic, mind is therefore quite alien to Jung's way of thinking.

This inherited potential consists of what Jung called *archetypes*. They are not experienced as such, he argued, but manifest themselves as symbolic images in myths, art, dreams and fantasies. The whole collection or interlocking system of archetypes Jung took to be the structure which gives sense and meaning to psychic life, for they contain 'the whole spiritual heritage of mankind's evolution' (CW8.342). Thus they act like maps projected by the psyche onto the world, and out of them arise all the most powerful and perennial ideas in art, religion, philosophy and science. Moreover, there are, he believed, 'as many archetypes as there are typical situations in life' (CW9.99), and the list of examples discussed by Jung include: anima, shadow, self, birth, child, hero, wise old man, and earth mother. They therefore represent typical key episodes in the drama of life, typical stories or *dramatis personae* which are repeated and replayed with infinite variations across the whole range of human history and culture, in myth, religion, art, even in science and philosophy. They therefore carry out a more than merely formal or rational function, ordering and shaping the data of experience, but are 'as much feelings as thoughts' (CW7.104), spontaneous elements of the whole personality, and hence constitute the very heart of human action and emotional life. In addition they carry a 'numinous' quality, a feeling of something special and even holy that appears to transcend the limits of ordinary experience. Thus the idea of God is itself an archetypal image, carrying with it a sense of mystery and awe.

Reference to their numinous quality does not imply a transcendent origin, for Jung, as I have already indicated, rejected any metaphysical interpretation, and held that archetypes are grounded firmly in biological instincts. To make this plain he argued that instinct and archetype 'meet in the biological conception of "the pattern of behaviour"', for just as the behaviour of organisms is not random but follows a programmed pattern, so also the pattern of human behaviour is shaped by archetypal forms, the latter being images that represent the meaning of the instinct. Thus while in animals the sexual instinct gives rise to identifiable and repeated patterns of behaviour, in the case of human beings it also gives rise to identifiable and repeated patterns of psychic and cultural symbolism. Archetypes, like instincts, have a regulatory function in that they 'intervene in the shaping of conscious contents by regulating, modifying and motivating them' (CW8.404). Here once again we can see that Jung is offering a picture of the psyche which views it, not as some kind of extra-terrestrial visitation, but as an integral part of the whole organic evolutionary process.

Jung did not invent either the idea or the term 'archetype', but adapted it from historical precedents which he scrupulously acknowledged and documented. The concept of an inherited foundational structure underlying the human psyche can, he believed, be traced back at least as far as Plato who maintained that the acquisition of knowledge represented a kind of *recollection* in which Forms or Ideas, learned prior to birth, were brought into play through the stimulus of sense experience. This was given a cosmological dimension in his dialogue *Timaeus* where Plato imagined that the creator-demiurge fashioned the world in accordance with eternally pre-existing models, a notion taken up by the Jewish philosopher Philo of Alexandria (b.10 BC) who, according to Jung, was the first to coin the term 'archetype' (CW9i.5). Thereafter we can perceive its influence on Christian thought in the theological writings of St Augustine, who held that the image of God is imprinted on each soul, and in the Hermetic tradition dating from the third century AD. In mediaeval scholastic philosophy, likewise, 'we find the notion that archetypes are natural images engraved on the human mind, helping it to form judgements' (CW8.275), and according to Jung the Indian concept of *karma* also prefigures his theory of archetypes in certain respects (see Coward, 1985, p.97).

The most immediate influence, however, was the philosophy of Kant, and Jung believed that his own concept of archetypes was both a derivative from and an extension of Kant's ideas. It was derivative in the sense that, as we saw in an earlier chapter, he accepted Kant's idea that the mind has an *a priori* structure which shapes our awareness and knowledge of the world. He recognized the shortcomings of a purely empiricist approach to knowledge and the need to postulate some form of regulatory agency within the knowing subject. He accepted therefore Kant's view that as well as the faculty of perception there is a faculty of *apperception* whose function is to give shape and meaning to the raw data of the senses. Like Kant he believed that archetypes must be understood in phenomenal rather than metaphysical terms, in other words as telling us about the necessary structure of experience rather than the essence of things. Just as for Kant we cannot know what space and time are like in themselves beyond our experience of them, so Jung believed that strictly speaking in itself the collective unconscious cannot be said to exist at all, but as a concept represents only the possibility of certain kinds of experience (CW15.126). In other words it does not refer to a mysterious hidden entity, but 'is a hypothetical and irrepresentable model' (CW8.6).

However, he went beyond Kant in maintaining, first, that the archetypes are not timeless structures embedded in the nature of mind as such, but have evolved over the long period of human, and indeed of animal, history in response to the actual experience of higher organisms, and, secondly, that they refer to the whole range of human experience, affective and evaluative as well as cognitive; they are, as Shelburne has put it, 'categories of the imagination' as well as of thought and perception (1988, p.38).

So much for the theory and its origins. What justification did Jung offer for it? Typically he used two types of mutually complementary arguments in support of his theory of the archetypes, the one concerned with the nature of the theory itself, the other with its empirical foundations.

The first argument involves a comparison between archetypal theory and theories derived from the biological sciences. The hypothesis of the collective unconscious is, he claimed, 'no more daring than to assume that there are instincts' (CW9i.92), for an instinct is merely a disposition to behave in a certain way rather than another. Is it possible, he asked, that the structures and behaviour of organisms in general are shaped by inherited patterns whereas the structures and behaviour of the human psyche are not? If we grant that the human mind is an integral part of the natural world, not cut off from it by the chasm of Cartesian mind–body dualism, then it would be absurd to suppose that in such a fundamental respect the psyche functioned quite differently from the body. The study of animals from insects to primates amply demonstrates the power of inherited instincts to programme unlearned behaviour. It is at least reasonable to suppose, therefore, that the psyche inherits certain structures in the same way that a living organism does. Furthermore, the mind, like the body, has evolved and we would therefore expect the individual psyche, like the individual body, to show marks of its phylogenetic origins, for '[just] as the human body represents a whole museum of organs, with a long evolutionary history behind them. so we should expect the mind to be organized in a similar way rather than to be a product without history' (CW18.522).

This may seem a somewhat tenuous argument, little more than an analogy. Yet a moment's reflection will show that it is typical of scientific arguments. No scientific investigation is capable of amassing all the data relevant to a hypothesis, but must always rely on extrapolation from a few cases. Evolution theory is a case in point. The prevailing Darwinian theory rests mainly on the evidence of a finite number of observed fossil remains which represent a minute fraction not only of the individual animals and plants that have existed, but also of the species that have constituted the totality of organisms. For the rest it is a matter of assumption – 'by analogy' – that the organisms and species that have not been observed conform to the same evolutionary pattern. In the last analysis it rests, as Bertrand Russell pointed out in his book, *The Problems of Philosophy* (1967), on an unproven assumption concerning the uniformity of nature. The same is true in physics, even, where vast uninvestigated regions of space and time are assumed to conform to the laws that are based on only the minute fraction of the cosmos that has actually been investigated.

The structure of Jung's argument is precisely the same, and is based on a similar assumption concerning the uniformity of nature, in this case the uniformity of physical and psychic activity. Moreover recent studies in the philosophy of science by such writers as Kuhn, Lakatos and Quine have suggested that scientific theories do not arise, stand, and fall as single entities but are part of wider theoretical domains comprising many interlocking theories, and that the primary concern of science lies not in the testing of individual theories but rather in the articulation and consistency of the whole domain. Jung's theory of archetypes may therefore be seen as part of an attempt to integrate psychology within the wider domain of theories within science as a whole.

Mere uniformity or consistency is not enough, however, for this principle by itself would validate almost any consistent hypothesis or set of hypotheses. What more is needed is some kind of *empirical* evidence, some observational data which, by confronting theory with fact, will transform a consistent into a plausible hypothesis. This leads us on to Jung's second argument which is concerned with the empirical basis of his theory. It was a very important stage in the formulation of the theory of archetypes when Jung came to realize that the 'chaotic assortment of images' that confronted him in his work with patients' dreams and fantasies 'reduced itself in the course of the work to certain well-defined themes and formal elements, which repeated themselves in identical or analogous forms with the most varied individuals' (CW8.401). But the noting and listing of archetypal motifs was not in itself sufficient for, as he admited, 'these can just as well be derived from acquisitions through language and education' (CW9i.92). In addition therefore it was necessary to show that these motifs can only, plausibly, be derived from archaic sources.

The earliest evidence that Jung obtained for this was derived during the first decade of this century from his treatment of psychotic patients. He found to his surprise that many of the fantasies and images of his patients resembled legends, myths and folktales, and that it was often impossible to relate the content of these fantasies to specific experiences of his patients. In 1912 he designated these 'primordial images', a term which was replaced in 1919 by 'archetype'. His subsequent clinical experience over many decades, allied with wide-ranging studies of the history of mythology, provided ample confirmation of this early work. While he was prompt to recognize that the contents of his patients' dreams frequently elicited material from their own past history, he also became convinced that many of these contents could only be explained by reference to the wider experience of mankind.

An early example of this occurred in 1906 when a schizoid patient of his reported seeing a vision of the sun which displayed a phallus and which he construed as being the origin of the wind. In 1910 Jung came across a study of the Mithraic cult by Albrecht Dieterich in which a vision was described in the following words: '"And likewise the so-called tube, the origin of the ministering wind. For you will see hanging down from the disc of the sun something that looks like a tube. And towards the regions westward it is as though there were an infinite east wind"' (CW8.318). Since the patient had been committed to hospital before the publication of the Greek text, and Jung only came across it in 1910, there seemed good reason, as he put it, 'to rule out the possibility of cryptomnesia [i.e. forgetting that he had read it] on his side and of thought-transference on mine' (CW8.319). The obvious parallel between the two could, he believed, only be explained in terms of some form of inheritance.

This explanation was reinforced by his studies in the history of mythology, folklore, comparative religion and alchemy which revealed a remarkable congruence of themes from a widely divergent range of sources. Like the German ethnologist Adolf Bastien before him, he was impressed by the fact that analogous images and motifs cropped up in cultures far removed from each other by geography and history, and that while specific cultural differences were readily observable, it was possible to discern recurrent patterns across the whole spectrum. These recurrent patterns included such themes as the eternal child, the earth goddess, the hero, and the wise old man. Now it was perfectly possible, Jung admitted, that in themselves these patterns could be explained by cultural migration or the power of tradition, but when added to the data collected from the contemporary dreams, fantasies and drawings of his patients, where there seemed to be no direct contact with archaic traditions or any possibility of learning through experience, it was only reasonable, he believed, to postulate some kind of inherited structure.

Here again the analogy with evolutionary biology is important. Much of Darwin's case concerning the evolution of man rested on the observation of structural similarities, or 'homologies' as biologists now call them, both between the anatomy and the behaviour of humans on the one side and of animals on the other. Now it is conceivable, as creationists argue, that these similarities are not causally related and that therefore there is no need to postulate an explanation for the one in terms of the other. But on the other hand it is on the face of it more plausible to suppose that the homologies indicate a biological continuity, and that the human characteristics have an evolutionary connection with those of the animals. No 'proof' is possible here, but at the same time the evolutionary hypothesis seems to give us a more comprehensive explanation of the facts than any of its competitors. The same applies to Jung's theory of archetypes. There is of course an alternative explanation, namely that the parallels between contemporary images and ancient myths are fortuitous; but it is more plausible to suppose that the link is an hereditary one.

The question of evolution, though, raises a thorny problem, namely: by what mechanism are the archetypes inherited. The issue here is the old one of Lamarckism versus Darwinism. Lamarck, it will be recalled, had argued that characteristics acquired by effort during an individual organism's lifetime could be passed on to offspring, whereas orthodox Darwinists (strictly speaking *Neo*-Darwinists, since Darwin himself adopted a form of Lamarckism) maintain that only genetic variations – now called 'mutations' – can be inherited. Are we to suppose, then, that psychic contents, acquired by previous generations, can be inherited by later ones? Must Jung adopt a form of supposedly long-discredited Lamarckism to make sense of his theory of inherited archetypes? Until recently it has been accepted almost without question that Jung, like Freud, was a Lamarckian. But while it is true that Jung was never well disposed towards Darwinism, and that both at Basel and at the Burghölzli he worked in a prevailingly Lamarckian culture, he never explicitly aligned himself with this theory.

The first point to make clear in response to this dilemma is that Jung explicitly rejected the notion that *ideas*, in the sense of mental contents such as images or thoughts, can be inherited. It is true that even after 1919 he continued to use the ambiguous term 'primordial image' in addition to 'archetype', and that he persisted in referring to archetypes both as images and as dispositions. But this was due more to his typical lack of terminological precision, a fault of which he was well aware, and does not make any significant difference to his theoretical position. He consistently maintained that it was the *disposition* to have certain ideas and images that was passed on from one generation to another, not the ideas and images themselves. The archetypes, he insisted again and again, 'are not inherited ideas but inherited possibilities'; the actual contents of consciousness 'are all acquired individually' (CW8.718–20).

> Archetypes are not determined as regards their content, but only as regards their form and then only to a very limited degree. . . . The archetype in itself is empty and purely formal . . . a possibility of representation which is given *a priori*. The representations themselves are not inherited, only the forms, and in that respect they correspond in every way to instincts, which are also determined in form only.
>
> (CW9i.155)

This may be likened to a computer operating system which acts as a general principle of organization, but does not prescribe exactly what is to be done at any particular moment (see Robertson, 1987, p.94).

This clearly dispenses with the accusation that the thoughts, ideas and beliefs of previous generations can be inherited. There is no question here of one generation developing, say, a hero myth and passing that myth on to the next generation through the genes. Nevertheless Jung did believe that archetypes as structures or forms are inherited, so we must now try to see exactly what he understood by this.

Jung's thesis is not at all easy to follow, and he formulated it in different ways over many years, but I think we can construe it in the following terms. We inherit a body which over long periods of time has evolved, by whatever mechanism, characteristics which are favourable to survival, such as the liver, lungs, heart, etc. We have also inherited a brain which has evolved, not organs, but dispositions to behave in certain favourable ways, such as the capacity to react to danger, to procreate or to obtain food. The specific behaviours associated with these dispositions have, in a sense, been learned, but it is not the specific memories of a fearful predator or a desirable mate that are passed on through the genes but rather an inbuilt and unconscious disposition to behave in certain ways given certain triggering conditions – or what the ethologist Niko Tinbergen has called 'innate releasing mechanisms'. Such dispositions, like bodily organs, have evolved over long periods of time by the gradual accretion of favourable characteristics and the elimination of unfavourable ones. Thus far we have an orthodox Darwinian story of evolution through natural selection.

Jung carried this one stage further by arguing that psychological characteristics have evolved in precisely the same way. Take the mother–child relationship. This is a powerful bond which has evolved over an immensely long period of time. It involves on the part of the child a repertoire of potential behaviour which is released under certain actual circumstances. Certain specific responses are learned, but in the early stages at least the general pattern of behaviour is genetically predetermined. But in addition to patterns of behaviour there also emerge in time patterns of psychic response, certain images and symbols which are projected onto the purely biological object of the mother. It is the disposition to develop such images and symbols which Jung called an archetype. In computer language the archetype is a hard-wired programme which is activated by actual inputs and which is to some extent modified by those inputs.

This argument is in fact very similar to the one employed by Darwin in *The Descent of Man*. In that book he argued that certain of the 'higher' abilities of conscious human life, such as language, the moral sense and the appreciation of beauty, could be explained in terms of evolution by natural selection. In the first place, Darwin argued, it was possible to discern in these types of behaviour clear homologies between human and animal behaviour which gave a *prima facie* plausibility to the evolutionary hypothesis: thus animals have the capacity to communicate in ways which seem to anticipate human language. In the second place such types of behaviour can be seen as endowing advantages in the struggle for survival, and thus while a human being has to learn a language within its own lifetime and does not in any sense inherit genetically a vocabulary from its ancestors, the *capacity* to learn a language may be viewed as a behavioural disposition that has evolved in exactly the same way as other types of behaviour. Similarly Jung argued that 'we have to start with the hypothesis that, so far as predisposition is concerned, there is no essential difference between man and all other creatures. Like every animal, he possesses a preformed psyche which breeds true to his species and which, on closer examination, reveals distinct features traceable to family antecedents'. Moreover such features are 'already present in the germ-plasm' (CW9i.152), and hence, according to Jung, they are the results of biological rather than cultural processes of inheritance.

Let us return to the question of whether Jung was a Lamarckian. In the absence of any clear statement from Jung on this matter it is not possible to come to any definitive conclusion. Stevens appears to be convinced that 'archetypes evolved through natural selection' (1982, p.17), though he does not produce any textual evidence for this claim. Samuels exonerates Jung from the accusation of Lamarckism on the grounds that Jung, after 1919, made it clear that he was talking about the inheritance of forms rather than of images (1985, p.25). But this is unconvincing since it assumes that the issue of the inheritance of 'forms' or 'patterns', as opposed to actual images, is unproblematic. Jung clearly took the view that patterns of behaviour are embedded in the genes as a result of some kind of repetitive behaviour over many generations, and that therefore the origin of the archetypes 'can only be explained by assuming them to be deposits of the constantly repeated experiences of humanity . . . [and are] recurrent impressions made by subjective reactions' (CW7.109). He offers in support the example of mankind's experience of the sun which, over its long history has given rise to various myths which go to 'form the sun archetype'. He admits that this account 'only pushes the problem further back without solving it', nevertheless the passage has a distinctly Lamarckian flavour for it suggests that the crucial factor is the 'repeated experiences' rather than any genetic change. This approach is reinforced in another work where he speaks of archetypes as '"pathways" gradually traced out through the cumulative experience of our ancestors' (CW8.99).

Now it would be possible to argue that these 'repeated experiences' are in their turn the results of random genetic changes and that archetypal behaviour is therefore the product of mutations which have given rise to forms of behaviour that are adaptively favourable. Thus in the example just quoted one might argue that certain kinds of psychic behaviour in the form of sun-related myth-making arose quite spontaneously as a result of genetic changes, and that it proved useful in the struggle for survival in that it evoked, say, a greater awareness of the physical environment. This is by no means implausible. Many sociobiologists now believe that social structures can be explained in terms of genetic variation along with adaptability to environmental conditions. However, much controversy surrounds this view and much work has still to be done to provide a plausible link between biological factors on the one side and behavioural factors on the other. Furthermore, since from the purely biological standpoint there is no evidence of any evolutionary changes in man for perhaps millions of years, the idea that the process of evolution is continuing to take place exclusively in the psychic sphere seems implausible.

An objection from a Jungian standpoint comes from a different quarter. For Jung the psyche is a *teleological* system and its central feature resides in its purposeful and goal-seeking nature: 'it is psychologically inadmissible', he wrote, 'to adopt the purely causal attitude to psychic phenomena' (CW8.45). Furthermore he was convinced that teleological explanations could not be eliminated from our attempts to understand the organic world as a whole. 'Life is teleology *par excellence*', he wrote, 'it is the intrinsic striving towards a goal, and the living organism is a system of directed aims which seek to fulfil themselves' (CW8.798). In the light of this it would be odd to ascribe to Jung a belief, namely Darwinism, which takes an explicitly mechanistic view of evolution and which offers an explanation of the evolution process in terms, not of purpose, but of chance. This is especially relevant in the case of the psyche to which Jung was at such pains to ascribe something more than just a subordinate, epiphenomenal, role.

However, it must be pointed out that the imputation of Lamarckism no longer carries quite the stigma that it did in the days when Neo-Darwinism enjoyed a status almost amounting to that of a religious dogma. Darwinism is itself undergoing evolution, and extreme positions on the question of the inheritance of acquired characteristics are now softened by a whole range of mediating views which make it possible to argue that a modified form of Lamarckism may yet have a role to play in some aspects of the evolutionary process.[1]

In my view this approach is not entirely satisfactory, even allowing for the possible rehabilitation of some form of Lamarckism. The idea that there has been a psychic evolution of mankind, whether or not by genetic mutation, during a period when the human body structures remained relatively stable, runs into a crucial difficulty, namely that of dispersion. If, as Jung suggests, archetypal features emerged over the past million or so years, then, given the relative isolation during that period of various groupings of *homo sapiens*, how did the newly emergent features come to be dispersed amongst the race as a whole and thereby come to constitute part of the human genetic endowment? If, say, the sun archetype appeared during relatively recent history, how did it come to be inherited by the race as a whole and not by only one segment of it?

A possible way out of this dilemma might come from the adoption of a distinction between 'open' and 'closed' behaviour patterns.[2] *Closed* behaviour patterns are genetically fixed in every detail, like the bee's honey dance in which the same pattern is repeated in all circumstances. In such a case there is little or no learning on the part of the individual bee. By contrast, *open* behaviour patterns lay down only an outline or structure within which a range of types of behaviour is possible. An example of this is the hunting behaviour of carnivorous mammals such as cats which can adapt themselves to a very wide variety of actual conditions, and may involve a degree of learning on the part of the individual animal. This is even more obvious in the case of humans whose sexual behaviour, for example, is very varied as between individuals, tribes or whole cultures, yet which is identifiable as a universal drive with recognizable shape and limits.

We may speculate, then, that from a genetic point of view the archetypes are part of the original genetic endowment of *homo sapiens* which has remained unaltered for millions of years, and which allows within certain structural limits the emergence of a variety of psychic behaviour in response to specific circumstances, whether internal or external. Thus, just as we do not need to invoke genetic mutations to explain the emergence within relatively recent times of, for example, new modes of linguistic expression, so too we can explain the emergence of the archetypes within human history in terms of open programmes with a secure genetic foundation. The behavioural programme which lies at the base of the archetypes was, according to this hypothesis, formed at the time of the evolution of *homo sapiens*, along with all the other specifically human characeristics, and, as an 'open programme', carried with it the potential for a wide variety of psychic behaviour which can be seen to fall into definite patterns. This interpretation is born out by Jung's claim that the 'universal similarity of human brains leads to the universal possibility of a uniform mental functioning' (CW7.456).

Much work remains to be done in elaborating the details of Jung's theory of archetypes; he himself referred to it as 'no more than a hypothesis', and as 'pioneer work which by its very nature can only be provisional' (CW9ii.27). This is not a problem peculiar to him since the whole field of human behaviour in its relation to evolution remains under-cultivated, and as I pointed out above Darwinian theory is itself under intense scrutiny at the present time. There still remain a number of unanswered questions, such as: exactly how do archetypes relate to genetic changes? Can new archetypes emerge, and if so can they make their appearance independently of strictly biological changes? Is the concept of an archetype too vague and too broad to carry any explanatory weight? What sort of evidence would count against it? But notwithstanding these doubts – doubts of a kind which typically assail any bold scientific conjecture – I hope to have shown in this chapter that Jung's theory, far from being, in Reich's phrase, 'mystically conceived', is a realistic attempt to address within the parameters of science a complex and elusive question concerning human behaviour.

# 10

# NATURE AND HUMAN NATURE

> In the collective unconscious you are the same as a man of another race.
>
> (C.G. Jung)

Jung has often been accused of neglecting the biological and instinctual basis of the human personality, of showing, unlike Freud, comparatively little interest in the 'lower' functions of human life, especially the sexual instinct, and of propounding a purely spiritualistic psychology. In the previous chapter I argued that, contrary to this prejudice, Jung's theory of archetypes was premised on the belief that the symbolic life of the mind was firmly rooted in biology and instinct. Some critics such as Steele have argued, however, that this whole approach is a mistaken one and that Jung's rather sketchy attempts to link archetypal inheritance with biology is superfluous. Steele believes 'Jung's work does not require any natural scientific support', and that the strength of argument concerning archetypes lay in his *hermeneutical* approach which rests entirely on the language of meaning, and that any attempt to intrude the causal language of the biological sciences into this domain would involve a kind of category mistake (Steele, 1982, p.331f. See also Neumann, 1954, for a similar view).

Furthermore, as Stevens points out, many recent followers of Jung have chosen to follow an 'esoteric path' which emphasizes the spiritual nature of the archetypes, and have been reluctant to 'elucidate the biological implications of Jung's theories', and in so doing have 'neglected the archetype's behavioural manifestations no less than its phylogenetic roots' (1982, p.29).[1] A tragic consequence of this, Stevens believes, has been a divorcing of analytical psychology from the mainstream of the behavioural sciences, and a confirmation in many people's minds of the supposed 'mystical' bent of Jung's thought.

I believe that the strength of Jung's whole approach lay in his attempt to integrate his theory of archetypes into a unified theory which embraced both the psychic and the biological realms, and hence that 'man must remain conscious of the world of the archetypes, because in it he is still a part of Nature and is connected with his own roots' (CW9i.174). According to Jung, as I interpret him, the human psyche is an integral part of the natural world and not an alien visitor to it. Body and mind constitute together a single whole, and hence the 'separation of psychology from the basic assumptions of biology is purely artificial, because the human psyche lives in indissoluble union with the body' (CW8.232).

In his earlier years Jung had regarded instinct and spirit as polar opposites or antinomies, but with the introduction of the idea of the *psychoid* in the 1940s he proposed that 'archetypal structures were fundamental to the existence of all living organisms, and that they were continuous with structures controlling the behaviour of inorganic matter' (Stevens, 1982, p.71). In other words the inherited archteype and the genetically structured organism were seen as special cases of the regulatory functions of living things in general which seek to reach a state of balance. As early as 1919 Jung had viewed archetypes as analogous to instincts, i.e. as performing similar functions in psychology and biology respectively. Later, according to Samuels, Jung revised this 'to advance the proposition that, far from being "correlates" of instinct, archetypes are just as fundamental', and that archetypes 'become seen as psychosomatic entities, occupying a midway position between instinct and image' (1985, p.27). Jung outlined this view in the following passage:

> The deeper 'layers' of the psyche lose their individual uniqueness as they retreat farther and farther into the darkness. 'Lower down', that is to say as they approach the autonomous functional systems, they become increasingly collective until they are universalized and extinguished in the body's materiality, i.e. in chemical substances. . . . Hence, 'at bottom' the psyche is simply 'world'.
>
> (CW9i.291)

The archetypes, therefore, represent the uniquely human means whereby instinctual, biological, energy is transformed into the meaningful symbolic life of the human psyche.

On this view the instincts and the world of the human spirit do not, as has so often been the case in Western thought from Plato to Sartre, stand in hostile and mutually exclusive opposition to each other. The concept of the psychoid was introduced as an attempt to construct a conceptual framework in which this opposition could be transcended, and in which the evolution of human consciousness could be firmly linked with the organic world within a unitary world-view.

A further consequence of the theory of archetypes is that it provides the basis for a theory of *human nature*, namely the view that underlying all the various manifestations of human behaviour, over the range of cultures and across the span of history, we can discern a common universal essence that is identifiably human. This notion runs sharply up against the prevailing orthodoxy in academic institutions throughout Jung's lifetime, which holds that, whether individually or socially, and unlike the animals, humans at birth are blank sheets on which virtually anything can be written. At one extreme of a whole spectrum of ideas lie the Existentialists who hold that individuals are entirely free to determine their own natures or essences. At the other extreme lie the behaviourists who maintain that patterns of human behaviour are entirely the result of social or environmental conditioning. What binds these views together is the belief that nurture, culture and individual effort, rather than nature in the form of genetics, are the determinants of human behaviour, and that in this respect there is an unbridgeable divide between the human and animal species.

By contrast, Jung held that human beings are not born *tabula rasa*, and hence capable of being shaped psychologically in a virtually indefinite variety of ways, but are already disposed by nature towards distinctive patterns of mental and behavioural life. These patterns consist, he argued, of an innate psychic structure which allows men to have experiences of a certain kind. Thus, for example, a man's experience of a woman is not shaped solely by his *actual* experience of women, for his 'system is tuned in to woman from the start, just as it is prepared for a quite definite world where there is water, light, air, salt, carbohydrate, etc.' (CW7.300).

The issue here is an ideological one in that it touches on a whole range of questions which are not just theoretical but have profound political undertones. There is amongst many thinkers a deep suspicion of any theory or doctrine which holds that there is such a thing as human nature and that this human nature is common to mankind by virtue of biological inheritance. Such a view not only detracts from human freedom, it is argued, but also provides a convenient justification for conservative, and even reactionary and repressive, political systems. Thus, to take a typical objection to certain ethological theories, if man is essentially by nature territorial or hierarchical, then there is little point in advocating the abolition of private property and social ranking since these are embedded in human nature. Similar objections would then apply to Jung, whose theory of archetypes might be seen as undermining such principles as liberty and the open society, and indeed Stevens has suggested that the academic ostracism of Jung was not so much the result of his supposed 'mysticism' as of his espousal of an officially discredited theory of human nature.

Central to this issue are two questions, both of which are to do with human freedom: (1) does a theory of inherited archetypes, tied to assumptions about biological instincts and a genetically inherited human nature, imply that our social behaviour is biologically preformed, much in the way that the behaviour of ants is; and (2) does such a theory imply that the actions of individuals are determined and hence that people are not free to choose their own destinies?

Despite his emphasis on the archaic preformation of psychic structures, Jung is quite categorical on the first of these questions: environmental factors are of equal importance to inherited ones in the shaping of human behaviour. The peculiar organization of the psyche, he declared, 'must be intimately connected with environmental conditions' (CW8.324), and to understand human psychology 'it is absolutely necessary that you study man also in his social and general environments', and consider 'different kinds of societies, different kinds of nations, different conditions' (quoted in Evans, 1976, p.151). He always insisted that the manner in which universal archetypal motifs manifested themselves depended on the particular cultural context in which they appeared. Thus while there is an inherited predisposition towards the development of mother–child images, the exact manner in which these appear depends on the particular environment, cultural and physical, as much as on the common genetic endowment. Or consider the case of astrology: there seems to be some disposition on the part of mankind to project images and meanings onto the heavens, yet we find a wide diversity of astrological theories across the range of cultures and historical epochs.

This point is especially worth emphasizing in relation to Jung's ideas concerning child development, an area that he has often been accused of neglecting. In fact he wrote extensively on the subject, and while he sought to avoid what he saw as Freud's excessive concentration on infancy, and especially on its sexual dimensions, he believed that the early stages of life were crucial in the development of the personality. It is not so much that he neglected childhood but that he saw it as only one phase in the whole cycle of life (his writings on this subject are collected in CW17).

Thus, on the one hand he was convinced that the psychic life of the child was capable of a remarkably wide range of autonomous development which could not simply be attributed to environmental conditioning: 'The psyche of the child', he wrote, 'is anything but a *tabula rasa*; it is already preformed in a recognizably individual way' (MDR, p.381); the world of the small child is teeming with images and thoughts which cannot be explained exclusively in terms of the child's experience. But on the other hand he insisted on the importance of environmental factors in the shaping of its personality. He believed that during its early years the infant was very largely dependent, from a psychological standpoint, on its parents, that its attitudes and feelings are largely determined by the parents, and where the latter betray pathological traits these will tend to be imprinted, more or less deeply, on the child (see CW17.80).

A similar point can be made in relation to Jung's comments about primitive societies. It will be recalled that, while he accepted the theory of Lévy-Bruhl that persons belonging to primitive cultures do not have full consciousness of their own identity, and live in a condition the latter misleadingly called *participation mystique*, he rejected the idea that this involved some kind of innate difference between the intellectual powers of primitive and modern man. The difference is wholly due to environmental factors, namely the relative state of cultural development of the two kinds of societies. Though primitives think differently from ourselves, these differences are in the final analysis due to historical factors rather than any supposed divergence in natural endowment. The same argument applies to societies which have a similar level of civilization to ours, such as the Chinese whose evident psychological differences from our own, Jung believed, cannot be explained on biological grounds.

In effect Jung was attempting to achieve some sort of balance or mediation between innate and environmental factors. 'Our psychology', he claimed, 'takes account of the cultural as well as the natural man, and accordingly its explanations must keep both points of view in mind, the spiritual and the biological' (CW17.160). This characteristic approach of Jung's is nowhere more evident than in his treatment of sexuality. It is important to clarify this point as Jung was accused by Freud of abandoning the biological basis of psychological behaviour by virtue of his rejection of the theory of infantile sexuality.

Now, Jung did *not* in fact reject sexuality as an important factor in psychic life, and as a powerful instinctual force rooted in biological functioning. Nor did he deny that sexual factors in childhood sometimes play a role in the formation of neuroses. What he objected to was Freud's *exclusive* reliance on the sexual instinct as an explanatory factor, and his attempt to reduce the variety and complexity of psychic life to the relative simplicity of the sexual drive. He spoke of the 'one-sidedness' of Freud's view, with its 'over-evaluation of sexuality', of its 'simplifying reduction' to a mechanistic-causal standpoint (CW8.35). He affirmed that he 'did not mean to deny the importance of sexuality in psychic life', but sought to 'set bounds to the rampant terminology of sex which threatens to vitiate all discussion of the human psyche' (MM, p.138). The sexual drive needs to be set alongside other drives which are of equal importance in the psychic life, drives that range all the way from the biological to the spiritual. Sex, in Jung's view, 'plays no small role among human motives, but in many cases it is secondary to hunger, the power drive, ambition, fanaticism, envy, revenge, or the devouring passion of the creative impulse and the religious spirit' (CW18.493). To reduce the psychic life to the sexual drive, he wryly suggested, would 'be tantamount to treating of Cologne Cathedral in a textbook of mineralogy, on the ground that it consisted largely of stones' (CW5.194).

A similar attempt at reconciliation between the biological and the cultural is evident in his treatment of the second of our two questions, namely that of free-will and determinism. Glover accused Jung of being 'rigid and mechanical' in his thinking about human behaviour, of seeing the stages of life as 'mapped out with a barrack-room indifference to individual development and human character', and of preaching a 'variety of predestination compared with which the psychic determinism of Freud can be regarded as sheer soaring optimism' (1950, p.138). This is a complete distortion of Jung's beliefs. While he totally rejected the existentialist view that we are free to determine our own natures, at the same time he wanted to avoid the alternative extreme of supposing that we are totally shaped by our instincts. He spoke often of our 'relative freedom', allotting it a limited yet crucial role in human behaviour, and saw the archetypes as setting 'narrow limits on [the] range of volition' (CW8.398).

In order to clarify Jung's views on this matter we will need to investigate the concept of *instinct* in more detail. We have seen that in his later years Jung came to view the archetype, not as a purely spiritual entity, but as a psychic function that had its roots in biological instincts. Psychic processes, he wrote, 'are somehow bound to an organic substrate', and as such 'they are articulated with the life of the organism as a whole and therefore partake of its dynamism – in other words, they must have a share in its instincts' (CW8.375). The archetypes themselves represent the conscious symbolic expression of unconscious instinctual drives whose origins lie in the purely organic realm. He summed up this view by saying that 'The archetypes are simply the forms which instincts assume' (CW8.339), and that therefore 'the [archetypal] image represents the meaning of the instinct' (CW8.398).

Now, considerable scepticism has been expressed in recent years concerning the idea of an instinct. It has frequently been condemned as a metaphysical concept or as obviating the possibility of persons claiming responsibility for their actions. For Jung the notion was not at all mysterious, but represented simply the idea of an inherited pattern of behaviour, and hence for him an archetype was simply a disposition towards a certain repertoire or pattern of psychic activity. As such it does not necessarily constrain behaviour, but provides a framework within which certain kinds of psychic expression become possible. It is, using Ernst Mayr's term, an 'open programme' which is genetically acquired yet permits a wide variety of behaviour depending on environmental circumstances.

Following a similar model sketched by Schopenhauer, Jung envisaged a kind of hierarchy, at the lower end of which we are totally constrained by our instincts and largely unconscious of them, and at the upper end of which as we evolve our conscious functions we gain increasing control and autonomy and may even act deliberately in conflict with our instincts. He spoke of the development of the psyche from its unconscious roots to its fully conscious flowering as 'an emancipation of function from its instinctual form and so from the compulsiveness which . . . causes it to harden into a mechanism' (CW8.377). There is, in this process of development, an 'increasing freedom from sheer instinct [so that] at the upper limit of the psyche . . . the instincts lose their influence as movers of the will' (CW8.379).

Cultural conditioning, likewise, can never entirely constrain our behaviour for, as with our biological instincts, it becomes with the full development of adult consciousness a force against which we can respond with our individual wills. Children, as we have seen, are according to Jung for many years locked within the psychological bondage of their parents' psyches, and while even in adulthood many individuals allow themselves to be carried along by collective pressures and opinions, nevertheless from puberty onwards, with the emergence of the self-conscious ego, there is a growing urge towards independence and self-direction. Like Nietzsche he drew a contrast between the heteronomous conformity of 'mass man', who allows himself to be engulfed by external constraints, and the person who, 'firmly rooted not only in the outside world but also in the world within' (CW10.462), acts autonomously or authentically. It is man's potential for the latter which provides the basis for Jung's notion of *individuation*, which will be examined in Chapter 12 below.

Thus, while always tied to instinct, the development of human personality 'brings with it the possibility of deviating from . . . inherited psychic structures . . . and hence from instinct' (CW8.724), and carries with it 'the distinctive power of creating something new' (CW8.245). To be sure 'we do not enjoy masterless freedom', but we do enjoy a measure of autonomy and conscious control over our lives which can be described as free will. However, the inner essence of this 'will' cannot properly be the subject of empirical investigation, Jung believed, and must be left to the philosophers.

Jung in his theory of archetypes has, in effect, offered us in outline a *theory of human nature* which, though based securely on biological foundations, allows for the possibility of individual development and spiritual growth which far transcends its origins. An important corollary of this argument was that by means of his theory of archetypes he was able to affirm *the unity of the human species*. The suggestion sometimes made that his theory of the collective unconscious encouraged some sort of racist philosophy involves a complete misunderstanding of his thinking (see for example Brown, 1961, p.106). In his Tavistock Lectures delivered in London in 1935 he insisted that the archetypes 'belong to a pattern not peculiar to any particular mind or person, but rather to a pattern peculiar to *mankind in general*', that they 'have nothing to do with so-called blood or racial inheritance, nor are they personally acquired by the individual. They belong to mankind in general, and therefore they are of a *collective* nature' (CW18.79, Jung's italics). From this he concluded that 'somewhere you are the same as the Negro or the Chinese. . . . In the collective unconscious you are the same as a man of another race, you have the same archetypes, just as you have, like him, eyes, a heart, a liver, and so on. It does not matter that his skin is black' (CW18.93).

We can sum this point up by saying that, while there is ambiguity in some of Jung's earlier statements on this matter, in his later writings he clearly rejected any idea that differences in the collective unconscious are based on racial inheritance. Any psychological differences between Jew and gentile, European and Chinese are due to the work of culture, not of genetics; all share a common inheritance of archetypal forms, though the contents that fill these forms may vary over time and place.

The whole question of human nature, of instincts, of race, and of culture is, of course, a minefield. Jung himself stepped into this minefield in the 1930s, and as a result of some injudicious remarks in 1934 – which he later deeply regretted – about the psychological differences between Jews and Aryans, came to be accused of racism and anti-semitism. The charge was an absurd one and has frequently been refuted (see for example: Jaffé, 1989, p.78f; Odajnik, 1976, p.86f; and G. Wehr, 1987, p.304f), and though the time and place of these remarks was insensitive, to say the least, they do at any rate accurately reflect his long-standing view that on top of a common universal archetypal inheritance lie identifiable psychological differences between one cultural grouping and another. As he himself pointed out, his remarks concerning the psychological differences between Jews and Aryans implied 'no depreciation of Semitic psychology, any more than it is a depreciation of the Chinese to speak of the peculiar psychology of the Oriental' (CW10.1014). He certainly maintained that individual cultures have unique identities, that they 'have their own peculiar psychology, and in some way they also have their own peculiar kind of psychopathology' (CW10.466), and had frequently drawn attention to such differences between European and Chinese peoples. But it is clear from the Tavistock Lectures quoted above, and indeed from the whole context of his writings at this period, that his theory of archetypes represented a commitment to the fundamental equality of all races.

The issue of Jung and the Nazis has been raised again recently by Masson (1989), who argues, in a style which is unbalanced and abusive, that Jung was not only anti-Semitic, but advocated a doctrine which showed affinity with fascist thinking, and actively consorted for reasons of personal aggrandisement with the Nazis in the years prior to the war. The first two accusations are totally without plausibility, and Masson offers no real argument in their support. Aniela Jaffé, herself a Jew and a close friend and colleague of Jung's from the mid-1930s to his death in 1961, points to Jung's association in that period with many Jewish people as both patients and colleagues, and to the help, advice, and financial support he gave to many individual Jews during the period of Nazi persecution (1989, p.78f). The accusation of collaboration is more complex. His own claim was that his association with the German Medical Society for Psychotherapy from 1933 to 1939 as its president was undertaken in order to preserve the nascent psychoanalytic movement from extinction, an undertaking which he recognized as having grave risks to his own reputation. Furthermore as president he succeeded in rescinding the Nazi ban on Jewish membership, stipulating that the Society be 'neutral as to politics and creed' (p.84), a policy which was reversed by the German authorities shortly after his resignation in 1939.

He certainly showed a close interest in the Nazi phenomenon and in Hitler's personality, but this interest was clearly more psychological than political. He was fascinated by the eruption of political mania in the 1930s, but unlike the vast majority of his contemporaries he saw it, not primarily as the consequence of Germany's recent history, but rather as the release of powerful archetypal forces which, due to the peculiarities of German culture, had remained unassimilated and hence full of awesome potential. It must be evident by now that Jung's whole personality and way of thinking were fundamentally opposed to Nazi ideology and politics. His commitment to the fundamental value of the individual and his deep suspicion of the dehumanizing capabilities of groups and crowds, combined with his catholic outlook and rejection of Eurocentrism, place him at the opposite end of the spectrum from the German National Socialists. His distaste for the latter was only matched by his dislike of Bolshevism which he saw as equally totalitarian and equally a threat to the spiritual values of the West.

Though in many respects Jung's theory of archetypes and the collective unconscious ran contrary to prevailing twentieth century orthodoxies, his construction of a theory of human nature bears interesting comparison with developments in recent years in a number of areas of behavioural studies. For example, in the field of ethology, i.e. the study of the social behaviour of animals, investigators such as Konrad Lorenz and Niko Tinbergen have pointed to a whole range of similarities between animal and human behaviour, thereby tending to place the animal and the cultural domains on a continuum, and hence to blur the traditionally sharp distinction between them. Sociobiologists such as E.O. Wilson, working in a parallel and closely related field, have also stressed the homologies between the social behaviour of animals and humans, and tend to view human behaviour patterns, like those of the animal species, as having evolved along Darwinian lines. Structural anthroplogy, of whom the chief exponent is Claude Lévi-Strauss, but which has also influenced the investigations of Jean Piaget into child development, maintains as a central tenet that social structures, such as those related to kinship, are not fortuitous products of individual societies, let alone individual persons, but are projections of systems embedded in the human psyche. Such systems are therefore universal in the sense that they represent the expressions in different cultures of patterns which in the last analysis may be explained in terms of the inherited structure of the human brain. Finally, structural linguistics, associated chiefly with the name of Noam Chomsky, and born of a union between anthropology, linguistics, and mathematical logic, claims that language acquisition is not to be explained merely as a learned or conditioned reflex, but that it must rest on unlearned structures which, again, are in the last analysis explicable in terms of neural inheritance. Such inherited linguistic structures or potentialities represent for Chomsky the distinctive mark of being human. What links these diverse fields and theories together is the rejection of the *tabula rasa* theory of the human mind and human behaviour, and the acceptance of universal inherited structures which, while not determining human behaviour, constitute the universal parameters within which behaviour may be seen as recognizably and essentially human. (For a fuller discussion of these ideas and their relationship with Jung, see Stevens, 1982, *passim.*)

Associating Jung with the recent work of ethologists and sociobiologists has its risks. They too have stepped into a minefield and have suffered accordingly, often accused of racism and dubbed as reactionaries and even fascists. Reactions of this kind to their way of thinking had its heyday in the 1960s and 1970s, especially in the highly charged atmosphere of American campuses. Since then it has become possible to take a calmer view of the matter. Mary Midgeley, in her wide-ranging exploration of this subject, has argued that their efforts to open up and explore the whole cluster of issues surrounding the question of human nature has been salutary. It has enabled us to look again at specific questions about the genesis of social behaviour patterns, and at the broad issue of the relationship between the human and the animal kingdoms. She argues strongly that to maintain a secure concept of human dignity 'we need some sort of notion of human nature', and that such a notion, 'far from threatening the concept of freedom, is absolutely essential to it'. She laments the fact that the 'rejection of the idea of human nature has become a dogma which in itself is a threat to human freedom'. Moreover the much-despised term 'instinct' can be shown to be not only harmless but actually quite useful if we construe it, not 'as a voice within' or as a 'supernatural being or entity', but as an inherited behavioural disposition (1979, pp.85, xviii, xix, 51).

At the same time she is critical of many aspects of ethology and sociobiology, pointing out that the one often naïvely extrapolates from animal to human behaviour, and the other offers a rather simplistic reductionist programme, and while the aim of her argument is to bring biology and psychology closer together, she is also concerned that the latter should not be reduced to the former. But not all ethologists and sociobiologists can be criticized on these grounds. It is true that earlier writers in these fields, such as Robert Ardrey and E.O. Wilson, are vulnerable to such charges, but determinism and reductionism are certainly not essential to these disciplines, and many in the field now explicitly reject them. J.H. Crook, for example, drawing on a wide range of research, argues that, while the sociobiological paradigm 'effectively relates man to behavioural evolution in the animal kingdom . . . and thus for the first time anchors the study of society in evolutionary biology', sociobiological explanations 'do not in the least explain the enormous variance in cultural manifestations' of human behaviour, and that they do not 'seek to reduce all descriptions of individual human action to biological causation'. On the contrary, sociobiology is concerned 'with the *boundaries* or the *framework* of human action and not with the here-and-now causation of personal events' (1980, p.186, my italics). Thus the genetic endowment of the human species, forged by the long process of evolution, does not constrain human behaviour within iron laws; it is more correct, Crook argues, to see this endowment as an 'open programme', as a 'flexible strategy', as a 'biogrammatical frame for action' (p.189).

Jung would, I believe, have concurred with this, and his own speculations in many ways anticipated much of Midgeley's argument as well as the non-reductionist views of recent sociobiologists. Far from being a recipe for mysticism, or a manifesto for racism, then, his theory of archetypes and the collective unconscious was a bold attempt to build the foundations of a theory of human nature, of a common universal humanity, firmly grounded in biology, and to find a way to overcome both the reductionism of a purely materialistic standpoint, and the dualism that fails to find any bridge between organism and psyche. It was also a way of acknowledging the great flexibility of human behaviour without at the same time denying its biological roots.

If not a racist, though, was Jung guilty of the less serious charge of 'reactionary'? Is it not inevitable that a theory of human nature based on inherited archetypes will define human action in such a way as to affirm the status quo and preclude radical change? If our psychic activity is set within a framework of inherited mental dispositions, then do not the prospects of any transformation in our condition seem excluded? This accusation is not wide of the mark, though it is one that can to some extent be turned to Jung's advantage. He himself was a liberal democrat by political persuasion, a lifelong defender of the individual against the state who, while critical of some of the dehumanizing tendencies of the modern state, felt a strong bond of sympathy with the small-scale liberal democratic institutions of Switzerland. He made no secret of his dislike for the revolutionary philosophy of Marxism and of his scepticism for any political theory based on the idea of the continuous progress of mankind. He believed, as we saw in Chapter 4, that the human psyche needs to be firmly planted in historical traditions, and hence he strongly criticized the Marxist tendency 'to destroy all tradition . . . [which] could interrupt the normal process of development for several hundred years and substitute an interlude of barbarism', and which, furthermore, could 'neuroticize the masses and prepare them for collective hysteria' (CW9ii.282).

But from this it does not follow that change is impossible or undesirable. Jung certainly had no time for Utopian schemes, whether from the right or the left of the political spectrum, which sought to transform and reshape human nature; such schemes only lead to vicious dictatorship, and in any case must inevitably elude our grasp since they are based on a mistaken understanding of the human psyche. This does not mean, however, that we are locked in an archetypal straightjacket and thereby prevented from contemplating and working towards social change. It is important, he believed, that we should not stick to old myths and well-tried formulae, but see these as requiring renewal with each generation. Each generation, he suggested, needs to retell its myths in its own way, and to shape its archetypal endowment for its own purposes: 'the old myth needs to be clothed anew in every renewed age if it is not to lose its therapeutic effect' (CW9ii.281). He was well aware, as we shall document in Chapter 12, that an archetypal inheritance, such as that of Christianity in the modern world, can lose its meaning and ossify into unacceptably rigid forms, and he himself saw it as his life's task to revivify this tradition, to breathe new life into it, not by turning the clock back or by propping up tottering institutions, but by turning to radically different cultures and alternative traditions such as Buddhism and Taoism which emphasized personal experience rather than conventional doctrine. There would have been little point in his undertaking this task if he was wedded firmly to the status quo, and indeed some theologians have viewed his efforts in this regard as dangerously subversive.

It might still be objected that the archetypes themselves represent a form of Western bourgeois ideology, a disguised shorthand for modern Western values, in particular those of the dominant and privileged classes, which have simply been extrapolated to embrace humanity as such. Thus the 'discovery' of a God-archetype might be little more than an unconscious reinforcement of prevailing belief-systems and hence of prevailing social structures. This is a possibility that cannot easily be dismissed, even on Jung's own premises. He was, as we saw earlier, very conscious of the fact that one's own psychological inheritance and make-up tends to shape one's beliefs, a view parallel to Marx's own theory of the social determination of consciousness, and hence he could hardly avoid the possibility that his archetypal theory represented a projection, if not of his class interests, at any rate of a certain psychological disposition of which he was a representative. It is not possible to examine here the full implications of this argument, for apart from anything else it might lead to the self-stultifying conclusion that no arguments whatsoever, including this one, escape ideological distortion. But leaving aside these philosophical questions, it must be said in mitigation of Jung that in his formulation of the archetypal theory he adopted a far from blinkered methodology, drawing on evidence from a very wide range of divergent cultural and historical sources, and seeking, at any rate at a conscious level, to maintain a critical stance with respect to the values and beliefs of his own culture. This does not, of course, guarantee total freedom from ideological bias, and indeed as we noted in an earlier chapter Jung might be accused of neglecting the link between belief systems and the institutions of political and social power, but it does give us some confidence in the at least *relative* objectivity of the theory.

There is in all of this a typical Jungian balance between opposing considerations. 'As above, so below': on the one side he was concerned to show that the symbolic activities of the human psyche, those activities that are so uniquely characteristic of the human species, have their roots firmly planted in nature, that they represent the 'meaning of the instincts', and thereby constitute a common universal principle that binds humanity into one. But at the same time our symbolic, and hence typically human, behaviour represents an emancipation from instinct, the expression of the essentially human goal of the fullest development of our unique individual potential. This goal Jung called the *self*, a concept to which we turn our attention in the next chapter.

# 11

# THE STRUCTURE OF THE PSYCHE

The self is not only the centre but also the whole circumference.
(C.G. Jung)

The concept of the self occupies a central place in Jung's model of the human psyche. In the Western intellectual tradition the self has usually been identified with the conscious ego, which in turn has been cast in a lead role in the total play of the human personality. Furthermore, the ego has often been viewed as a kind of substance, by analogy with physical substance, and while recognizing that it may be influenced by its wider environment, there has nevertheless been a tendency to see the ego as the central power in the psychic realm, with other factors remaining subordinate to it. Thus in the psychologies of the seventeenth and eighteenth centuries the ego was viewed as the central rational core of the human person, with the passions and instincts revolving round it like satellites. A major exception was David Hume who denied the existence of a central pontifical ego and, like Jung to some extent, identified the self with the whole range of mental – albeit conscious – activity. Freud himself was an heir to the earlier tradition to the extent that he viewed the ego as 'the central agency of the personality' (see Samuels, 1985, p.55).

Jung proposed a very different model which represented a revolutionary gestalt switch in our perception of the relationship between ego and self. Progoff has described this as nothing less than a 'Copernican Revolution' in psychology, and quotes Jung himself as remarking that the ego revolves around the self 'very much as the earth rotates around the sun' (1953, p.153). Where traditional thinking saw the ego as – to use the gestalt terminology – the 'figure' and the rest of the self as the 'ground', Jung saw the total self as the primal source, with the ego emerging as a secondary phenomenon. The self is, according to Jung, 'an unconscious prefiguration of the ego. It is not I who create myself, rather I happen to myself'. Thus the 'ego stands to the self as the moved to the mover, or as object to subject, because the determining factors which radiate out from the self surround the ego on all sides and are therefore supraordinate to it' (CW11.391). Here again Jung's general approach has much in common with that of Nietzsche who spoke of 'The absurd overestimation of consciousness', and who ridiculed the idea of the conscious ego 'as the supreme kind of being, as God' (1967, para.529). These ideas have, furthermore, had considerable influence on recent poststructuralist talk of 'decentring the self', of unseating the self from its imperial position in modern humanist thinking (see for example Lacan, 1977, p.30f).

Let us now look more closely at Jung's conception of the psyche. In the first place he drew a sharp distinction between self and ego. While he confined the term 'ego' to the centre of consciousness, he taught that the 'self' is the totality of psychic function. 'By ego', he wrote, 'I understand a complex of ideas which constitutes the centre of my field of consciousness and appears to possess a high degree of continuity and identity' (CW6.706), whereas 'I have chosen the term "self" to designate the totality of man, the sum total of his conscious and unconscious contents' (CW11.140), a totality in which the ego plays a role subordinate to that of the self. The self, furthermore, 'is not a static quantity or constant form', but is rather 'a dynamic process', 'an active force' whose essence is one of continual transformation and rejuvenation (CW9ii.411). It is not so much a thing, therefore, as a tendency or goal, a unifying principle which represents the archetypal image of personal fulfilment.

We begin with the ego. It is first of all the centre of consciousness, and as such is the mediator of memory and the sense of a continuing self-identity. Ego and consciousness were for Jung complementary, even synonymous, terms, for 'no consciousness can exist without a subject, an ego to which its contents are related. . . . Nor can we imagine a consciousness without an ego' (CW9i.506). It also embraces the ideas of will and reason. To some extent this conception of the ego is echoed in Lacan's belief that the ego is a 'false construction', a mere linguistic representation which arises from the process of 'mirroring' that takes place between infant and mother (1977, p.30f). How then does Jung's theory differ from traditional notions of the ego?

In the first place it is not, as Jung put it, an *a priori* existence but emerges like a growing organism from the unconscious womb of the psyche. In a word, it is a process with a *history*. It is not an immutable substance, like a psychic atom or particle, but rather a function or process which is developing and which emerges from the interaction between the unconscious and the external environment. 'The ego-centre', Jung stated, 'crystallizes out of the dark depths in which it is somehow contained *in potentia*' (CW9i.503). It has no existence in its own right but evolves from childhood in response to existential demands. It may, in the fully developed adult, become a relatively autonomous function, but at the same time it remains tied, 'as the moved to the mover', to the unconscious.

Secondly the relation of the ego to the unconscious is one of constant struggle in which now the ego and now the unconscious attains supremacy. On the one hand the ego may be 'ousted from its central and dominating position and thus [find] itself in the role of passive observer', which may lead to the fragmentation or even the dissolution of the ego. Or on the other hand there is the situation in which the ego identifies itself with the total self, thereby engendering a falsely inflated and dangerous sense of power and self-mastery (CW8.430). The aim of the self, as we shall see, is to mediate between these extremes by bringing the conscious ego and the unconscious forces that lie around and beneath it into some kind of balance or harmony, and thereby to seek wholeness.

This idea of a struggle between rational consciousness and the irrational depths of one's personality has a long history in Western philosophy. Plato's influence here as elsewhere is paramount. In a number of dialogues he depicted the soul as being in a constant state of strife in which the 'higher' rational faculty struggles with the 'lower' passions for supremacy. Like Jung he viewed the ultimate goal of this struggle as one of harmony and balance, yet at the same time he was in no doubt that in order to achieve this balance it was necessary for the lower parts of the soul to become subordinate to the higher. A similar assumption underlay Aristotle's idea of the soul, and, backed by the added authority of St Paul, became accepted almost without question by Christian theologians and by philosophers until the nineteenth century. The first major challenge to this view came from Schopenhauer. He argued that the rational intellect is not, despite its pretensions, wholly in command of the situation, but is like a small boat bobbing about on the surface of the great ocean of the unconscious. Jung's conception of the relationship between ego and self is in many ways an elaboration of Schopenhauer's revolutionary ideas, though as we shall see there are also some important differences.

One important difference lay in the fact that while Schopenhauer's philosophy led him to propound a doctrine of resigned pessimism, even of ego-annihilation, Jung in two important respects maintained the optimistic spirit of the Platonic tradition. In the first place he conceived the self in its relationship with the ego as being essentially purposeful, as having a goal. Indeed he sometimes spoke of the self as *the* goal. This goal he called 'individuation', and the means whereby it is to be achieved the 'transcendent function'. These ideas will be examined in more detail in the next chapter, but here we must note that the struggle he depicted as taking place within the self is precisely that which gives meaning to our existence, and hence is not, as it was for Schopenhauer, a pointless struggle-to-death. Moreover this goal or purpose is not something that lies beyond the self or the world, like the heaven of traditional Christian theology, but rather lies in the process whereby the self emerges from potentiality into fuller and more satisfying actuality. It is in essence the process of *self-realization*, a term which has become widely used in recent years and for which Jung's thinking provides a useful theoretical framework. It is a model which was first elucidated by Aristotle and which allows us to understand human life as a purposeful unfolding from within rather than as the passive consequence of forces, natural or divine, from without.

In the second place Jung believed that the goal of self-realization could not be achieved by the dissolution of the ego. Here we must turn our attention eastwards, for Schopenhauer himself had come independently to a solution of the problem of life not altogether different from that of certain Buddhist traditions. The solution consisted in the recognition that the source of suffering lies in the attachment to a belief in the absolute existence of the substantive individual ego. The solution to the problem of suffering, therefore, lay in the extinction of this belief and the attainment of an ego-less state. Now, Jung was prepared to travel some way along this road, for he saw in Eastern philosophy a recognition of the centrality of the self and the subordinate status of the ego. In the West, he argued, we have tended to identify psyche with ego, rational consciousness. The East, on the other hand, can teach us that there are other dimensions that we can explore. But he drew up short of the possibility, envisaged in Vedanta Yoga, of the total dissolution of the ego, of consciousness without a subject. 'There can be no consciousness where there is no-one to say "I am conscious"' (CW9i.506). He did not doubt the existence of mental states that transcend ordinary consciousness, but he could not imagine a conscious state that did not relate to a subject (CW11.774).

Some critics such as Alan Watts have taken Jung to task for clinging to his Western prejudices and for failing to realize that his stand on this question was nothing more than a projection onto mankind of the Western egocentric mode of consciousness. 'How a mere convention of syntax, that the verb must have a subject, can force itself upon perception and seem to be the logic of reality!' Watts exclaims (1973, p.94f). This objection undoubtedly has some force, and it points to a persistent wariness on Jung's part, which we noted in a previous chapter, about taking over undigested ideas from the East. However it is worth noting that his stand on this question reflected his fundamental commitment to the tradition of Western individualism, and to the belief that in the last analysis individuals cannot be thought of as dissoluble into an undifferentiated One or World Soul. The mystic in Jung was drawn to the Vedanta principle of all-is-one, but the scientist in him was clear that this is a metaphysical belief that has no place in an empirical investigation of the psyche.

It also reflected his insistence on taking a balanced position between the opposing demands of the *many* and the *one*, of plurality and unity. The self is both many and one, and cannot be reduced to either of these polarities. This provides us with a useful framework in which to explore in more depth Jung's model of the self, and we will examine each of these polarities – plurality and unity – in turn.

For Jung the idea of the unity of consciousness was a 'naive assumption'. He was convinced from an early age that the psyche contains within itself a plurality of centres and functions and is by no means an undifferentiated unity. We saw earlier that as a young man he discovered, as he put it, 'to my utmost confusion that I was actually two different persons. . . . One was the son of my parents, who went to school and was less intelligent, attentive, hard-working, decent, and clean than many other boys. The other was grown up – old in fact – sceptical, mistrustful, remote from the world of men, but close to nature, the earth, the sun, the moon, the weather, all living creatures, and above all close to the night, to dreams' (MDR, pp.61–2).

This fragmentation within himself was confirmed by more objective observations at the start of his professional career. As a medical student he had taken part in séances involving his cousin, Hélène Preiswerk who displayed some bizarre characteristics of multiple personality, an experience which had a lasting effect on his view of the psyche, and which he used as the basis of his doctoral dissertation presented to the University of Zürich in 1902. There was much interest at the turn of the century, both popular and scientific, in the phenomena of multiple and split personality. Robert Louis Stevenson's famous novel, *The Strange Case of Dr Jekyll and Mr Hyde*, published in 1886, was only one of many fictional accounts from that period, and Flournoy's study of the spiritualist medium Helen Smith was widely discussed and had an important influence on Jung's own development. In his dissertation he came to the conclusion that the hallucinatory personalities speaking through his cousin were in fact elements of her own repressed personality seeking to come to birth. It was conceivable, he surmised, 'that the phenomena of double consciousness are simply new character formations, or the attempts of the future personality to break through' (CW2.136).

These ideas were further developed during his early years at the Burghölzli Hospital, in particular through his studies of schizophrenics and his use of the word-association tests. Jung came to the conclusion on the basis of this work that the psyche is composed of fragmentary personalities which he called *complexes*, each complex being a fabric of ideas and images held together first by a pervasive 'feeling tone' and second by relations of meaning and significance. Thus a father complex is a network of related feelings, thoughts, images, etc., centred around the nuclear idea of the father, and having a certain life of its own partially independent of the rest of the personality.

Jung's belief that a complex is a fabric of *meaning*, rather than of things or events, placed his psychological thinking, right from the early period, in marked contrast with empiricist/associationist tradition. Ever since the eighteenth century it had been the ambition, first of philosophers, then of psychologists, to demonstrate that the human mind can be understood as a system of forces by analogy with a physical system; behaviourism is a twentieth century expression of this tendency. Now it is true that Jung took over the concept of physical energy from science and used it, under the name of 'libido', by way of analogy in his own domain. But his work with schizophrenics convinced him that the links that bind the human psyche together are links of quite a different sort from those which bind together physical systems. He realized that the essence of the human mind lies in the meaning and significance of its operations rather than in the causal connections that might hold between them. Thus a complex is like a little narrative, relatively self-contained yet part of a larger story, in which the events must be understood in terms of their meanings rather than any physical relationship. Hence 'the psyche . . . is a series of images in the true sense, not just an accidental juxtaposition or sequence, but a structure that is throughout full of meaning and purpose' (CW8.618).

Making use of an important concept from twentieth century philosophy, we may say that for Jung the characteristic feature of human consciousness lies in its *intentionality*. This concept was first used in its modern psychological sense in the late nineteenth century by Franz von Brentano who had an important influence on the development of the phenomenological movement *via* his pupil Edmund Husserl. Brentano had argued that what distinguished human consciousness absolutely from the realm of physical things and events lay in the fact that it necessarily points beyond itself, that consciousness is always consciousness *of* something; it is this feature of 'aboutness' that he called intentionality. Now unfortunately Jung does not appear to have taken a close interest in the work of Husserl, or of his pupil Heidegger whose 'impenetrable' style repelled him, but it is clear that like them he conceived the psyche in terms of meanings, that psychic contents are always about something in the way that a linguistic phrase or sentence is about something.[1]

But complexes are not just fragments of meaning, for they 'behave like independent beings' (CW8.253), and are invested with the emotive life of personalities. Their significance is not just an abstract one, but, in marked contrast with Freud's impersonal 'id', they have something of the quality of a human person. James Hillman went so far as to claim that Jung's most important discovery lay, not in the complex, or the archetype, but 'in his radical personification of the psyche'. Whereas philosophers had hitherto conceived the forces within the personality as quasi-events, 'Jung described them as persons', a move which 'harked back to Renaissance, Hellenic, and archaic thought forms', and to polytheistic mythologies (1975, p.20f). The various complexes, along with the archetypes such as shadow and anima, that make up the structural components of the personality, were for Jung like so many partial personalities, or 'splinter psyches' as he called them, an idea which he contrasted ironically with our 'true religion [of] a monotheism of consciousness' which is 'coupled with a fanatical denial of the existence of fragmentary autonomous systems' (CW13.51).

His early clinical work with schizophrenics had inevitably led Jung to see the fragmentation of the personality in pathological terms. Many of the patients he observed at that time were suffering from severe personality disintegration, often bordering on insanity, in which there was sometimes no apparent connection between one part of the personality and another. However, one of Jung's most important achievements was to discover in this strange witch's cauldron the elements of a theory of the *normal* psyche, and to argue that some kind of dissociation and fragmentation is a necessary condition for psychic growth and health, and even in his schizophrenic patients he saw their fantasy worlds as, at bottom, positive attempts to cope with reality.[2] The autonomous complexes, he came to believe, are not just lapses from the proper and normal unity of the psyche, but are aspects of its essential nature. In 1936 he wrote that the psyche's tendency to split is fundamentally 'a normal phenomenon' which 'need not be a question of hysterical multiple personality, or schizophrenic alterations of personality, but merely of so-called "complexes" that come entirely within the scope of the normal' (CW8.253). In abnormal cases they may appear as inner voices or even as some sort of possession that may take hold and dominate, but for the most part they represent the inner dynamic tensions of the psyche which play an essential role in personal growth.

The personification of the psyche became even more evident to Jung in the course of his elaboration of the theory of archetypes. The symbolic figures that inhabit our dreams and that appear in a variety of forms in myth and legend are, he believed, nothing other than the outer manifestation, the projection, of the partial characters that populate our own psyches. Like Feuerbach, the Hegelian philosopher who had such an influence on Marx, he held that the galaxy of deities and supernatural forces that populated the pre-scientific and pre-Christian cosmos were merely reflections of the complex inner life of mankind.

The account of the self in terms of a plurality of complexes and personality fragments is, however, only a partial view of Jung's theory. To speak of the self is necessarily to speak of a tendency towards *unity* and *wholeness*. As I have already insisted, this unity is not one which dissolves all differences into a mystical oneness, but is rather a matter of balance and equilibrium within a system which is in a state of dynamic tension. In the final pages of this chapter we will try to gain a better understanding of Jung's sometimes misunderstood conception of psychic wholeness.

In the first place he stated unequivocally that 'there are no isolated psychic processes', explicitly rejecting thereby the old empiricist notion, 'dating back to Condillac', that mental contents can be broken down into isolated atomic bits (CW8.197). All our perceptions, thoughts and feelings are embedded within the total matrix of our personality, for not only are all our actions influenced by a whole host of others, but the very notion of a thought or image isolated from all others makes no sense. He saw that any attempt to analyse an image, fantasy or dream in isolation from the whole personality was an impossible task since their very identity depended on the whole psychic environment. A mental image is not just an image in the ordinary sense but, as in a hologram, has stamped on it the quality of the whole personality.

On this question Jung had much in common with Gestalt psychology. This school emerged in the late-nineteenth and early-twentieth centuries as a reaction against the piecemeal analysis of mental states into constituent parts typical of the associationist schools of psychology. It argued that the activities of the psyche cannot be broken down into parts, and that individual mental contents had to be seen in terms of the whole psychic context in which they occurred. As the German word *Gestalt* ('form' or 'pattern') implies, the emphasis was on the shape, form or configuration of mental states, in which a particular 'figure' depended for its significance on the total 'ground' in which it was located. Jung was certainly aware of the work of Max Wertheimer, who founded the Gestalt school, and may have been influenced by him in his approach to the word-association tests, but, surprisingly, thereafter he showed no interest in this school, at any rate on the evidence of his published works.

There are also interesting links with the great French philosopher Henri Bergson (1859–1941). He was the most famous philosopher of his day, and is mentioned approvingly by Jung on a number of occasions, particularly in relation to his idea of libido which he compared with Bergson's concept of *élan vital*. Bergson was a leading critic of the mechanistic philosophy, advocating an alternative organic cosmology which conceived nature in terms of dynamic, evolutionary process (Bergson, 1911). His thinking represented a fundamental challenge to the orthodox idea that, at bottom, nature consists of a collection of things or substances, and proposed instead that 'things are events of a special kind, temporary crystallizations of images . . . movement is the real and original stuff the world is made of, whereas the picture of the universe as consisting of distinct material objects is an artefact of intelligence' (Kolakowski, 1985, p.45). Furthermore, he maintained, the human mind also must be thought of in terms of process and change rather than of substance. Under the influence of William James' idea of the 'stream of consciousness', he came to see consciousness as a process of continuous indivisible flow in which there are strictly speaking no divisions, only a continuous stream of interlocking events.

This way of looking at the psyche could be described by the now somewhat overworked term 'holistic', a word first coined in 1926 by Jan Smuts. Jung had begun to use the words 'unity', 'totality' and 'wholeness' in relation to the psyche as early as 1913 (see CW4.556), and in 1936 he actually referred to his approach as 'holistic' in the sense that it involved 'the systematic observation of the psyche as a whole' (CW6.966). It was an attitude reflected very strongly in his clinical work where he frequently spoke of the need to address the patient as a whole person rather than as isolated pieces of behaviour or single dreams, and pointed towards the idea of wholeness as the key to psychic health. In the following passage, written in 1931, this idea was even extended to the wider realm of medicine in general:

> Medicine until recently has gone on the supposition that illness should be treated and cured by itself; yet voices are now heard which declare this view to be wrong, and demand the treatment of the sick person, and not of the illness. The same demand is forced upon us in the treatment of psychic suffering. More and more we turn our attention from the visible disease and direct it upon the man as a whole. We have come to understand that psychic suffering is not a definitely localized, sharply delimited phenomenon, but rather the symptom of a wrong attitude assumed by the total personality. We can therefore not hope for a thorough cure to result from a treatment restricted to the trouble itself, but only from a treatment of the personality as a whole.
>
> (MM, pp.222–3)

As I have already indicated, the concept of a psychic whole did not imply for Jung totally undifferentiated unity – 'a dark night in which all cows are black', to use Hegel's ironical characterization of Schelling's idealist metaphysics – but rather a dynamic *balance between opposites*. 'I see in all that happens', he declared, 'the play of opposites' (CW4.779). This is a theme which ran through the whole of Jung's thought, one which links him with some of the less orthodox traditions of European thought, and provides a bridge between these traditions and recent speculations about the bilateral nature of the brain and related mental functions (see Ornstein, 1973).

There are many influences on Jung in this regard, but amongst the most important are: first the ancient Greek philosopher Heracleitus, whose concept of *enantiodromia* – the tendency of things to turn into their opposites – is frequently cited by Jung; secondly the Neoplatonic and hermetic idea of the circular cosmic journey from primal oneness, through division and opposition, and back to the original unity; thirdly the philosophers of the Romantic period, especially Schelling with his idea that all things flow back and forth from positive and negative poles, and that the very nature of mind or consciousness presupposes an opposition between subject and object; and fourthly in poets such as Goethe, with his principle of systole–diastole – the universal inward–outward rhythm of living things, and William Blake whose *Marriage of Heaven and Hell* is built around the notion of cosmic and psychic opposites (on Jung's link with Blake, see CW6.460).

Jung, then, viewed the self as an arena of struggle and conflict between polar opposites, but also as a self-regulating system seeking equilibrium through the interplay between these opposing forces: 'There is no balance, no system of self-regulation, without opposition. The psyche is just such a self-regulating system', seeking a balance between various opposing tendencies: between the tendencies towards unity and plurality, between the conscious and the unconscious, the male and female elements within the psyche, between reason and instinct, convention and nature, good and evil (CW7.92). Thus the psyche shows, in Frey-Rohn's words, 'not only a tendency to polarization but also an inclination to strike a balance, even to establish continuous states of equilibrium' (1974, p.170).

As a 'self-regulating system' the psyche strives to achieve a state of equilibrium through its own natural forces. In other words equilibrium is not something imposed from without, but rather comes from within – it is 'endogenous' rather than 'exogenous' – and is a natural tendency of the psychic organism. This idea has come to full flower in modern *systems theory*, an approach that has been developed over the past few decades, bringing together insights from biology, ecology, cybernetics and engineering.[3] Frijof Capra has argued that the systems approach is at the heart of a revolutionary transformation in outlook, a 'paradigm shift', which is taking place at the present time, and which he believes was in many ways foreshadowed by the thought of Jung. The systems view, he writes,

> looks at the world in terms of relationship and integration. Systems are integrated wholes whose properties cannot be reduced to those of smaller units. Instead of concentrating on basic building blocks or basic substances, the systems approach emphasizes basic principles of organization. . . . Every organism . . . is an integrated whole and thus a living system. . . . The same aspects of wholeness are

> exhibited by social systems – such as an anthill, a beehive, or a human family – and by ecosystems that consist of a variety of organisms and inanimate matter in mutual interaction.
>
> (1982, p.286)

Systems of the kind mentioned here are often called cybernetic systems. The term, coined by Norbert Wiener (1948) and derived from the Greek *kybernan* meaning 'to govern', refers to the fact that through various feedback devices a system such as an organism is able to control its own inner states and to achieve a state of equilibrium, or homeostasis, despite the relative autonomy of its constituent parts. Thus in an ecosystem the various animals, plants, and physical factors each act in their own way, yet, when they are looked at systemically, one can see a tendency towards self-correction, balance and overall integrity. Furthermore, systems are intrinsically dynamic in nature, flexible rather than rigid structures, in which fluctuations and temporary imbalances occur, a feature which allows for great flexibility and which opens up a large number of options for acting internally and interacting externally.

The connection here with Jung's model of the psyche is evident, and emphasizes once again the importance of his depiction of the self on the analogy of a living organism. Just as living systems have the ability to adapt to a changing environment through homeostatic mechanisms, so too the human psyche, by its ability to achieve unity and stability within margins of fluctuation and disturbance, can survive and flourish. The cybernetic nature of his thinking is evident in the following passage:

> The intrinsically goal-like quality of the self and the urge to realize this goal are . . . not dependent on the participation of consciousness. . . . In reality, the entelechy of the self consists in a succession of endless compromises, ego and self laboriously keeping the scales balanced if all is to go well. Too great a swing to one side or the other is often an example of how not to set about it.
>
> (CW11.960)

Thus while the self-conscious ego emerges out of the total self, it is the interaction of the whole personality, rather than the action of a sovereign ego, that gives the self its potential for unity and wholeness. Indeed, 'that an ego was possible at all appears to spring from the fact that all opposites seek to achieve a state of balance' (MDR, p.379).

This is a principle that had wide ramifications for Jung and links together a number of themes that pervade his work, ranging from considerations of society to speculations about the cosmos. But perhaps the most significant implication of all lay in his idea of *individuation*. The quest for psychic unity through the reconciliation of opposites is nothing less than the coming to self-hood, the realization of all that lies potentially within the psyche, and thereby the goal and meaning of human existence. This goal he called individuation.

# 12

# INDIVIDUATION AND THE QUEST FOR MEANING

Individuation is now our mythology.

(C.G. Jung)

The concept of individuation – the *principium individuationis* as it is sometimes referred to – has a long history. It is to be found in the works of Aristotle, Plotinus, Aquinas, Leibniz and Schopenhauer, and refers to the discrimination of individual entities out of the general or universal. In earlier times it had a strictly logical connotation, but in the philosophy of Schopenhauer it acquired a rather special meaning. We saw in an earlier chapter that he believed the world is the product of will, a blind force or energy, which unfolds and objectifies itself through an ascending series of grades of increasing individuality, beginning with matter and the universal forces of nature, and rising through plants and animals to mankind who represents the most fully individuated manifestation of will. But though mankind represents the 'highest grade' of the will, this exalted and refined individuality offers not peace or fulfilment, but restless, agitated, ever-unfulfilled desires, insatiable striving, and a self-destructive egoism that inevitably leads to misery, suffering and death. In the absurd tragi-comedy of life, Schopenhauer tells us, 'no-one is happy, but every man strives his whole life long after a supposed happiness which he seldom attains, and even if he does it is only to be disappointed with it' (1970, p.52).

In many ways the philosophy of Schopenhauer was the culmination and apotheosis of Romantic philosophy, with its picture of life as a great journey, an odyssey of cosmic and human transformation. The idea of a transformational journey is closely connected with the *principium individuationis*. It can be traced back at least as far as the Roman Neoplatonist philosopher Plotinus (c. AD 205–62) who envisaged the world as engaged in a cyclical journey involving an emanation from the original One, a fall into division, multiplicity and individuality, and finally an 'epistrophe' or return to the original unity. This idea was developed in the mediaeval period and became a cornerstone of Renaissance thinking when it was integrated with Christian, Jewish, and Hermetic traditions. It was elaborated more fully in the sixteenth and seventeenth centuries by two thinkers who had a great influence on Jung, Paracelsus and Boehme, who linked the whole Plotinean circle with the ideas of alchemy and identified the stage of emanation from the One with the Christian idea of the Fall.

In Hegel and Schelling the cyclical journey is the journey of the Spirit, a cosmic process embracing the whole history of the world and of mankind, whose end is the reconciliation of all opposites, the overcoming of all separate individuality in the Absolute. This overcoming does not destroy all prior differentiation but incorporates it within a higher synthesis; in Hegel's words: 'the abundance of content, simplified into determinateness, returns into itself . . . nothing is lost, all principles are preserved'. A similar conception is to be found in the work of contemporary poets such as Goethe, Blake, Byron, and Wordsworth (see Abrams, 1971, for a detailed account of this aspect of Romantic thought). In Schopenhauer's philosophy the great journey amounts to a cosmic farce which ends in misery and death. His work represents an extreme form of Romantic pessimism, for life has no meaning or purpose, and the best we can do is to disguise its horror from ourselves by various palliatives such as the contemplation of works of art, altruistic sentiment, or the pursuit of saintly indifference to life.

While endorsing much of Schopenhauer's analysis of the human situation, and his refusal to postulate some ultimate transcendent purpose to human striving, Nietzsche rejected his nihilistic conclusions. The goal of life, as Nietzsche came to see it in his mature philosophy, lay in the affirmation of human will and in the path of self-overcoming. While there is no purpose beyond us, we ourselves are creators of purpose, and through our creations in the fields of art, science and philosophy, we project meaning onto an otherwise meaningless cosmos. Most people are content to be carried along by the flow of life, thereby disguising from themselves its ultimate futility, but some are able to fulfil a higher destiny for mankind by facing into the darkness without cringing and by affirming their own value as world-makers. This is the essence of Nietzsche's controversial teaching concerning the *Übermensch*, the overman, who stands for the rejection of mediocrity and conformism, and for the joyful commitment to life in all its shades of light and dark, for the capacity to say 'yes' to the best and the worst in life, even though they might recur everlastingly.

Despite his closeness to Schopenhauer in so many respects, Jung here showed greater affinity with Nietzsche, and especially with the figure of Zarathustra who symbolized Nietzsche's affirmation of life and refusal of despair. His interpretation of *Thus Spake Zarathustra* as a revelation or upwelling from Nietzsche's own unconscious, and of the concept of overman as the psychological goal of self-realization, anticipated some more recent re-evaluations of Nietzsche in a number of important respects. Thus Walter Kaufmann, in his path-making book on Nietzsche published in 1956, argued that the idea of Julius Caesar as an example of overman should be viewed, not in the light of his external political triumphs, and hence as a model for the wielders of political power, but rather of his inner struggle to overcome congenital weakness. More recently Ofelia Schutte, while rejecting the identification of any historical figure with overman, sees it as a symbol of the drive towards self-transformation, towards 'the wholeness of the spirit that is missing from alienated life', and as 'a metaphor for what it means to transcend the dualism and alienation of the human condition' (1984, pp.120–3). And the French philosopher Michel Haar speaks of the overman, 'not as the master of the slave, but as master of himself' (Allison, 1985, p.22. For a psychological interpretation of Nietzsche based on Jungian insights, see Frey-Rohn, 1988).

Where Schopenhauer saw individuation as mankind's most terrible burden, a kind of punishment for our very existence, Jung, like Nietzsche, saw it as the opportunity to find meaning. Though it may carry with it heavy responsibilities and dangers, nevertheless it was for Jung a way towards healing and wholeness. It does not promise the ultimate perfection of Plotinus' 'One', or Hegel's 'Absolute', nor even Nietzche's history-redeeming overman, but it held out a realistic goal of personal transformation and growth, of integration and self-realization. The central core of Schopenhauer's problem – his Romantic *Weltschmerz*, or world-pain – lay in his belief that only perfection and absolute completeness and oneness can satisfy, and since these are impossible delusions, *nothing* can satisfy. Life is a cheat since it teases us with intimations of perfection, yet denies us the means to attain it. Jung's concept of individuation begins with the assumption that perfection is not possible, and that while we might hold it before us as a goal, we must know that what makes the journey worthwhile is the journey itself with all its vicissitudes, rather than some ultimate destination. 'The meaning and purpose of a problem seem to lie not in its solution', he wrote, 'but in our working at it incessantly' (CW8.771).

Jung's whole treatment of the question of individuation arose, as it did for the Romantics and for Nietzsche, out of a sense of historical crisis. It will be recalled that in a lengthy chapter on Schiller in *Psychological Types* he discussed the latter's belief that the problem for modern man is that of fragmentation, specialization, one-sidedness, estrangement, and lack of the sort of psycho-cultural unity which the Ancient Greeks supposedly possessed (CW6.101f). While rejecting Schiller's typically Romantic inclination to believe in a Golden Age in the past when human nature was at one with itself and the world, Jung saw his own age as one of inner disharmony and self-alienation. It is not just that individuals require healing, the whole of society is sick, a diagnosis that had echoes in the writings of a whole series of critics of modern mass society, from Kierkegaard, Marx, and Weber in the nineteenth century, to Fromm, Toynbee and Mumford in our own.

Jung's analysis of modern humanity's alienation was based on a broad historical perspective. The problem began with the Protestant Reformation of the sixteenth century which rent the 'lovely veil' of psychic unity that characterized Catholic mediaeval Europe, a veil which was then torn to shreds by the rise of modern science which has destroyed all traditional myths and metaphysical certainties, and has turned our attention from things of the spirit outwards towards the material world. The world, as Max Weber put it, has become 'disenchanted', it has suffered a catastrophic loss of its encompassing, vivifying myths. Scientific rationalism tends to offer us a 'statistical world picture [which] displaces the individual in favour of anonymous units that pile up into mass formations . . . which robs the individual of his foundation and dignity' (US, pp.13–16). Science and Protestantism, furthermore, helped to create the climate for the rise of capitalism and of mass society which have together resulted in 'a sort of collective possession' which in the twentieth century has reached the proportions of a 'psychic epidemic' (p.5). In 1937 he wrote of 'the incredible savagery going on in the so-called civilized world', and of 'the powers of the underworld . . . which in former times were more or less successfully chained up in a gigantic spiritual edifice where they could be of some use, [and which] are now creating, or trying to create, a State slavery and a state prison devoid of any mental or spiritual charm' (CW11.83).

Though war and the threat of war was at that time accentuating this condition, the most important outward source of the spiritual crisis lay, according to Jung, in the growing subordination in modern times of the individual to large impersonal organizations, especially the all-devouring state. He spoke of the 'craze for mass organization [which] wrenches everyone out of his private world into the deafening tumult of the market place, making him an unconscious, meaningless particle in the mass' (CW18.1345), and lamented the policy of the modern state which is to deprive the individual as far as possible of the capacity for autonomous moral decision (US, p.14).

The concept of individuation was Jung's unique way of confronting this issue. As Peter Homans has pointed out, individuation 'was not designed just as a psychotherapeutic strategy, isolated from its social context [but] was addressed with equal seriousness to the problem of modernity, understood as mass man in mass society' (p.179). Though there is strictly speaking no such thing as a 'Jungian Sociology', Homans argues, 'Jung's psychology fits lock and key with an enormous and incredibly amorphous body of literature that has been subsumed under the rubric "the theory of mass society"' and his diagnosis of modernity in terms of depersonalization and loss of autonomy represents an important contribution to the analysis of the contemporary cultural situation (1979, p.173f). Indeed, contrary to those who see Jung solely in terms of other-worldly and esoteric concerns, the 'preoccupation with the plight of modern man constitutes a fundamental theme in Jung's mature thought' (p.178).

In adopting this strategy Jung was flying deliberately in the face of the prevailing orthodoxy which held that sociological problems must be dealt with at the level of society, and that questions concerning identity and alienation must be seen as social rather than individual problems. Odajnyk points out that according to Jung it is the individual who 'is, in fact, the pivot around which consciousness, society, and history develop . . . a society or a state derives its quality from the mental condition of the individuals composing it' (1976, pp.67–8). Jung himself wrote that: 'In the last analysis, the essential thing is the life of the individual. This alone makes history, here alone do the great transformations take place, and the whole future, the whole history of the world, ultimately springs as a gigantic summation from these hidden sources in individuals' (CW10.315).

He tended, rather as Nietzsche did, to see society as little more than a thin veneer stretched over the surface of primitive instincts, and the *persona* as a kind of false self that, while not necessarily pathological as such, may lock us into a social role if identified with too closely. The persona, he wrote, 'is, as its name implies, only a mask of the collective psyche, a mask that feigns individuality, making others and oneself believe that one is an individual, whereas one is simply acting a role' (CW7.245), a view remarkably close to Sartre's notion of *mauvaise foi* (bad faith) according to which a person escapes the burdens of individuality and freedom by adopting a rigid and socially contrived pattern of behaviour. The remedy for the problems of mass society therefore lay not primarily in political or social action but rather in a return to the spiritual needs of the individual, to a rediscovery of the self. Individuation is thus the only fundamental long-term remedy for the predicament of modern man.

The loss of authentic religious experience in the modern world, and the progressive codification of religious doctrines and practices, furthermore, has had a crucial effect in engendering in the individual a sense of meaninglessness. Jung felt the impact of this in his own consulting room, and referred to the considerable number of patients who came to see him, 'not because they were suffering from a neurosis, but because they could find no meaning in life or were torturing themselves with questions which neither present-day philosophy nor religion could answer' (MM, p.267). For such people religion had lost its authority and justification, they no longer felt themselves redeemed by the death of Christ, and yet despite this, Jung maintained, 'there has not been one whose problem in the last resort was not that of finding a religious outlook on life'. This was not, he hastened to add, a matter of 'a particular creed or membership of a church', but rather of that which lay at the heart of religious experience, namely a sense of wholeness and purpose (p.264).

Jung also feared that in a post-Christian epoch all sorts of demons, thought to have been disposed of, yet still active in the unconscious, could expose humanity to dangerous psychic storms. The period of the Enlightenment, which saw the devitalization of Christianity and the disposing of the gods as mere projections, closed with 'the horrors of the French Revolution' and culminated in the 'uprising of the unconscious destructive forces of the collective psyche' witnessed during the First World War in 'mass murder on an unparalleled scale' (CW7.150). As early as 1918 Jung had warned that the thin veneer of culture, 'this pleasing patina', could easily be rent asunder by the powerful primitive forces that lie beneath it. He saw this as especially problematic for the Germans whose lower, darker, barbaric half 'still awaits redemption', and he was concerned that '[as] the Christian view of the world loses its authority, the more menacingly will the "blond beast" be heard prowling about in its underground prison, ready at any moment to burst out with devastating consequences' (CW10.17). This prophetic warning was amply fulfilled before two decades were out.

The only effective remedy to mass-mindedness, to the depersonalizing effect of modern collective social institutions, and to the threat of nihilism, Jung believed, lay in the growth of self-awareness and the maturing of the individual psyche. We must now examine this notion in more detail.

The 'heart and essence' of individuation consists in the task of *self-knowledge*, and its overriding demand is to '*be yourself!*', in accordance with your own nature, and not another's, to be authentic rather than in bad faith. But what is your *self*? It is, as we saw in the last chapter, 'the sum total of [an individual's] conscious and unconscious contents' (CW11.140), and hence individuation means nothing less than the demand consciously to realize or actualize one's full potential. It means, in Jung's words:

> the optimum development of the whole individual human being [for which task] a whole lifetime, in all its biological, social and spiritual aspects, is needed. Personality is the supreme realization of the innate idiosyncracy of a living being. It is an act of high courage flung in the face of life, the absolute affirmation of all that constitutes the individual.
>
> (CW17.284)

This means being a 'yea-sayer', as Nietzsche put it, in contrast to the nay-saying quietism which he found in Schopenhauer's philosophy. Echoing this, Jung wrote that 'the development of personality . . . is a matter of saying yea to oneself, of taking oneself as the most serious of tasks, of being conscious of everything that one does, and keeping it constantly before one's eyes in all its dubious aspects' (CW13.24) Following a serious illness in 1944, he spoke of the need he felt on recovery to 'affirm one's existence', and to affirm 'things as they are', to say 'an unconditional "yes" to that which is, without subjective protest . . . acceptance of my own nature as I happen to be' (MDR, p.328). Furthermore, the path of self-actualization requires the active collaboration of the conscious ego, and hence it is a matter of moral choice and of will. Individuation is not something that happens to one automatically, but must be sought out and striven for 'as an act of high courage flung in the face of life'.

But this is only part of the story for Jung. He did not believe that the role of will lay in taming and subduing the instinctual part of one's nature, as in the Platonic/Christian tradition. Nor, as in Sartre's philosophy, did he view it as the sovereign legislator of the personality. And he had deep reservations concerning Nietzsche's inflated, all-conquering 'will-to-power'. Rather, he saw the will as facilitating the emergence of the instincts into consciousness, mirrored in the form of emotions, images and fantasies, and in integrating them into the fully functioning self. In 1916 he named this process the 'transcendent function'. He spoke of it as a kind of dialogue, carried on through images rather than words, in which the conscious and unconscious functions transcend their old positions of mutual indifference, or even hostility, and enter into partnership. It meant getting in touch with and respecting the impulses and images that arise from one's innermost nature, and a harmonizing of the psyche by correcting what he called the 'overvaluation of consciousness', a characteristic feature, he believed, of modern Western civilization with its inordinate faith in science and rationality. The individuation process involves a whole range of interactions across what Erich Neumann has called the 'ego-Self axis' (1954), including the polarities of conscious–unconscious, persona–shadow, extravert–introvert, anima–animus. It will be useful to look briefly at the last of these as an example of how the individuation process might work.

The pair of concepts, anima–animus, is one of the best known aspects of Jung's thought, and has provoked much controversy in recent years. They are viewed by Jung as innate, archetypal dispositions that constitute part of the dynamic structure of the human psyche, and correspond respectively to typically feminine and masculine qualities. Jung's essential thought here is that both sexes contain elements of the other: 'in the unconscious of every man there is hidden a feminine personality, and in that of every woman a masculine personality' (CW9i.511), but whereas in a woman the female qualities predominate, the male elements are usually unconscious and are projected onto members of the opposite sex; and correspondingly for a man. 'Every man carries within him the eternal image of woman, not the image of this or that particular woman, but a definite feminine image. . . . Since this image is unconscious, it is always unconsciously projected upon the person of the beloved. . . . The same is true of the woman' (CW17.338). The 'transcendent function' means the possibility of transcending this one-sided situation, withdrawing projections, and owning and integrating the transexual element into oneself. This process, which he believed to be mainly the task of the second half of life, was necessary for the development of a well-adjusted, balanced personality in which the hitherto unconscious contrasexual element is allowed to express and fulfil itself.

This model has been subjected to much debate and criticism. Though Jung's ideas in general have found great appeal for women, perhaps due to his emphasis on meaning rather than mechanism, and on imagination, feeling and intuition (see D. Wehr, 1988, p.6), his own stance and style have often been labelled sexist, and his views concerning the anima seen as limiting and even damaging for women. Now there is no doubt that as a man Jung displayed many of the cultural prejudices of his age, and despite his evident affinity for women, both personally and professionally, he showed some decidedly old-fashioned prejudices, about intellectual women in particular, describing them deprecatingly as prone to being 'animus-driven'. Nevertheless I believe that he has made important contributions to the female/male debate by drawing attention to the need, both within individuals and society, to integrate elements of both sexes, and to seek a balance between male and female characteristics. Seen within the context of the history of Western thought, his ideas represent a major realignment of our views on gender, and as Zabriskie has put it they 'have been enormously important in assisting the re-entry and reintroduction into modern consciousness of the feminine principle' (Barnaby and D'Acierno, 1990, p.275). They have also been important in helping us to see that male/female relationships, and the attraction between the sexes, cannot be reduced to the physical level but need to be understood also in psychological terms (see 'Marriage as a Psychological Relationship', CW17.324f).

Critics have suggested that he failed to look sufficiently deeply into the cultural as opposed to the biological origins of stereotypical male or female characteristics. He certainly tended to assume that the male/female distinction as it appears in Western male-dominated society is a universal archetype, and to that extent he was caught up in the prejudices of his culture. But the importance of his contribution lay, in my opinion, in seeking to re-evaluate what in our culture is seen as typically feminine, interpreting it in psychological and symbolic rather than biological terms, and seeking to give it an equal status alongside and in harmony with the masculine. What he was saying was that unless the female and the male principles could engage in a psychic dialogue of equals, then there is no hope of achieving wholeness, either within individuals or within nations. It was not for him the old 'battle of the sexes', a contest which tends to confirm and ossify social prejudices, but the creative tension between psychological principles which cut across entrenched gender boundaries. Female/male integration was for him therefore of archetypal significance, a key to the reconciliation of all opposites and therefore to the attainment of selfhood.[1]

Individuation, then, involves the bringing-to-be of a more fully realized, liberated self. This is the task of a lifetime and has to be seen as part of Jung's whole organic conception of the psyche. It is therefore first and foremost a *natural* process, one which arises fundamentally from an inner unfolding, a self-directed development, not one imposed artifically from without. Whereas other, later, self-actualization theorists such as Maslow thought of this process as peculiarly human, Jung actually considered it to be a function that we have in common with all living things. He wrote that 'Individuation is an expression of that biological process . . . by which every living thing becomes what it was destined to become from the very beginning' (CW11.460). Following Aristotle's terminology, he described the self as an 'entelechy', i.e. a natural process that has an inherent tendency to achieve its own goal of psychic wholeness.

Natural growth in the organic world involves passing through a series of broadly predetermined stages from germination to maturity. So too with the self. There have been many attempts to delineate a series of stages through which human life progresses from the cradle to the grave, perhaps the most famous being Shakespeare's 'seven ages of man', in *As You Like It*, which begin with the infant 'Mewling and puking in the nurse's arms', and ends with the second childhood of old age, 'Sans teeth, sans eyes, sans taste, sans everything'. What is distinctive about Jung's contribution to the genre, as Staude has argued, is his holistic approach in that whereas most 'theories of human development have emphasized either physical, emotional, cognitive, or moral development', Jung's theory 'is exceptional and important because he was one of the first psychologists to consider the development of the person holistically as well as across the entire life-span' (1981, p.71). This view is endorsed by Samuels who credits Jung with introducing a model which includes the inner and outer worlds, the cultural context, the religious viewpoint, as well as a biological and evolutionary aspect (1985, p.171).

Jung divided life into four periods: childhood up to puberty in which the individual is largely governed by instinct; adulthood from puberty to mid-life in which the ego separates itself from the unconscious, establishes its autonomy, and engages with others in the community; the mid-life stage in which the emphasis is on the adaptation to the internal rather than the external environment; and old-age which is the 'preparation for the ultimate goal of death'. Individuation, as the natural process of becoming a whole human being, occupies the whole of life and occurs at all stages, for 'the optimum development of the whole individual human being . . . a whole lifetime, in all its biological, social and spiritual aspects is needed' (CW17.289). In fact he sometimes, rather confusingly, identified individuation with the process of personality development as such, as when he remarked that 'individuation is practically the same as the development of consciousness out of the original state of identity' (CW6.762). Nevertheless it is especially during the mid-life stage, from the age of about thirty-five onwards, that individuation becomes a major task to be undertaken consciously, indeed a task so demanding that only a minority of people have the courage and will to embark on it.

Jung's relative neglect of the phenomenon of personal growth during the first half of life has suggested to some that individuation has no place during those earlier stages. However it would seem more plausible to interpret this as a rectification of the imbalance of attention that has been paid to the two halves of life respectively by psychologists. No doubt with Freud largely in mind, he pointed to the 'boundless expansion of the kindergarten [which] amounts to complete forgetfulness of the problems of adult education', and while it would be foolish 'to underestimate the importance of childhood', the need in our age for emphasis on adult education was becoming increasingly urgent (CW17.284).

There has been some controversy in recent years on the question of whether individuation is strictly speaking a *natural* process which everyone undergoes, or a special vocation for the few. Jacobi goes so far as to distinguish two kinds of individuation: the 'natural' process occurring autonomously without conscious direction, and the 'artificial' process consciously sought and perhaps aided by analysis (1967, p.15f). This controversy, and Jacobi's distinction, are perfectly understandable in view of the fact that Jung concentrated most of his attention on individuation as a deliberate undertaking in the second half of life, relating it strongly to the practice of dream analysis and active imagination, and omitted to develop in any detail his claim that it is a process taking place throughout life. But it is possible to see Jung's ideas on this question as perfectly self-consistent. As with the archetypes, we have in the case of individuation a natural activity which unfolds in accordance with an 'open programme', to use Ernst Mayr's term again. Like all living things, the human personality has an inherited programme according to which its major characteristic features emerge and take shape in a definite progression over a lifetime. It is, in Progoff's phrase, an 'unfoldment from within' (1973, p.62), and in Jung's words it is 'a natural process: it is what makes a tree turn into a tree' (JS, p.206). Furthermore the systemic processes whereby the psyche endeavours to attain some sort of equilibrium between the forces at tension within it also carry out their essential function at every stage of a person's life, a process that does not require the continuous co-operation of consciousness. Without this a normal healthy life would be impossible. The decision on the part of an individual to pursue the path of self-development, whether in mid-life or at any other stage, therefore, is not an 'artificial' process, but is the perfectly natural exercise of conscious human will which is throughout all of life engaging with one's biologically inherited behaviour patterns. By way of comparison, there is nothing artificial about the decision to keep oneself physically healthy, despite the fact that nature has its own methods for achieving that end.

Individuation is a 'natural' process in another sense, namely that it does not necessarily require the help of religious doctrines or institutions. The emergence of the self is, as Homans put it, 'a natural and spontaneous process, not dependent on traditional theological dogma' (1979, p.186). Nevertheless he recognized that the religions of the world all serve the universal human need for self-development and integration, and that for many people the path towards wholeness must be laid out within the framework of a religious faith. Indeed it is only in the modern context, with the growth of secularism and the loss of traditional bonds of cultural identity, that individuation becomes clearly detached from its religious roots. This explains in part his abiding concern with Christianity in spite of his public statements of agnosticism, for he identified in its doctrines and practices a powerful pre-scientific statement of the psychological notion of individuation. Hence, while Jung saw this idea as having roots in Christianity, he was concerned to re-interpret its spirituality in post-Christian terms. By the same token of course, individuation may be facilitated by, but is not identical with, the theory and practice of psychotherapy.

Jung is sometimes criticized for putting forward a somewhat elitist concept of personal growth, and for admitting that only a select few have the capacity for individuation. He does indeed sometimes speak of it, in terms clearly reminiscent of Nietzsche, as a 'vocation' that 'destines a man to emancipate himself from the herd', and as an 'unpopular undertaking, a deviation that is highly uncongenial to the herd, an eccentricity smelling of the cenobite', it being small wonder therefore that 'from earliest times only the chosen few have embarked on this strange adventure' (CW17.298).

We have already noted his kinship with that Existentialist tradition of thought from Kierkegaard ('the crowd is untruth') to Sartre ('hell is other people') which exalts the individual above the mass and which sees the mass as the greatest threat to the freedom and autonomy of the individual person. But there is a significant difference between Jung's position and theirs. It is important to reiterate that individuation in its broadest sense was for Jung a perfectly natural and universal process 'by which individual beings are formed and differentiated . . . having for its goal the development of the individual personality' (CW6.757). To this extent every human being who passes beyond the infantile stage is engaged in the process of individuation, and hence 'it is theoretically possible for any man . . . to achieve wholeness' (CW17.307). Furthermore the state of collectivity in which the individual is absorbed within a wider social and moral reality is not intrinsically hostile to individuation but is a natural and necessary stage of human development, and hence the adaptation to collective norms is a necessary condition for further psychological growth: 'If a plant is to unfold its specific nature to the full, it must first be able to grow in the soil in which it is planted' (CW6.760).

For some, though, the natural unfolding of individuality is not enough, and a higher goal is sought. In this regard Jung is at one with the Existentialists, for he sees this higher goal, not as involving some new kind of breed or mutation, but rather as the result of a deliberate act of will on the part of the individual. Just as Nietzsche firmly rejected any Darwinian interpretation of his idea of the higher man, i.e. as the product of future evolution, so too Jung saw the path of individuation, not as the emergence of a new species, but as the path of self-development chosen by the individual. This does not imply that in individuation the conscious rational ego takes over and directs the process. Sartre's belief that 'Man is what he makes himself' does not at all concur with Jung's theory, for while the individuation process requires ego-consciousness, and indeed may even serve to strengthen it, the work of becoming fully human is the work of the whole personality, the self, of which the conscious willing ego is only a fragile component; indeed the process is, he suggests, in some sense 'always a defeat for the ego' (CW14.778).

This chosen path may of course conflict with collective norms, but it is not for that reason essentially narcissistic and anti-social. Indeed for Jung 'relationship to the self is at once relationship to our fellow man, and no one can be related to the latter until he is related to himself' (CW16.445). Jung insisted that the path of individuation is not the path of *individualism* in its narrow, negative sense, but one which can enhance rather than diminish social awareness and responsibility. Individualism is an unnatural, even pathological, process characterized by an inflation of the ego. By contrast individuation is a path which relativizes, rather than exalts, the ego, and through its accommodation with the unconscious puts the ego into balance rather than competition with collective factors. In other words, the wholeness which is the goal of individuation is one which transcends the narrowness of ego-consciousness, and puts the individual in touch with those elemental forces which bind them to the universal features of humanity. As Jung put it: 'Individuation does not shut one out from the world, but gathers the world to oneself' (CW8.432). Indeed society is a necessary condition for individuation for 'one cannot individuate without other human beings. One cannot individuate on top of Mount Everest or in a cave where one doesn't see people for seventy years; one can only individuate with or against something or somebody' (NZ, p.102). Moreover, the very vitality of a society depends, not on the anonymity and uniformity of its members but on their ability to aim at a higher self-hood. Here again Jung sees the matter in terms of balance between opposite tendencies: 'only a society that can preserve its internal cohesion and collective values, while at the same time granting the individual the greatest possible freedom, has any prospect of enduring vitality' (CW6.758), sentiments with an impeccably liberal-democratic pedigree.

In a similar vein, Jung has sometimes been accused, along with psychotherapists in general, of encouraging an unhealthy degree of narcissistic self-regard, which not only narrows the horizons and diminishes the resources of the individual, but also saps the vitality of the community. This is a complex issue which cannot be adequately dealt with in a few sentences. But it must be emphasized once again that for Jung the self, which is the goal of individuation, is not to be confused with the isolated satisfaction-pursuing ego which has underlain much discussion in modern political and economic theory, but is seen as a much richer phenomenon rooted in nature and in the collective symbolic inheritance of mankind. Furthermore, Jung was aware of the dangers of excessive dependence of patient on therapist, and the consequent attenuation of the former's capacity for responsible action in the world, and for this reason encouraged the practice of interruptions to the regular schedule of therapeutic sessions.[2]

Plainly Jung's theory of individuation is an *ethical* theory which goes beyond a purely descriptive or scientific account of the personality. Though he is describing the natural process of human development, he is at the same time offering a goal, prescribing what in Aristotelian terms is the *good* for mankind. Self-actualization, therefore, is not a purely neutral scientific concept but one charged with moral significance; the acorn not only *becomes* the oak, but in doing so it is achieving what is right and good. On the face of it this might seem to conflict with the belief that individuals have in some sense an obligation to liberate themselves from conformity to the rules of society. But it will be clear from all that has been said so far in this chapter that Jung is in no sense offering a set of moral prescriptions, a code of conduct, or a set of rules to live by, whether in conformity or in conflict with those of society, for 'there is no recipe for living that suits all cases' (MM, p.69). On this question Jung finally parted company with Kant, for here, as in the epistemological realm, Jung showed a strong tendency towards relativism. The great German philosopher had argued that the universal moral law is inscribed, as it were, in the mind of each rational being, and its precepts can be grasped through the activity of reason alone. Jung on the contrary took the view that 'good and evil are categories of our moral judgement, [and] therefore relative to man' (CW18.1657). He saw that the making of moral judgements was a necessary condition of being human, and that the possession of a conscience is a univeral archetypal endowment; echoing Sartre he admitted that our very freedom means that we must make choices between good and evil, and that 'nothing can spare us the torment of ethical decision' (MDR, p.361–2). But though we are moral beings, there are no moral rules that can be established objectively for all rational beings.

Various reasons for this are to be found scattered throughout his writings. In the first place human life is too complex, and the questions we must face too paradoxical: 'No rules can cope with the paradoxes of life. Moral law, like natural law represents only one aspect of life' (CW18.1430); thus, just as there is no single unequivocal viewpoint that physics can adopt to make sense of the physical world, so too in the moral sphere we must accept the partial, onesidedness of our viewpoints. Secondly there is no decision-procedure that enables us to formulate a single set of moral rules: 'The formulation of ethical rules is not only difficult but actually impossible because one can hardly think of a single rule that would not have to be reversed under certain conditions' (CW18.1413). And thirdly, moral judgements, like all judgements, are constrained by the psychological perspective of the individual making them, they always 'reveal the subjective point of reference . . . [and] always implicate the subject, presupposing that something is good or beautiful *for me* (CW10.825, Jung's italics). But 'once we know how uncertain the foundation is, ethical decision becomes a subjective, creative act' (MDR, p.361).

The central feature of Jung's moral outlook lay in his emphasis on the moral autonomy and responsibility of the individual, an outlook which is evident in his oft-stated conviction that each patient must be encouraged to find their own unique way, and that the therapist's role is to facilitate rather than to prescribe. The absence of any absolute moral standards did not imply for him, any more than it did for Nietzsche, an out-and-out amoralism, an acceptance of the maxim that 'anything goes'. Quite the contrary, for without the guidance of objective standards the responsibility for deciding on moral issues falls squarely upon us, and it is a responsibility that each of us must carry with the utmost seriousness. The greatest immorality lies, not so much in the independence of the individual as in the threat to individual moral autonomy by the demands of society, ecclesiastical as well as civil. He recognized the need for society to establish rules of conduct, but a society composed of 'de-individualized persons' will, he warned, easily succumb to the amoralism of a ruthless dictatorship (US, p.55).

Individuation, then, is a unique, individual way, a lifepath as in Taoist philosophy that each of us must make for ourselves and follow, rather than a rule for all. 'There is no single definite way for the individual which is prescribed for him and would be the proper one' (*Letters I*, p.132). But though in some senses the pursuit of this way is solitary and detaches us from the comforting norms of the crowd, it is also a way that is firmly rooted in nature. Unlike the angst-ridden path that must be trod by the Existentialist, 'condemned to be free' in the words of Sartre, the journey which Jung describes is one which keeps us in close touch with our natural roots. However high our spiritual aspirations, the energy we use in our quest is drawn from the same source as that of all other living processes. This energy is expressed, as we saw in an earlier chapter, in archetypal images which are themselves the mental, symbolic sublimates of instinctual processes. The goal of integration, therefore, does not take us outside or beyond the living world of nature, but is an expression at the human level of processes which are universal in nature. Individuation is therefore a healing process – one which makes whole – not only within the soul of the individual person, but between humanity and the natural world.

There is no final healing for life, no ultimate cure. 'Complete redemption from the sufferings of this world is and must remain an illusion' (CW16.400). This is true for Jung in the narrower sense that the method of psychotherapy cannot provide a patient with a permanent remedy. It was nothing more than a 'widespread prejudice that analysis is something like a "cure" to which one submits and then is discharged healed'; the best that can be said of the process is that it provokes a 'readjustment of psychological attitude', 'a renewal of personality', perhaps even 'a way of attaining liberation by one's own efforts, and of finding the courage to be oneself' (CW8.142,184,193). In the broader sense, too, the dialectical movement of life to and fro between opposites has no final resolution, no Hegelian Absolute in which all opposites are reconciled: 'The life of the unconscious goes on and continuously produces problematical situations. . . . There is no change which is unconditionally valid over a long period of time. Life has always to be tackled anew' (CW8.142). However, 'unattainability is no argument against the ideal, for ideals are only signposts, never the goal' (CW17.291); 'The essential thing is the *opus* which leads to the goal: *that* is the goal of a lifetime' (CW16.400).

The end, though, is death. Western philosophy has for the most part ignored this inescapable fact of life, its attitude perhaps best summed up in Wittgenstein's remark that 'Death is not an event in life', and hence not something about which we can meaningfully speak. A conspicuous exception is to be found amongst Existentialist thinkers. Thus for Heidegger death is a liberating goal, the ultimate possibility of human existence. The fact of my death is indicative of my uniqueness as a human being for no-one else can die for me. Death is mine in a very particular and intimate way: it individualizes me, and hence renders my life unique. There is of course a negative side to this, emphasized more by Kierkegaard and Sartre, for death is also the termination of all possibilities for me, and therefore, because of its very arbitrariness, ultimately absurd. Freud in his later years had spoken of a 'death-instinct', as an impulse towards the destruction of life, in contrast with eros, the impulse towards life. Jung sought to reconcile these opposites by arguing that death is 'a goal and fulfilment' of life, not its mere negation, and that the second half of one's life is in effect a preparation for death. Ageing therefore is not mere degeneration, old age more than just a passive waiting for the end, for life's purposes can be found in all its stages. Life, he affirmed,

> is an energy process. Like every energy process it is in principle irreversible and is therefore directed towards a goal. That goal is a state of rest. In the long run everything that happens is, as it were, no more than the initial disturbance of a perpetual state of rest which forever attempts to re-establish itself. Life is teleology *par excellence*; it is the intrinsic striving towards a goal, and the living organism is a system of directed aims which seek to fulfil themselves. . . . The curve of life is like the parabola of a projectile which, disturbed from its initial state of rest, rises, and then returns to a state of repose.
>
> (CW8.798)

The individual life is therefore in microcosm the great cyclical journey of the macrocosmos conceived in ancient times by Plotinus: from unity to diversity and back to unity again. It is a natural cycle, and just as the rhythm of birth–maturation–death is inherent in all living organisms, so too is it in the life of the human psyche.

What of life beyond death? Neither science nor philosophy can tell us anything of this, it is a metaphysical question not susceptible to rational decision. But, Jung observed, it would be foolish to suppose that the world is limited to our subjective categories of space and time. Telepathic phenomena indicate that we cannot rule out the possibility that there exists a non-spatio-temporal form of psychic existence, a suggestion reinforced by the relativization of spatio-temporal categories within modern physics. Furthermore, he pointed out, a 'large majority of people have from time immemorial felt the need of believing in the continuance of life', and though this does not in itself constitute evidence for immortality, it does suggest that a basic, perhaps archetypal, need lies hidden here, from which he concludes that 'From the standpoint of psychotherapy it would therefore be desirable to think of death as only a transition – one part of a life-process whose extent and duration escape our knowledge' (MM, p.129). Hence, just as the life-cycle of an organism is part of a wider system of living things, so too the life-cycle of the individual psyche may be seen as participating in a greater whole, of which the great mythic, religious, and philosophical speculations of mankind concerning immortality and rebirth are so many symbolic expressions. An examination of this wider vision of Jung's will be our next, and last major, task.

# 13

# ONE WORLD

> The latest conclusions of science are coming nearer and nearer to a unitary idea of being.
>
> (C.G. Jung)

The characteristic feature of human life, Jung believed, is that it must be explained in terms of meanings, purposes and reasons, not merely of events or causes. Individuation means that the psyche is essentially *goal-* or *aim*-directed, and must therefore be understood in *teleological* terms, in the language of ends and purposes. According to Jung this is the case for living things in general: 'Life', he wrote, 'is directed towards a goal. . . . Life is teleology *par excellence*; it is the intrinsic striving towards a goal, and the living organism is a system of directed aims which seek to fulfil themselves' (CW8.798). So too the human psyche, the microcosm which mirrors the macrocosmic world of living things: 'the nature of the human mind compels us to take the finalistic [i.e. the teleological] view. It cannot be disputed that, psychologically speaking, we are living and working day by day according to the principle of directed aim or purpose as well as that of causality' (CW4.687).

Jung was not content, however, merely to *assert* the teleological nature of the psyche as an empirical fact. To make sense of this idea he felt it necessary to show how this claim could be located within a wider view of nature. He was essentially a holistic thinker, one who was inclined to see the interconnectedness of things, and though, as I pointed out early on in this book, he did not seek to construct a system, the search for a unified world-view runs as a sub-theme throughout his life's work. But standing in the way of any thinker bold enough to seek such a unitary world-view is an old philosophical conundrum, namely how to fit together into a single philosophy the world of meanings and purposes on the one side and the world of things and events on the other.

This issue, let us remind ourselves, was first posed for the modern world by Descartes. The Cartesian philosophy, which provided the underpinning to so many aspects of modern thought, made an absolute distinction between the physical and the mental worlds. These constituted two distinct types of reality: the physical defined in terms of space, and the mental in terms of consciousness. This was an effective division of labour from the point of view of the natural sciences, and served well as a methodological device enabling scientists to get on with the job of understanding the mechanical workings of nature without being diverted by intractable metaphysical issues; Jung himself admitted that from a pragmatic standpoint such a division was 'absolutely necessary if we are to gain reliable knowledge of the world' (CW14.662). It enabled science to leave on one side, not only questions of mind and spirit, but also questions of meaning and purpose, for the physical world could now be understood in purely causal terms without reference to teleology, as essentially inert, mindless stuff that has neither meaning nor purpose other than any that we care to project upon it.

But from a philosophical point of view this division is decidedly unsatisfactory, for not only does it leave us with a rather untidy picture of a world which seems to be composed of two mutually exclusive realms of being, but it also allows us to make no sense of the apparent interaction between these two worlds which we observe every day in the shape of conscious human behaviour. If, as seems to be the case, our minds and bodies interact, then it makes no sense to speak of two quite distinct substances or domains, for if they can interact they must have some properties in common with each other, and hence belong to the same world.

Now Jung did not, by strict philosophical standards, have a satisfactory solution to this problem. But he did see the urgent necessity to address it, and realized that a solution could be offered only by the development of a radically new world-view, for it clearly could not be solved in the context of the traditional Cartesian/Newtonian paradigm. Like the German Romantic philosophers before him, he saw that only a unitary picture of the world, which offered complementary places for mind and body, and which allowed for the operation of both causes and purposes, would be satisfactory. The search for such a unitary picture is again at the end of the twentieth century back on the agenda, and it will be useful to see what contributions Jung made to this.

He addressed the Cartesian dilemma repeatedly in his writings. In his early days as a colleague of Freud he had toyed with various versions of epiphenomenalism, and suggested that 'all conscious contents . . . are reflections of processes in the brain' (CW8.608), but subsequently he came to the conclusion that, though mind and body have distinct characteristics and cannot be reduced the one to the other (we noted his arguments for this in an earlier chapter), they are nevertheless intimately related within a single cosmos. 'Mind and body', he wrote in 1926,

> are presumably a pair of opposites and, as such, the expression of a single entity whose essential nature is not knowable. . . . We cannot rid ourselves of the doubt that perhaps this whole separation of mind and body may finally prove to be merely a device of reason for the purpose of conscious discrimination – an intellectually necessary separation of one and the same fact into two aspects, to which we then illegitimately attribute an independent existence.
>
> (CW8.619)

This view was reinforced in his mind by the evident empirical fact that 'psychological events, whether conscious or unconscious, are bound up with the organic nervous system' (*Letters I*, p.87), and the evident connections between mind and matter which 'point to their underlying unitary nature' (CW14.767). Psyche and matter, he concluded, 'exist in one and the same world, and each partakes of the other, [for] otherwise any reciprocal action would be impossible' (CW9ii.413). Indeed it is possible, he conjectured, that further advances in psychophysics would establish a complete parallel between the two spheres. The separation of mind and body is therefore a convenient and understandable fiction, an 'artificial dichotomy . . . based far more on the peculiarity of intellectual understanding than on the nature of things' (MM, p.85). They are in reality 'two different aspects of one and the same thing' (CW8.418).

The notion that mind and body are but two different aspects of one and the same continuous reality has a history in modern philosophy going back at least as far as to Leibniz and Spinoza, both of whom were concerned to escape the dilemma of Cartesian dualism. The immediate influence on Jung however is once again that of Arthur Schopenhauer, whom Jung referred to as the 'godfather to the views I am now developing' (SY, p.16). Central to Schopenhauer's philosophy was the belief that the divisions and discriminations between types of natural entities was more a function of the needs of the human intellect than of reality in itself. This clearly had implications for the distinction between mind and body, and between the mechanistic and the organic. He argued that these distinctions too are constructed by the mind, and that it was more correct to see mind and body, not as two separate substances, but rather as two complementary aspects of one and the same continuous reality. All events, he concluded, 'stand in two fundamentally different kinds of connection . . . firstly in the objective, causal connection of the natural process; secondly [in the] subjective connection which exists only in relation to the individual who experiences it' (quoted from Schopenhauer in SY, p.16). This conclusion bore the evident stamp of Kant's thinking, but it is interesting to note that it also bore close comparison with the Indian Vedanta philosophy, a tradition with which Schopenhauer was familiar.

The seeming plurality and diversity of things is therefore underpinned, according to this view, by unity; the world is one world – *unus mundus*, a cosmos constructed of a single continuous unified fabric extending from matter at one end to spirit at the other. In his last book, *Mysterium Coniunctionis*, Jung wrote that the mediaeval idea of the *unus mundus* is a 'probable hypothesis' that is 'founded on the assumption that the multiplicity of the empirical world rests on an underlying unity . . . everything divided and different [belonging] to one and the same world' (CW14.767). In such a system it is possible to find a place for the material and the mental, and for the mechanistic and the teleological, without separating them into distinct ontological spheres.

Once again it must be emphasized that this bond with pre-scientific thought did not mean that Jung was prepared to abandon the twentieth century and return to the metaphysical notions of a bygone age. One of the significant features of his struggle with dualism and his attempt to find a place for meaning and purpose within the universe was that, though he drew inspiration from the Aristotelian/mediaeval world-view as an *unus mundus*, as well as from German Idealist philosophy, he was also aware of the need to reconcile his conception of the psyche with the scientific outlook of his own age. Revolutionary developments in physics in the first half of this century presented Jung with the opportunity to work towards this reconciliation. As early as 1912 Jung had referred to the 'strange encounter between atomic physics and psychology', and had come to the conclusion that '[the] microphysical world of the atom exhibits certain affinities with the psychic', affinities which, he claimed, had also 'impressed themselves even on the physicists' (CW17.164). The essence of the solution which Jung proposed lay in the first place in the opening up by modern physics of the possibility of alternative forms of explanations to those proposed within the system of classical Newtonian physics, built as it was on the foundations of mechanical causality.

As we saw in Chapter 2, he was particularly impressed by the fact that modern physics was obliged to offer seemingly contradictory accounts of reality, to make what he called 'antinomian statements . . . such as the nature of light or of the smallest particles of matter, which physics represents both as corpuscles and as waves' (CW14.715). He suggested that this idea of *complementarity*, as it became known, might help in understanding the relation between the physical and the psychical. Niels Bohr, the chief architect of quantum theory, had argued that in our attempts to describe physical phenomena, such as light, we may be obliged to accept that two distinct and mutually exclusive descriptions are applicable to one and the same set of phenomena. In the same way, Jung argued, a causal account of a phenomenon – say a human action – does not necessarily exclude an explanation in terms of meanings and purposes. 'Physics determines quantities . . . psychology determines qualities without being able to measure quantities. Despite that, both sciences arrive at ideas which come significantly close to one another' (CW8.440). In the wider context he claimed that our attempts to make sense of and to conceptualize the world, whether at the level of physics or of common sense, inevitably lead us into applying contrary concepts to the world – e.g. mind and body, wave and particle, yin and yang, male and female, to name but a few.

Another relevant consideration arising from developments in physics concerned what Jung referred to as the 'possibility of getting rid of the incommensurability between observer and observed' (SY, p.133). In modern physics, he argued, the role of the observer had become crucial, in contrast with classical physics where the observer had to all intents and purposes been ignored, an idea which may well have been planted in his mind during the early part of the century when he had frequent conversations with Einstein. Thus, physics 'has demonstrated that in the realm of atomic magnitudes an observer is postulated in objective reality, and that only on this condition is a satisfactory scheme of explanation possible'. From this he inferred that the psychic factor could not be excluded from the physicist's world-picture, and that hence the old mental/physical dichotomy had to be abandoned. 'This means that a subjective element attaches to the physicist's world picture, and secondly that a connection necessarily exists between the psyche . . . and the space-time continuum', the upshot being once again the 'bridging over [of] the seeming incommensurability between the physical world and the psychic' (CW8.440).

Furthermore it is important to recall that for Jung scientific laws and theories do not constitute copies or pictures of nature, but are models or instruments which, while allowing us to fit together and make sense of the data of experience, do not offer any kind of insight into the innermost workings of nature. We noted in an earlier chapter that Jung's underlying Kantian predispositions led him to the view that all generalizations about nature, including those of the physical sciences, are read into, rather than from, nature, and hence '[there] are no "absolute" natural laws to whose authority we can appeal' (SY, p.9). This view, foreshadowed at the end of the last century in Nietzsche's claim that all systems of knowledge, whether myth or science, religion or philosophy, are so many *perspectives* on the world, none of which can claim absolute validity, has become increasingly acceptable to scientists and philosophers of science during the course of this century. The old idea that scientists 'discover' the laws which are in some sense 'obeyed' by natural phenomena has been superseded by the view that science *creates* hypotheses which allow us to make sense of and make predictions from our empirical observations.

This general line of thought recurred many times during the final decades of Jung's life when, it seems, he felt at last able to speculate more freely about his long-cherished belief in a holistic world-view. It was approached from one angle, as we have seen, in his discussion of the idea of *unus mundus*, and from another in his concept of the psychoid which he had developed in the 1940s as a way of linking archetypes with biological instincts. But it is in a short book entitled *Synchronicity*, first published in 1951, that he gave his conjectures fullest scope, and began to pull together and to clarify some of the ideas that had for many years been fermenting in his mind.

The immediate task of this book was to explain the phenomenon of *meaningful coincidence*. Throughout his life Jung had noticed the occurrence of coincidences, meaningful conjunctions of events, which he regarded as inadequately explained by pure chance or by the laws of classical physics. The most striking examples of these were cases of telepathy, precognition and extra-sensory perception for which some statistical evidence had been accumulated. He drew attention to the work at Duke University of J.B. Rhine who, in a long series of carefully constructed experiments in which subjects were given the task of guessing the identity of cards, produced results which consistently exceeded chance probability. Such experiments, and related cases of extra-sensory perception, Jung suggested, 'confront us with the fact that there are events which are related to one another . . . *meaningfully*, without there being any possibility of proving that this relation is a causal one' (SY, p.27). It would make sense therefore to postulate a new *acausal* principle of explanation, namely synchronicity, to supplement the more typical causal explanation. This did not mean that in the event of a meaningful coincidence the laws of causality were in some miraculous way suspended, but rather that in such circumstances the account we give of events must be drawn from two seemingly opposed, but complementary, languages, namely that of causes on the one hand and that of meanings on the other, neither being adequate on its own.

The theoretical side of the argument of *Synchronicity* rested on two claims. First of all, he contended, the new sciences of relativity and quantum theory had blown apart the Newtonian model of nature with its belief that the world comprises solid physical entities which are tied together by rigid mechanical laws within an absolute spatio-temporal framework. 'The discoveries of modern physics have', he wrote, 'brought about a significant change in our scientific picture of the world, in that they have shattered the absolute validity of natural law and made it relative. Natural laws are *statistical* truths' (SY, p.7). He then went on to argue that the new physics has opened up the possibility of non-causal principles in nature. It is obvious, he thought, that the experimental method traditionally employed in science will tend to establish a picture of mechanical regularity; in other words our understanding of nature is 'more or less influenced by the kind of questions asked'. What is becoming increasingly evident, however, is that our mechanistic conception is 'hardly anything more than a psychologically biased partial view' (SY, p.8), and that even within the compass of science itself it is possible to employ in our descriptions of the world several different kinds of model.

His aim was not to supplant the traditional principle of causality, any more than it is the aim of modern physics to completely discard Newton, but rather to offer it as an additional complementary principle, 'seeking to fill in the open spaces left by statistical laws', as Progoff puts it (1973, p.99). This 'open space' allowed the possibility of applying other, non-causal, explanations to events, and even for the return of teleology, and it was into this space that he introduced his idea of synchronicity. The influence of Kant is once again strong here, for 'space', 'time', and 'causality' are concepts which do not, properly speaking, denote data of experience, but are 'hypostatized concepts born of the discriminating activity of the conscious mind . . . the indispensable co-ordinates for describing the behaviour of bodies in motion', and are therefore 'essentially psychic in origin' (SY, p.28). To this triad of classical physics he added the concept of synchronicity, a fourth *a priori* condition of experience which, like the other three, makes no claims of a transcendent kind (see SY, p.133f).

Moreover, he saw the elevation of causality as a supreme principle of explanation as a modern Western myth, and concluded that it represented a psychologically and historically conditioned point of view. Though in his later years he drew the mediaeval notion of the *unus mundus* into his discussions of this question, his ideas concerning synchronicity first began to take shape in the 1920s in the course of his study of the ancient Chinese Taoist text, the *I Ching*. There he encountered an understanding of reality wholly at variance with the modern Western picture. At first it seemed baffling and incomprehensible, but as he entered more deeply into it he came to realize that it was based on a consistent view of the world, one which saw it in terms, not of causal, but of meaningful connections. He saw that it represented a technique 'for grasping the total situation', a method 'characteristic of China', and which, in contrast with the Western habit of 'grasping details for their own sake', sought to comprehend the details 'as part of the whole' (SY, p.49). Such a method, he believed, pointed to a way of understanding nature which was completely excluded by classical physics, but which might well find a complementary place in the emerging post-Newtonian culture.

The initial aim of introducing this new hypothetical concept was the relatively restricted one of accounting for a limited class of phenomena, namely that of meaningful coincidences, taking advantage of the demise of the rigidly deterministic assumptions of classical physics. But Jung went further than this and, with the lessons of his study of the *I Ching* in mind, speculated that it might have wider implications, suggesting that synchronicity might be regarded as 'a special instance of general acausal orderedness' (SY, pp.139–40), and that it might represent an *a priori* principle of order alongside the principle of causality. He even suggested that it might serve as the foundation for an explanation for biological morphogenesis – the replication of living structures (p.132), an idea that has recently been developed by Rupert Sheldrake (1981). Such an extension to encompass general acausal orderedness, which would mean abandoning the idea that synchronicity is a relatively rare phenomenon associated mainly with parapsychological phenomena, might cast light, he speculated, on the age-old problem of the relationship between the mental and the physical realms; Jung pursued this speculation with enthusiasm.

Typically, in the context of the Cartesian paradigm, the relationship between mind and body has been seen as a *causal* one: mental events affect physical events and vice versa. Jung himself held such a view at one time, but when he came to write *Synchronicity* he was forced to admit that 'it is hard to see how chemical processes can ever produce psychic processes . . . how an immaterial psyche could ever set matter in motion' (SY, p.124). In support of this he pointed to the fact that in certain kinds of 'out-of-body' experiences, a person may enjoy vivid 'hallucinatory' experiences, while from all the physiological evidence appearing to be in a coma and hence to be lacking in the appropriate cerebral functioning (p.124f). The concept of synchronicity presented him with a new way of looking at this old problem. Meaningful coincidences occur relatively rarely, but if we take them seriously, Jung argued, then in order to understand them it is necessary that we postulate a principle which postulates a meaningful, rather than a causal, relationship between events. But the relatively frequent everyday occurrence of coincidence between physical and mental events might be seen to fall under the same principle. Such a principle does not provide any insight into the underlying nature of things in themselves, any more than causality does, but it does represent what Jung called 'an intellectually necessary principle which could be added as a fourth to the recognized triad of space, time, and causality' (SY, p.132).

Jung noted an interesting precedent to his application of synchronicity theory to the mind–body issue in Leibniz's theory of pre-established harmony, a theory which required that God pre-ordains from all eternity the correspondence between the two totally distinct sequences of mental and physical events (see SY, p.112f). Though the idea of two parallel but causally unrelated series was attractive to Jung, and bore a formal resemblance to his own theory, the metaphysical implications of Leibniz's theory were unacceptable to him. The theory of pre-established harmony required the activity of a transcendent architect-deity who contrived the whole process in advance, and hence fell a victim to Jung's principle that of 'what lies beyond the phenomenal world we can have absolutely no idea' (CW8.437). Also unacceptable to him were the deterministic implications of Leibniz's theory which envisaged a kind of two-clock universe, the two clocks – physical and mental – being synchronized in advance by God. For Jung the two principles, causality and synchronicity, must be seen as conditions of experience, 'intellectually necessary' to our understanding of the world, not constitutive of reality as such. If there is an underlying force in the universe keeping body and soul working in harmony, we cannot know it; in the last analysis it is, as Jung put it, borrowing a phrase from Kipling, 'just so!'.[1]

The upshot of Jung's speculations on these matters is that, taking account of the revolution in scientific thought in our century, the threat of the old dichotomy between a physical world subject to causal laws and a mental world of meanings and purposes had receded. He recognized that it was now possible to view the cosmos as a whole, not as two uneasily conjoined realms, but to see mind and matter, living and non-living, mechanical and purposeful as all part of a continuum; the mediaeval idea of the *unus mundus*, allied to Schopenhauer's double-aspect theory, appeared to be reborn therefore in the vesture of modern microphysics, a development which pointed to the re-unification of the subject matters of physics and psychology (CW14.768–9). Microphysics, he observed,

> is feeling its way into the unknown side of matter, just as complex psychology is pushing forward into the unknown side of the psyche. Both lines of investigation have yielded findings which can be conceived only by means of antinomies, and both have developed concepts which display remarkable analogies. If this trend should become more pronounced in the future, the hypothesis of the unity of their subject matters would gain in probability.
>
> (CW14.768)

This meant that for Jung the psychic world of meaning and purpose was not a cosmic orphan, wandering like a suppliant seeking recognition on the fringes of the 'real' world, but a legitimate world in its own right, and one which, with the world of life and matter, formed a single cosmos.[2]

These ideas remained for Jung little more than conjectures, and bear all the marks of confusion and ambiguity that attend intellectual endeavour at the frontiers of knowledge. He was well aware of their speculative and provisional nature, and saw them as an outline of a theoretical framework which needed considerable elaboration to turn it into a genuine scientific theory. 'Our hypotheses', he admitted, 'are uncertain and groping, and nothing offers us the assurance that they may ultimately prove correct' (CW14.787). They do not offer 'in any way a final proof', but are just 'work in progress' (SY, p.58). Furthermore it was, he claimed, a strictly *empirical* theory, designed to account for experimentally observed fact. It was not in any sense a transcendental or metaphysical explanation, for 'a "transcendental cause" is a contradiction in terms' (p.42), and indeed he saw it as 'no more baffling or mysterious than the discontinuities of [modern quantum] physics' (p.141).

He was not entirely alone in such speculations. He noted that even in his own day scientists of the calibre of Sir Arthur Eddington and Sir James Jeans were thinking along similar lines, for both had recognized that the demise of the mechanical model of nature opened the way to a unitary world-view embracing both matter and spirit. Indeed Jeans even went so far as to suggest in the 1930s that the universe was beginning to look more like a thought than a thing! These speculations have gathered in pace and respectability since Jung first put them forward. Paul Davies after noting that physics has 'long since abandoned a purely reductionist approach to the physical world', points out that 'in recent years . . . holistic philosophy has begun to have a more general impact on physical science' (1983, p.64), and goes on to argue that quantum theory, a pillar of the new physics, 'provides the most convincing scientific evidence yet that consciousness plays an essential role in the nature of physical reality . . . [and] contains some astonishing insights into the nature of the mind' (p.100).

One of the most interesting attempts to spell out this insight in more detail is to be found in the work of the quantum physicist David Bohm who has suggested that matter and consciousness can now be understood in terms of a general notion of order, thereby opening the way to 'a new notion of unbroken wholeness, in which consciousness is no longer to be fundamentally separated from matter'. The essential nature of consciousness is 'unfolding' and 'transformation', he argued, for an understanding of thoughts, feelings and emotions can only be articulated in terms of the unfolding of what is merely implicit in the present moment. But this constitutes a 'striking parallel' to the kind of activity we find in the subatomic world where a particle must now be understood, not as a thing, but as a perpetually unfolding process (1981, p.196f). The principle of synchronicity may thus be an instance of what Bohm has called the 'implicate order', namely the idea that each region of reality contains a total structure 'enfolded' within it (p.149f).

This brings us back full circle to the notion that the psyche must be seen, not as an entity participating in causal connections, but as a living process, as the unfolding of all that is implicit within it. These early insights of Jung were formulated in the first decades of this century, at that crucial period for modern science when physics was simultaneously engaged in revolutionizing our conception of reality. The full implications of these changes in science have taken a long time to mature, but we are gradually realizing that the new physics has provided us with a fresh opportunity to integrate into our world-view that peculiar and elusive quality of mind – its tendency to generate meaning and purpose. Jung, from the standpoint of psychology, has made a major contribution towards this integration, a contribution which in many ways anticipated subsequent developments, and whose full implications are still to be unfolded.

# 14
# CONCLUSION

> The only question is whether what I tell is *my* fable, *my* truth.
>
> (C.G. Jung)

Where, then, does Jung stand in relation to modern thought? It might seem that, despite his suspicion of systems and of doctrines, his inclination towards a holistic philosophy is nothing but a regression to old-fashioned metaphysics, a reversion to the need for some secure and protective narrative that will enable us to feel more at home in our earthly sojourn. Furthermore it is a story which plainly gives a privileged position to the human psyche, and hence may be yet another version of the story of Western man's need for domination. Jung's preoccupation with antiquated mythologies and religions may then turn out to be just a weary return to safe old creeds, just another piece of mystification and reactionary special pleading, maybe not at all the radical, heretical sublimation of modern thought that I have argued for.

My response to this is that we should take Jung seriously, at his word, and work with his claim that what he is offering is a *myth*, not a final truth, a *perspective*, not a doctrine. Let us pose the question: is the concept of synchronicity intended to unmask the true essence of the world, or is it just a convenient fiction? It is sometimes suggested that in his later years Jung cut loose from his Kantian straitjacket and allowed himself the freedom to wander into the realms of the transcendent with such ideas as synchronicity, the psychoid, and in such works as *Answer to Job* and *Mysterium Conjunctionis*. Do these mature reflections represent a return to a pre-modern attitude, or can they be construed in such a way as to speak to our post-modern, post-Christian consciousness?

Addressing this question to 'Jung', namely to the set of texts which we have at our disposal, leads to no unequivocal answer. Just as Freud burnt his letters to make things difficult for his biographers, so Jung has constructed a variety of elusive viewpoints to confuse his interpreters. Nevertheless I believe that it is this very variety and elusiveness that is the key that we must make use of. I have argued in this book that Jung was a problem thinker, a dialectitian who saw in the continuous play of varied and often opposing viewpoints and stories the only honest way in which human beings can approach the world and who, unlike the great dialectitian Hegel, saw no possible end to this play. While Nietzsche's 'eternal return' promised the rigours of endless repetition, Jung's concept of the self held out the sublime, if troubling, promise of the unending creation of worlds beyond worlds.

At the end of his long life Jung admitted that 'There is nothing I am quite sure about. I have no definite convictions – not about anything really', and that 'Life is – or has – meaning and meaninglessness', quoting the saying of Lao-Tzu: 'All are clear, I alone am clouded' (MDR, p.391–2). But in these valedictory remarks he was not uttering the final wearied sighs of a disillusioned spirit, but summing up in quiet affirmation the conviction of a lifetime, namely that the infinite variety of the world and the mysterious depths of the psyche cannot be boxed up in a set of formulae or be recited as a set of unshakeable doctrines.

The testimony to this is the great sprawling *opus* that was Jung's lifetime's work. In it we find much confusion and contradiction. In the present book I have pointed to, without elaborating in detail, some of the difficulties that the reader of this *opus* will encounter. His pioneering concepts of archetype and of synchronicity, to name but two, are, by his own admission, nothing but 'work in progress', rough-hewn conjectures that must be shaped and reshaped by future generations of thinkers; he himself spoke of 'many beginnings unfinished', and of the 'manifold possibilities for further development' (CW18.1137) which his ideas demanded, not to mention the 'philosophical clarification' which as a self-appointed empiricist he felt obliged to forswear.

There are omissions, too. Despite his affirmation of the holistic nature of the psyche, and of the importance of the interpersonal and the social to psychic being and health, he showed in his writings little sense of the social, economic and political forces which enter into our discourse and which help to shape the way we construct the world. While at one level he was aware of the shaping power of inherited archetypal structures, at another level his concern for the autonomy of the individual led him to underestimate the more devious ways in which the iron of political and social authority can enter the human soul. Linked to this is an apparent failure to translate talk of the interpersonal dimension into a fully fleshed-out picture of the way human beings really are and relate to each other in the world. His assertions of human embodiment and of human sexuality, which I have been careful to emphasize in this book, sometimes have an overly academic quality and lack the richness of phenomenological detail that he accorded to the world of dreams, fantasies and symbols. And his continued attachment to the language of Christian theology, in spite of personal scepticism, suggests that he underestimated the extent to which we have been moving towards a post-Christian, multi-cultural society.

But as well as – perhaps even because of – the confusions, the omissions, and the shortcomings, we find, too, in this *opus* ideas which address directly our contemporary condition: his serious dialogue with what Foucault has called 'subjugated knowledge', with the despised and marginalized aspects of our modern culture – with the feminine, the oriental, the schizoid, the mythic, with fantasy, alchemy, magic, astrology, theology; his rejection of modern Western hegemony, whether political or ideological, and his refusal to give any privileged status to Western consciousness; his fear of the oppressive force of mass organizations; his doubts about language as the begetter of false abstractions, and his corresponding affirmation of the imaginal and the symbolic; his doubts about the ideology of progress based on the rationalization of human life and the application of a mechanical, determinist philosophy; his distrust of grand theories and of the whole philosophical search for a grounding in universal and inescapable certainties; his method, too, with its sense of irony, its refusal to take its own formulations quite seriously, its awareness of the contingency, fragility and relativity of his own language. In these respects Jung stands with us at the point where the modern world, with all its spectacular achievements, now seems emptied of its charms and lacking in its old persuasiveness, and obliges us to search for new ways and new purposes. Even the 'omissions' I have noted can be viewed as timely criticisms of the one-sidedness of the modern world with its obsession with what is common, social, universal, and its comparative neglect of the unique inner spiritual world of the individual. It may be that the great Enlightenment project which we call the modern world was only possible because we have ignored or suppressed the anarchic, heretical world within.

The endless play of life and thought – between which in any case it is impossible to make any clear distinction, for each is mediated by the other – this great cosmic dance is essentially brought to life and made real by the very presence of the human psyche in the world. The myth of the divinely created world, as with the myth of sub-atomic particles, can only make sense to us if we weave round that myth the idea that it is human consciousness that brings meaning – and meaninglessness – to it. 'We are the music-makers, the dreamers of dreams', to borrow the words of the poet O'Shaughnessy, the weavers of tales and of myths. 'Individuation', 'types', 'archetypes', 'synchronicity', 'one world' – all are of the stuff that dreams and myths are made of, and all are projections of the endlessly creative activity of the human psyche.

The creation of meaning and its projection onto the cosmos is a peculiar privilege of human beings: 'Existence is only real when it is conscious to somebody' (CW11.575), and as far as we can discern 'the sole purpose of human existence is to kindle a light in the darkness of mere being' (MDR, p.358). By virtue of consciousness 'man is raised out of the animal world, and by his mind he demonstrates that nature has put a high premium precisely on the development of consciousness' (p.371). This is the new myth which Jung proposes in the face of the death of all gods, namely that we ourselves become the myth-maker, that the development of the psyche itself, not anything beyond or above or ahead of it, is the point of our journey. The loss of the legitimizing function of orthodox myths and narratives, tragic though it may seem, actually opens the way for the re-empowerment of the individual, and the recovery of human autonomy.

But does this mean that we ourselves become gods, that we simply perpetuate the old humanist myth of our inherent superiority by becoming lords of creation? Are we actually capable of carrying the cosmogonic responsibility that this new myth lays upon us?

Jung is careful to warn us of the dangers of the inflation of the conscious ego and of the rational will that such an attitude might entail. He saw these dangers in Nietzsche and in Nietzsche's creation, Zarathustra, where the will to power, uncoupled from roots in nature, community and history, can only end in madness. By contrast, his model of the human psyche, as I have been careful to emphasize throughout this book, recognizes that the psyche is not identical with ego or with will, but is a living organism sustained by its deep connections with nature and with the history of the human race. His seemingly endless, and to some critics unnecessary, hermeneutical gaming with mediaeval alchemy, and his obsession with the theological minutiae of a religion he probably no longer believed in, now become clear: they represent his refusal to abandon history and to leave the human psyche without support and protection. The myth of individuation offers a path that leads back into, not away from, the accumulated experience of mankind.

While, therefore, much of Jung's work can be seen as a 'deconstruction' of some of the central myths of the modern – and the ancient – world, his sense of rootedness and continuity prevented him from adopting completely what many now call a 'postmodern' stance. His work continued to address what F.L. Baumer has called the 'perennial questions', questions about God, nature, human nature, meaning, and history, and to emphasize the continuities of human history and the universality of human nature. In this sense our final judgement about his place in modern thought must fail, appropriately enough, to offer us a single unequivocal perspective.[1]

That sense of rootedness and of belonging-in-the-world, which had throughout his life been in painful tension with a sense of separation and alienation, is the consolation that he grasped at on the final page of his autobiography. There, despite the clouds of unknowing that seemed especially dark in his old age, he could still affirm that 'there is much that fills me: plants, animals, clouds, day and night, and the eternal in man. The more uncertain I have felt about myself, the more there has grown up in me a feeling of kinship with all things.'

# NOTES

## 1 FREUD AND JUNG

1 A timely volume of essays attempting to assess Jung's cultural impact has recently been published (Barnaby and D'Acierno, 1990). The work of James Hillman comes nearest to a 'rereading' of Jung, though it is still from within the circle of analytical psychology.

2 'Hermeneutics' is the art or science of textual interpretation, and will be discussed more fully in Chapter 3.

## 3 PHILOSOPHICAL FOUNDATIONS

1 Compare W.V.O. Quine, a central figure in recent philosophical debates in the USA and Britain: 'physical objects and the gods differ only in degree and not in kind. Both sets of entities enter our conception only as cultural deposits.' Belief in physical objects is justified only 'as a device for working a manageable structure into the flux of experience' (1963, p.131).

2 Other writers who have sought to draw Jung close to the hermeneutic tradition include: Hogenson, 1983; Rauhala, 1984; Steele, 1982; and Stein, 1985.

## 4 HISTORICAL PERSPECTIVES

1 The question of relativism has become a highly contentious issue in recent philosophical debates. See for example: Bernstein, 1983; Feyerabend, 1978 and 1987; and Winch, 1958.

## 5 ROMANTICS AND IDEALISTS

1 I am indebted to Michael Whan for this point. Jung's deconstruction of Hegel is in some ways parallel to that of Marx who endeavoured to uncover the hidden ideological agenda within Hegel's philosophy.

## 6 SPIRITUAL TRADITIONS, EAST AND WEST

1 The issue of the dual nature of God, as a projection of the dual nature of the human psyche, is the subject of Jung's late work, *Answer to Job*.

2 On the question of alternative traditions see: MM, Ch.10; SY, Ch.3; Hardy,

1987, p.93f; Hoeller, 1982, p.25f; and the writings of Frances Yates. The philosopher Richard Rorty has been influential in advocating experimenting with alternative philosophical vocabularies as a way of reassessing our prevailing assumptions (1989, p.80). Feyerabend has also been a strong advocate of the reassessment of the relationship between orthodox and marginalized cultures (1978).

## 7 PSYCHE AND ITS PLACE IN NATURE

1 Jung's argument here is specifically related to 'consciousness' rather than to the wider concept of 'psyche'; we will examine the relationship between these two in Chapter 11. I am treating 'consciousness' in its broad sense of awareness in general, though Jung sometimes confusingly uses it to refer more narrowly to *self*-consciousness.

2 In recent years similar ideas have been expressed in a number of quarters; see for example Popper & Eccles, 1977, passim; and Crook, 1980, pp,18 & 27, who suggests that the evolutionary advantage of consciousness lies in its supreme capacity to organize and integrate.

## 9 ARCHETYPES AND THE COLLECTIVE UNCONSCIOUS

1 It is worth noting that Freud was a self-confessed Lamarckian; see his *Moses and Monotheism*, and Odajnyk, 1976, p.178f.

2 I am indebted to Mary Midgeley for her discussion of the implications of this distinction (1979, p.52f). Her whole approach to instincts and to the question of human nature fits very closely with Jung's theory of archetypes. Stevens argues along similar lines (1982, p.52).

## 10 NATURE AND HUMAN NATURE

1 Probably he has in mind James Hillman who, rather than seeking to develop a scientific approach to the archetypes, proposes that we understand science from an archetypal standpoint. See Hillman, 1975, *passim*, and Shelburne, 1988, Ch.5.

## 11 THE STRUCTURE OF THE PSYCHE

1 Freud actually attended Brentano's lectures on philosophy at the University of Vienna in the 1880s and his dream theory might well have been partly shaped by this experience. It should be noted that there is a wide chasm between Jung and the phenomenologists on the question of the unconscious, the existence of which the latter deny. Neither does Husserl's idea of the '*epoché*' match with Jung's more holistic concept of the psyche.

2 This idea was later developed by R.D. Laing (1965), and in many respects Laing's whole approach to schizophrenia is close to that of Jung.

3 See: von Bertalanffy, 1968, for a useful account of systems philosophy in general; Bateson, 1980, for its application to biological and psychological domains; and Stevens, 1990, for its relevance to Jung.

## 12 INDIVIDUATION AND THE QUEST FOR MEANING

1 For a full discussion of these issues see: Lauter & Schreier Rupprecht, 1985; Ulanov, 1971; and D. Wehr, 1988. See also: Barnaby & D'Acierno, 1990, p.275f; Steele, 1982, p.337f; Stevens, 1990, p.210f; and Whitmont, 1969, p.170f.

2 The issue of narcissism as a modern cultural phenomenon has been discussed by, amongst others, C. Lasch, 1984, and as a psychological concept by H. Kohut, 1958.

## 13 ONE WORLD

1 Leibniz was himself probably influenced by Chinese Taoist thinking which in his day was making an impact on European thought and in which Leibniz took an interest, though due to his theological presuppositions Leibniz was less in harmony with Taoist thinking than Jung.

2 Philosophically, the mind–body, the mechanism–teleology, and the causal–purposive issues are, of course, distinct. Jung's theory of synchronicity could perhaps be seen as a conceptual framework within which all these issues can be addressed.

## 14 CONCLUSION

1 For a discussion of Jung as a postmodern thinker see Barnaby & D'Acierno, 1990, p.307f. The term 'postmodern' may be taken to refer to the current disillusionment with the culture of 'modernism', in particular with the ideals (first clearly enunciated during the eighteenth-century Enlightenment) of: certainty in knowledge, universality of moral and aesthetic values, progress through scientific rationalism and technology, and humanistic anthropocentrism. A key text here is Lyotard, 1984. See also Appignanesi, 1989.

# BIBLIOGRAPHY

Please note that references to Freud's works are to the Pelican Freud Edition, published by Pelican, London.


Abrams, M.H. (1971) *Natural Supernaturalism: Tradition and Revolution in Romantic Literature*. Open University Press, London.

Allison, D.B. (ed.) (1985) *The New Nietzsche: Contemporary Stages of Interpretation*. MIT Press, Cambridge, Mass., and London.

Appignanesi, L. (ed.) (1989) *Postmodernism: ICA Documents*. Free Association Books, London.

Avens, R. (1980) *Imagination is Reality: Western Nirvana in Jung, Hillman, Barfield and Cassirer*. Spring Publications Inc., Dallas.

Bakan, B. (1958) *Sigmund Freud and the Jewish Mystical Tradition*. Beacon Press, Boston.

Barnaby, K, and D'Acierno, P. (eds) (1990) *C.G. Jung and the Humanities: Towards a Hermeneutics of Culture*. Routledge, London.

Bateson, G. (1980) *Mind and Nature: A Necessary Unity*. Collins, Glasgow.

Bergson, H. (1911) *Creative Evolution*. Macmillan, London.

Bernstein, R. (1983) *Beyond Objectivism and Relativism: Science, Hermeneutics and Praxis*. Basil Blackwell, Oxford.

Bohm, D. (1981) *Wholeness and the Implicate Order*. Routledge, London.

Brome, V. (1980) *Jung: Man and Myth*. Paladin Books, London.

Brown, J. (1961) *Freud and the Post-Freudians*. Penguin Books, Harmondsworth.

Buber, M. (1953) *Eclipse of God: Studies in the Relationship between Religion and Philosophy*. Victor Gollancz, London.

Burckhardt, J. (1929) *Civilization of the Renaissance in Italy*, 2 vols. Harper and Row, New York.

Capra, F. (1982) *The Tao of Physics*. Collins, London.

Cassirer, E. (1962) *An Essay on Man: An Introduction to the Philosophy of Human Culture*. Yale University Press, New Haven and London.

Chomsky, N. (1966) *Cartesian Linguistics*. Harper and Row, New York.

Collingwood, R.G. (1961) *The Idea of History*. Oxford University Press, London.

Coward, H. (1985) *Jung and Eastern Thought*. State University of New York Press, Albany.

Crook, J.H. (1980) *The Evolution of Human Consciousness*. Clarendon Press, Oxford.

Darwin, C. (1871) *The Descent of Man*. D. Appleton & Co., New York.

Davidson, D. (1980) *Essays on Actions and Events*. Oxford University Press, London.

Davies, P. (1982) *Other Worlds: Space, Superspace and the Quantum Universe*. Dent, London.

—— (1983) *God and the New Physics*. Penguin Books, Harmondsworth.

—— (1987) *The Cosmic Blueprint*. Penguin Books, Harmondsworth.

Dry, A. (1961) *The Psychology of Jung*. Methuen, London.

Edinger, E. (1972) *Ego and Archetype*. Putnam, New York.

—— (1979) 'Depth Psychology as the New Dispensation', *Quadrant*, 12/2, pp.4–25.

—— (1984) *The Creation of Consciousness: Jung's Myth of Modern Man*. Inner City Books, Toronto.

Ellenberger, E.F. (1970) *The Discovery of the Unconscious: The History and Evolution of Dynamic Psychology*. Basic Books, New York.

Evans, R. (1979) *Jung on Elementary Psychology: A Discussion between C.G. Jung and Richard I. Evans*. Routledge, London.

Feyerabend, P. (1975) *Against Method: An Outline of an Anarchistic Theory of Knowledge*. Verso, London.

—— (1978) *Science in a Free Society*. Verso, London.

—— (1987) *Farewell to Reason*. Verso, London.

Fordham, M. (1958) 'Analytical Psychology and Religious Experience'. The Guild of Pastoral Psychology, Guild Lecture No.46.

Foucault, M. (1970) *The Order of Things: An Archaeology of the Human Sciences*. Tavistock Publications, London.

Freud. S. (1895) 'Project for a Scientific Psychology', in N. Bonaparte, A. Freud and E. Kris (eds) (1954) *The Origins of Psychoanalysis, Letters to Wilhelm Fliess, Drafts and Notes 1887–1902*. Imago, London.

—— (1900) *The Interpretation of Dreams*. Pelican Freud, Vol.4.

—— (1913) *Totem and Taboo*. Pelican Freud, Vol.13.

—— (1914) *On the History of the Psychoanalytic Movement*. Pelican Freud, Vol. 15.

—— (1927) *The Future of an Illusion*. Pelican Freud, Vol.12.

—— (1939) *Moses and Monotheism*. Pelican Freud, Vol.13.

—— (1988) *The Freud/Jung Letters*. See McGuire (1988).

Frey-Rohn, L. (1974) *From Freud to Jung: A Comparative Study of the Psychology of the Unconscious*. Putnam, New York.

—— (1988) *Friedrich Nietzsche: A Psychological Approach to his Life and Work*. Daimon Verlag, Einsiedeln.

Gadamer, H.G. (1975) *Truth and Method*. Sheed & Ward, London.

Glover, E. (1950) *Freud or Jung*. George Allen & Unwin, London.

Grunbaum, A. (1984) *The Foundations of Psychoanalysis: A Philosophical Critique*. University of California Press, Berkeley.

Haeckel, E. (1901) *The Riddles of the Universe*. Harper, New York.

Hardy, J. (1987) *A Psychology with a Soul: Psychosynthesis in Evolutionary Context*. Routledge, London.

Hearnshaw, L.S. (1987) *The Shaping of Modern Psychology*. Routledge, London.

Hegel, G.W.F. (1910) *The Phenomenology of Mind*. George Allen & Unwin, London.

Heidegger, M. (1980) *Being and Time*. Basil Blackwell, Oxford.

Hillman, J. (1972) *The Myth of Analysis: Three Essays in Archetypal Psychology*. Harper and Row, New York.

—— (1975) *Re-Visioning Psychology*. Harper and Row, New York.
Hoeller, S.A. (1982) *The Gnostic Jung and the Seven Sermons to the Dead*. The Theosophical Publishing House, Wheaton, Ill.
Hogenson, G.B. (1983) *Jung's Struggle with Freud*. University of Notre Dame Press, Notre Dame and London.
Holt, D. (1987–8) 'Alchemy: Jung and the Historians of Science'. *Harvest*, 33, pp.40–60.
Homans, P. (1979) *Jung in Context: Modernity and the Making of Psychology*. University of Chicago Press, Chicago.
Hostie, R. (1957) *Religion and the Psychology of Jung*. Sheed & Ward, London and New York.
Hughes, S.S. (1979) *Consciousness and Society: The Reorientation of European Social Thought 1890–1930*. Harvester Press, Brighton.
Hume, D. (1958) *A Treatise of Human Nature*. Clarendon Press, Oxford.
Husserl, E. (1958) *Ideas: General Introduction to Pure Phenomenology*. George Allen, London.
Jacobi. J. (1967) *The Way of Individuation*. Meridian, New York.
Jaffé, A. (1983) *The Myth of Meaning in the Work of C.G. Jung*. Daimon Verlag, Zürich.
—— (1989) *From the Life and Work of C.G. Jung*. Daimon Verlag, Einsiedeln.
James, W. (1890) *The Principles of Psychology*. Holt, New York.
—— (1907) *Pragmatism: A New Name for Some Old Ways of Thinking*. Longman, London.
Jones, E. (1964) *The Life and Work of Sigmund Freud*, One vol., edited and abridged by L. Trilling. Penguin Books, Harmondsworth.
Jordanova, L.J. (1984) *Lamarck*. Oxford University Press, Oxford.
Jung, C.G. (1953-83) *The Collected Works of C.G. Jung*, edited by H. Read, M. Fordham and G. Adler, translated by R.F.C. Hull. Routledge, London, and Princeton University Press, Princeton.
—— (1973 & 1975) *Letters*, edited by G. Adler and A. Jaffé, translated by R.F.C. Hull. Vol.I: 1906–1950; Vol.II: 1951–1961. Routledge, London, and Princeton University Press, Princeton.
—— (1974) *The Undiscovered Self*. Routledge, London and New York.
—— (1978) *Man and his Symbols*. Pan Books, London.
—— (1980) *C.G. Jung Speaking: Interviews and Encounters*, eds W. McGuire & R.F.C. Hull. Pan Books, London.
—— (1983) *Memories, Dreams, Reflections*, recorded and edited by A. Jaffé. Fontana, London.
—— (1985) *Synchronicity: An Acausal Connecting Principle*. Routledge, London.
—— (1988) *The Freud/Jung Letters: The Correspondence between Sigmund Freud and C.G. Jung*. See McGuire (1988).
—— (1989) *The Seminars: Nietzsche's Zarathustra: Notes of the Seminar Given in 1934–9*, edited by James L. Jarrett. Routledge, London, and Princeton University Press, Princeton.
Kant, I. (1956) *Critique of Pure Reason*. Macmillan, London.
Kaufmann, W. (1956) *Nietzsche: Psychologist and Antichrist*. Meridian Books, New York.
Kohut, H. (1958) *The Self and the Humanities: Reflections on a New Psychoanalytical Approach*. Norton, New York.
Kolakowski, L. (1985) *Bergson*. Oxford University Press, London.
Kuhn, T.S. (1962) *The Structure of Scientific Revolutions*. University of Chicago Press, Chicago.

Lacan, J. (1977) *Écrits: A Selection*. Tavistock Press, London.
Laing, R.D. (1965) *The Divided Self: An Existential Study in Sanity and Madness*. Penguin Books, Harmondsworth.
Lasch, C. (1984) *The Minimal Self: Psychic Survival in Troubled Times*. Norton, New York.
Lauter, E. & Schreier-Rupprecht, C. (1985) *Feminist Archetypal Theory: Interdisciplinary Re-Visions of Jungian Thought*. University of Tennessee Press, Knoxville.
Lovejoy, A.O., (1974) *The Great Chain of Being*. Harvard University Press, Cambridge, Mass.
Lyotard, J-F. (1984) *The Postmodern Condition*. Manchester University Press, Manchester.
McCully, R.S. (1987) *Jung and Rorschach: A Study in the Archetype of Perception*. Spring Publications, Dallas.
McGuire, W. (ed.) (1988) *The Freud/Jung Letters: The Correspondence between Sigmund Freud and C.G. Jung*, translated by R. Manheim and R.F.C. Hull. Harvard University Press, Cambridge, Mass.
Magee, B. (1983) *The Philosophy of Schopenhauer*. Clarendon Press, Oxford.
Masson, G. (1989) *Against Therapy*. Collins, London.
Midgeley, M. (1979) *Beast and Man: The Roots of Human Nature*. Methuen, London.
Needham, J. (1954–84) *Science and Civilization in China*. Cambridge University Press, Cambridge.
Neumann, E. (1954) *The History and Origins of Consciousness*. Routledge, London.
Nietzsche, F. (1956) *A Genealogy of Morals*. Doubleday, New York
—— (1961) *Thus Spake Zarathustra*. Penguin Books, Harmondsworth.
—— (1967) *The Will to Power*, ed. Walter Kaufmann. Random House, New York.
—— (1968) *The Twilight of the Idols*. Penguin Books, Harmondsworth.
—— (1973) *Beyond Good and Evil*. Penguin Books, Harmondsworth.
—— (1986) *Human all too Human*. Cambridge University Press, Cambridge.
Odajnyk, V.W. (1976) *Jung and Politics: The Political and Social Ideas of C.G. Jung*. New York University Press, New York.
Ornstein, R.E. (1973) *The Psychology of Consciousness*. Viking Press, New York.
Papadopoulos, R.K. and Saayman, G.S. (eds) (1984) *Jung in Modern Perspective*. Wildwood House, Hounslow.
Peters, R.S. (ed.) (1962) *Brett's History of Psychology*. George Allen & Unwin, London.
Pico Della Mirandola (1965) *Oration on the Dignity of Man*. Bobbs Merrill, Indianapolis.
Popper, K.R. & Eccles, J.C. (1977) *The Self and its Brain*. Springer International, Berlin.
Progoff, I. (1953) *Jung's Psychology and its Social Meaning*. Dialogue House Library, New York.
—— (1973) *Jung, Synchronicity and Human Destiny: C.G. Jung's Theory of Meaningful Coincidence*. Julian Press, New York.
Quine, W.V.O. (1963) 'Two Dogmas of Empiricism', in Lewis, H.D. (ed.) *Clarity is not Enough*. George Allen & Unwin, London.
Rauhala, L. (1984) 'The Basic Views of C.G. Jung in the Light of Hermeneutical Metascience', in Papadopoulos, R.K. and Saayman, G.S. (1984), q.v.

Rickman, H.P. (1988) *Dilthey Today: Appraisal of the Contemporary Relevance of his Work*. Greenwood Press, New York.
Ricoeur, P. (1970) *Freud and Philosophy: An Essay on Interpretation*. Yale University Press, New Haven.
Rieff, P. (1973) *The Triumph of the Therapeutic: Uses of Faith after Freud*. Penguin Books, Harmondsworth.
Roazen, P. (1979) *Freud and his Followers*. Penguin Books, Harmondsworth.
Robertson, R. (1987) *C.G. Jung and the Archetypes of the Collective Unconscious*. Peter Lang, New York.
Rorty, R. (1980) *Philosophy and the Mirror of Nature*. Basil Blackwell, Oxford.
—— (1989) *Contingency, Irony and Solidarity*. Cambridge University Press, Cambridge.
Russell, B (1967) *The Problems of Philosophy*. Oxford University Press, Oxford.
Rychlak, J.F. (1984) 'Jung as Dialectitian and Teleologist', in Papadopoulos, R.K. and Saayman, G.S. (1984), q.v.
Rycroft, C. (1972) *A Critical Dictionary of Psychoanalysis*, Penguin Books, Harmondsworth.
Samuels, A. (1985) *Jung and the Post-Jungians*. Routledge, London.
Schiller, F. (1982) *On the Aesthetic Education of Man*. Clarendon Press, Oxford.
Schnädelbach, H. (1984) *Philosophy in Germany, 1831–1933*. Cambridge University Press, Cambridge.
Schopenhauer, A. (1883) *The World as Will and Idea*. Two vols, Routledge, London.
—— (1970) *Essays and Aphorisms*, selected by R.J. Hollingdale. Penguin Books, Harmondsworth.
Schutte, O. (1984) *Beyond Nihilism: Nietzsche without Masks*. University of Chicago Press. Chicago.
Shelburne, W.A. (1988) *Mythos and Logos in the Thought of Carl Jung: The Theory of the Collective Unconscious in Scientific Perspective*. State University of New York Press, Albany, New York.
Sheldrake, R. (1981) *A New Science of Life: The Hypothesis of Formative Causation*. Paladin, London.
Skolimowski, H. (1981) *Eco-Philosophy: Designing New Tactics for Living*. Marion Boyars, Boston.
Solomon, R. (1980) *History and Human Nature: A Philosophical Review of European History and Culture, 1750–1800*. Harvester Press, Brighton.
Staude, J-R. (1981) *The Adult Development of C.G. Jung*. Routledge, London.
Steele, R.S. (1982) *Freud and Jung: Conflicts of Interpretation*. Routledge, London.
Stein, M. (1985) *Jung's Treatment of Christianity: The Psychotherapy of a Religious Tradition*. Chiron, Wilmette, Ill.
Stern, P. (1976) *C.G. Jung: The Haunted Prophet*. Brazillier, New York.
Stevens, A. (1982) *Archetype: A Natural History of the Self*. Routledge, London.
—— (1990) *On Jung*. Routledge, London.
Storr, A. (1973) *Jung*. Collins, London.
Taylor, C. (1964) *The Explanation of Behaviour*. Routledge, London.
Teilhard de Chardin, P. (1959) *The Phenomenon of Man*. Collins, London.
Toulmin, S. (1982) *The Return to Cosmology: Postmodern Science and the Theology of Nature*. University of California Press, Berkeley and Los Angeles.
Ulanov, A.B. (1971) *The Feminine in Jungian Psychology and in Christian Theology*. Northwestern University Press, Evanston.
Vaihinger, H. (1924) *The Philosophy of 'As If'*. Routledge, London.

Vickers, B. (ed.) (1984) *Occult Scientific Mentalities in the Renaissance*. Cambridge University Press, Cambridge.
von Bertalanffy, L. (1968) *General Systems Theory*. Brazillier, New York.
von Franz, M-L. (1975) *C.G. Jung: His Myth in our Time*. G.P. Putnam, New York.
von Hartmann, E. (1869) *Philosophie des Unbewussten*. Duncker, Berlin.
Watts, A. (1973) *Psychotherapy East and West*. Penguin Books, Harmondsworth.
Wehr, D.S., (1988) *Jung and Feminism: Liberating Archetypes*. Routledge, London.
Wehr, G. (1987) *Jung: A Biography*. Shambala, Boston and London.
Westman, R.S. (1984) 'Nature, Art and Psyche: Jung, Pauli, and the Kepler-Fludd Polemic', in Vickers, B. (1984), q.v.
White, V. (1952) *God and the Unconscious*. Collins, London.
Whitmont, E.C. (1969) *The Symbolic Quest: Basic Concepts of Analytical Psychology*. Princeton University Press, Princeton.
Wiener, N. (1948) *Cybernetics*. John Wiley & Sons, New York.
Wilson, C. (1984) *C.G. Jung: Lord of the Underworld*. The Aquarian Press, Wellingborough.
Winch, P. (1958) *The Idea of a Social Science*. Routledge, London.

# NAME INDEX

# SUBJECT INDEX

For Product Safety Concerns and Information please contact our EU representative GPSR@taylorandfrancis.com
Taylor & Francis Verlag GmbH, Kaufingerstraße 24, 80331 München, Germany

www.ingramcontent.com/pod-product-compliance
Ingram Content Group UK Ltd.
Pitfield, Milton Keynes, MK11 3LW, UK
UKHW021303190926
475701UK00009B/630

* 9 7 8 1 1 3 8 8 0 2 0 9 4 *